Castles, Keeps, and Leprechauns

◆ ◆ ◆

Phyllis Méras

CONGDON & WEED, INC.

New York • Chicago

Library of Congress Cataloging-in-Publication Data

Méras, Phyllis.
    Castles, keeps, and leprechauns : tales, myths, and legends
of historical sites in Great Britain and Ireland : a traveler's
companion / Phyllis Méras.
      p.   cm.
    ISBN 0-86553-186-2 : $17.95
    1. Historic sites—Great Britain.   2. Historic sites—
Ireland.   3. Tales—Great Britain.   4. Tales—Ireland.
5. Legends—Great Britain.   6. Legends—Ireland.
7. Great Britain—History—Miscellanea.   8. Ireland—
History—Miscellanea.   I. Title.
DA660.M48   1988
398.2′2′0941—dc19   88-23340
                                                CIP
                                             (Rev.)

International Standard Book Number: 0-86553-186-2
                                       0-8092-0186-2Z
                                       (Contemporary Books, Inc.)

Published by Congdon & Weed, Inc.
A subsidiary of Contemporary Books, Inc.
298 Fifth Avenue, New York, New York 10001
Distributed by Contemporary Books, Inc.
180 North Michigan Avenue, Chicago, Illinois 60601

Published simultaneously in Canada by Beaverbooks, Ltd.
195 Allstate Parkway, Valleywood Business Park
Markham, Ontario L3R 4T8 Canada

For John
And for Jennifer and Kenneth, travelers of tomorrow

ACKNOWLEDGMENTS

I am grateful to many for their aid in the preparation of this book—in particular to Andrew Glaze, H. Constance Hill, Mary McCaughey, Larry Ryan, Betty and Herb Silverman, Suzanne Sirignano, and Nancy Convery Young for research; to Sara Crafts, Nancy Luedeman, Susanna Sturgis, and Pat Ware for secretarial work.

For copyediting and fact checking, I am indebted to Edmund Antrobus, Elisa Cohen of Morris Silver Associates, Maebeth Fenton, Ruth Gottlieb, Anne Murray, Robert Titley of the British Tourist Authority, Orla Carey of the Irish Tourist Board, and Marie Macklin, Rosemary Evans, and Michael Roberts of the Northern Ireland Tourist Board.

Also contributing from their various fields of knowledge were Stanley Burnshaw, Hazel Carr of the Scotch Whiskey Association, Bridget Cooke, Olga Davies of the Wales Tourist Board, William A. Davis, Harvey Ewing, Patric Farrell, Richard Freedman, Ian Glass, Herbert Kenney, Al Kilborne, Mary McGovern, Ivo and Cynthia Meisner, Madelyn Merwin, Bedford Pace and Robin

Prestage of the British Tourist Authority, George, Alan, and Chèle Reekie, Ella Reston, Ray Hyde of the Guinness Import Company, Bernie O'Rourke of Belleek Ireland Incorporated, Laura Lee of the Waterford Crystal Company, Edwin Safford, Linda Stewart, and John E. Wallace.

Thanks are due also to Hilda Bijur, Anne Bowie, Robert Cocroft, Thomas B. Congdon, Jr., Grace Franklin, Ivan Fuldauer, David and Mary Alice Lowenthal, John and Bonnie Méras, Helen Milonas, Polly Woollcott Murphy, Rebecca Shanor, and Frances Tenenbaum.

And patient while the book was in process were Alan Kerr, Charles McC. Hauser, Jack Major, and the late Michael P. Metcalf of the *Providence Journal*; Joyce Dauley, Mary Jane Ertman, and Anne Morgan of Wellesley College; as well as my husband, Thomas Cocroft.

For miscellaneous tasks, thanks are due to Florence Brown and Nis Kildegard of the *Vineyard Gazette* and to Jean Rossi and Marianne Durgin.

Research facilities were provided by the Boston Public Library, the British Tourist Authority, Kathy Norton and Dorothy McGinniss of the Chilmark (Massachusetts) Public Library, the Providence (Rhode Island) Public Library, the Vineyard Haven (Massachusetts) Public Library, the Wellesley College Library, Ann Fielder and Mickey Barnes of the West Tisbury (Massachusetts) Public Library, Arnold Greenberg of The Complete Traveller Bookstore in New York City, Book Den East in Oak Bluffs, Massachusetts, and Roma Ryan Books in Belfast, Northern Ireland. But above all I consulted the remarkable private libraries of the late Donald A. Roberts and the late Truman Deforris Ross.

CONTENTS

Castles, Keeps, and Leprechauns

INTRODUCTION

It is the events that occur in a place that make it memorable. When I stand in London's Highgate Cemetery at the grave of Elizabeth Rossetti, I see her husband, poet-painter Dante Gabriel Rossetti. He stands there seven years after Elizabeth's death. She is being disinterred, and he is removing the love poems that he had had buried with her.

I cannot help but smile at Trinity College, Cambridge, at the thought of the poet Byron, a student there, keeping a pet bear cub in his rooms.

At Brighton's Royal Pavilion I can almost hear eighteen-year-old Queen Victoria shyly singing operatic songs in the Music Room.

And so, in the pages that follow, I have collected anecdotes of my favorite sites throughout the British Isles. Some stories are historical, some mythological, some purely apocryphal, but all have enriched the place about which they are told.

This does not pretend to be a complete compendium of stories worth telling, nor of sites worth visiting in the

British Isles. It is a very personal selection. The sites and their accompanying stories have been arranged by region in England, Scotland, Wales, Northern Ireland, and the Republic of Ireland; then alphabetically by city or town.

Some of these anecdotes have been gathered during the years that I have spent as a travel writer for major newspapers. Others have been researched from histories, diaries, and biographies; still others have been recounted by church vergers, innkeepers, publicans, and guides. All have added a new and greater dimension to my travels. I hope they will add to yours.

1
ENGLAND

BAKEWELL

Chatsworth House

In the great Tudor house that once stood on the site of this 175-room, 21-kitchen house, Mary, Queen of Scots became a prisoner in 1568 on order of her cousin, Queen Elizabeth. Her "jailers" were Bess of Hardwick and Bess's husband, the Earl of Shrewsbury. At first the women shared a love of embroidery together. But when four-times-married Bess accused her husband of having had a love affair with Mary and Mary learned of the accusation, the furious Scottish queen dispatched a note to Queen Elizabeth. In it, she listed all the disagreeable statements that Bess had ever made about Elizabeth. Happily for all (for Mary still had nineteen years to live), the letter was intercepted before it reached the queen.

BATH

Tradition has it that when he was a youth, Bladud, who became the father of King Lear, traveled abroad for a time. But it was not a happy trip, for by the time the prince, for whom there were the highest expectations, returned to Britain, he was suffering from leprosy.

As was the custom of the day, he was banished and became a swineherd. To his horror, the pigs, too, began to show the lesions of the dread disease. Then one morning the pigs disappeared. When Bladud found them they were wallowing in mud beside a hot spring. A few days later, the prince-swineherd was astonished to see that the skin of his pigs was no longer blemished, but firm and pink. He went in search of the swamp and spring again and, finding them, bathed himself in the spring waters. A few days later, his sores, too, were healed. In time, the prince-swineherd became the king it had been intended that he be, while the hot spring that had healed him became the site of this spa city.

◆ ◆ ◆

When the artist Thomas Gainsborough arrived here in 1760, it was only to stay a little while. To finance his stay, he painted pictures of some of the illustrious guests. That first year, his small fee of five guineas seemed reasonable. But when he left fourteen years later, the much sought-after artist had raised his fee to forty guineas. No one complained. After all, gossip and art critics alike were whispering over the "Blue Boy" that he had painted here.

◆ ◆ ◆

Though she wrote about it with brilliance in her novels *Northanger Abbey* and *Persuasion*, Jane Austen never liked Bath. Shortly before her father decided to move here, her aunt, Mrs. Leigh Perrot, whose home this was, was accused of stealing lace from a shop and put on trial. Perhaps Jane's dislike of Bath stemmed from this. Had her aunt not been acquitted, the sentence could have been fourteen years' "transportation" to Australia—hardly a happy thought at the turn of the nineteenth century.

◆ ◆ ◆

Poor Queen Anne, who had to be carried to her coronation in 1702 because of the gout she suffered, was a hopeful frequenter of these medicinal baths. But when she brought her husband here and he died soon after, she blamed the baths.

◆ ◆ ◆

When he arrived here in 1705 with a party of gamblers, Richard Nash certainly couldn't have been called a gentleman. Born into the middle class, he had studied law briefly at Oxford but much preferred gaiety and games to serious endeavors. On a dare, he was said to have once ridden naked through the streets of a village on a cow. With gambling burgeoning at this posh watering place, a man so daring was worth fostering.

And Bath did foster Beau Nash, as Richard Nash came to be called. It wasn't long before the young gambling man had become the "King" of Bath, establishing a dress code, improving lodgings, and hiring musicians for the resort's dancing "assemblies." Beau Nash died a gentleman indeed.

Assembly Rooms: THE BALL ROOM

When George II's somewhat obstreperous daughter, Princess Amelia, came here on a holiday, she would have liked to dance all night. But the rules of Beau Nash, the "King" of Bath, did not allow dancing after eleven o'clock. One night when the music stopped and seventeen-year-old Amelia, stamping her foot, insisted that it begin again since, after all, she was a princess, Beau Nash stepped in.

"Yes, madam," he sternly replied, "but I reign here." The chastised princess went away to bed.

Bath Abbey

Fifteenth-century Bishop Oliver King was convinced it could be nothing but a direct message from God. In a dream, he had seen angels climbing up a ladder to Heaven, then down again, and a voice had said, "Let an Oliver establish a crown, and a King restore the church."

So he began to build this abbey and had sculpted on the west front representations of the ladder he had dreamed the angels climbed.

1 Royal Crescent

Among the illustrious guests here in 1780 was Marie Thérèse Louise de Savoie Carignon, a lady-in-waiting to France's Queen Marie Antoinette. She came with her physician and many servants to seek a cure for her nervousness and her allergies. At opposite ends of the spectrum, the fragrance of violets and the sight of shellfish made her sick.

But she liked England and returned to France in 1781 to convince her beloved queen and king to escape the French Revolution by returning to England with her.

They didn't make it. Nor did she. Imprisoned as an aristocrat, Marie Thérèse was dragged from her cell by an angry mob, robbed, and beheaded.

11 Royal Crescent

On March 18, 1772, it was from this house that the twenty-one-year-old Richard Brinsley Sheridan, a handsome Irish roué who liked to write, fled with the eighteen-year-old singer, Elizabeth Linley.

Neither of their fathers approved the match. Even the bride-to-be wasn't certain she was in love with Sheridan. But her bridegroom's solicitousness on their honeymoon journey made her really fall in love, she later confessed to him. As it turned out, the elopement was nearly the death of the youthful playwright-to-be (*School for Scandal, The Rivals*). Elizabeth was such a charmer that many men had paid her court. When one of them insulted Sheridan publicly, he responded by a challenge to a duel. Before the affront was righted, there were two duels. In the second one, fought at Kingsdown near here,

Sheridan was badly injured. It was only after several weeks in the hospital that his sword wounds were healed and Sheridan was able to return to his pretty bride.

BEESTON

Beeston Castle

Three times treasure hunters have delved to the bottom of the 370-foot-deep well seeking the treasure Richard III is said to have hidden in it.

Because he had supporters here and knew it would be safe, Richard hid a fortune in silver here in 1485 before he went to war.

The treasure certainly has been safe. The king did not return (*See* Market Bosworth, Bosworth Field), and it was four centuries before the first treasure seeker came hunting for the silver cache. He found nothing. Nor did the 1935 or 1970 treasure hunters, who came equipped with the latest treasure-hunting devices.

While skeptics say the treasure was a tall story from the beginning, others maintain that demons guard the riches of "that demon" Richard. (*See* London, Tower of London: Bloody Tower.)

BERKELEY

Berkeley Castle

In 1327, King Edward II resolutely refused to die of the natural causes his captors wished for.

A man of strength and valor, a fine horseman, the deposed king survived even though rotting carcasses were thrown into a pit beneath his cell in hopes the odor and the vermin from them would kill him.

Finally, his captors could wait no longer and armed with a red-hot poker, they pinned him to a table in his clammy cell here and disemboweled him.

BIDFORD-ON-AVON

At the Falcon Inn that once stood here, William Shakespeare entered a drinking contest on behalf of his neighboring town of Stratford.

He lost. Will Shakespeare and his Stratford friends began to stumble home. But they made it only as far as a roadside crab apple tree, under whose sheltering limbs they slept off their overdose of ale.

BINSEY

St. Margaret's Churchyard: THE TREACLE WELL

One summer afternoon in 1862, Charles Dodgson (who wrote as Lewis Carroll), his friend Robinson Duckworth, and Alice, Lorina, and Edith Liddell, the three young daughters of the dean of Oxford's Christ Church (*See* Oxford, Christ Church College), rowed up the Thames past this village. As he rowed, Dodgson spun a tale for the girls about this well. He told of a dormouse who knew three little girls, Elsie, Lacey, and Tillie, who lived at the bottom of a treacle well—a well of thick, tasty molasses. (*Treacle* here means both *molasses* and *healing*, as in the nickname for this well.)

Fully enrapt, the girls listened to his story. Dodgson was inspired by their enthusiasm to put the tale on paper. It became the Mad Hatter's Tea Party in *Alice's Adventures in Wonderland.*

◆ ◆ ◆

In response to the prayers of the Princess Frideswide that pagan King Algar, whom she had blinded, be able to see again (*See* Oxford, The Cathedral: St. Frideswide's Shrine), St. Margaret is said to have created this well whose water performed miracles. Legend has it that the water from it, applied to the Anglo-Saxon king's sightless eyes, soon cleared his clouded vision.

BLADON

St. Martin's Churchyard

When the Sunday worship service was over here, little Winston Churchill (*See* Woodstock, Blenheim Palace) would run furiously up the hill outside, leaping back and forth across the ditches. It was as if, the older generation said, the boy were trying to prove something to himself.

BOSTON

Guildhall

All that separatists William Bradford and William Brewster and their followers wanted was to leave England for some place where they could worship in peace. But the government of James I considered anyone who did not worship according to the tenets of the Church of England to be a traitor. Inexplicably, such so-called traitors needed permission from the king to emigrate. The separatists of the northern village of Scrooby decided they would try escaping without permission.

They came to this east coast port in 1607, and some of them persuaded a Dutch sea captain to take them across the sea to Holland. He collected their money. Then, while they waited aboard his ship for it to set sail, he told Boston officials of their plan to flee.

The separatists were arrested, and in this hall, Bradford and Brewster were tried and imprisoned for a month for their "crime" of wishing to leave England. But eventually they did leave, to be among the founders of the Plymouth Bay Colony. (*See* Plymouth, Barbican: Mayflower Stone.)

St. Botolph's Church

For centuries, the top of this "stumpy" 275-foot-high tower above the sea was kept illuminated at night as a

beacon for seamen. But in 1633 when its vicar for twenty-
one years, John Cotton, left for America, it is said that
the light went out.

BRIGHTON

The Royal Pavilion

When eighteen-year-old Queen Victoria came here on her
first visit in 1837, she shyly sang operatic songs in the
Music Room with her mother.

◆   ◆   ◆

One of the merriest evenings that George IV spent in
this Chinese pavilion that he and his architect John
Nash created was the December night in 1823 when the
Italian composer Gioacchino Rossini came to visit. He
delighted the king by not treating him like a king. Sitting beside His Majesty at the concert that had occa-
sioned his visit, Rossini casually twirled his hat around
on one finger. And the king pleased Rossini by not act-
ing like a king. Arm in arm, without ceremony, His
Majesty introduced the composer to the orchestra.

Rossini was so delighted, indeed, with his reception
that he ended the concert by playing the pianoforte himself.

BROADWAY

Middle Hill House

Owner of this house in the early nineteenth century, Sir
Thomas Phillips wished, he said, to own a copy of every
book in the world. Although he never fulfilled his
dream, he acquired enough of a library so that today,
more than a century and a half later, there are still books
and manuscripts in his collection that are being sold.

CAMBRIDGE

Christ's College

Devout Lady Margaret Beaufort, grandmother of Henry
VIII and founder of this college, kept rooms here. To

assure that she could attend services but would not have to face the clamor of the students, an oriel window in her rooms looked down on the chapel below.

Not that there *was* much clamor or rowdiness among the students. In accordance with her rules, no drinking parties were allowed here; no dogs or hawks could be kept; there was to be no playing of dice or cards; no carrying of weapons; and no engaging in trade.

Great St. Mary's

During the persecution of the Protestants in 1557 by Queen Mary Tudor, the Bishop of Chester said that it was essential that this church be properly cleansed of heresy. By hallowing this unoffending structure with a mixture of salt, water, ashes, and wine, he did it.

◆ ◆ ◆

Listening here to a discussion of the pros and cons of monarchy, an energetic young Elizabeth I could not hear some of what was being said on stage, so she shouted loudly at the speakers, "Speak up!" When she found that she still could not hear, the queen rose from her throne, marched up, and joined the participants on the stage.

Jesus College

Scolded for idleness and encumbered with debts, the youthful Samuel Taylor Coleridge embarked on a six-week drinking binge in his second year here. When it was over, he left Cambridge to join the cavalry, enlisting under the unlikely pseudonym of Silas Tomkyn Comberbache.

But soldiering was not for the poet. He continually fell off his horse and bored his comrades by extensively quoting from Euripides. Before any harm could come to him, his brothers bought his discharge from the Fifteenth Light Dragoons, paid his debts, and saw that he returned to the university.

King's College Chapel

When Anne Boleyn was still his beloved queen, Henry VIII had their initials carved into the wooden altar screen here. The initials are H.R.A.S., which stand for the Latin "Henricus Rex" and "Anna Spousa." Presumably, Henry had too much on his mind after her beheading in 1536 (*see* London, Tower of London: King's House) to bother having Anne's initials removed.

Magdalene College: SECOND COURT—PEPYS LIBRARY

Perhaps because he liked the beer here so much on his visits in adulthood, the diarist Samuel Pepys left his entire library to this college where he had studied as a youth. There were books, prints, and manuscripts in his collection. Most important was his six-volume diary, handwritten in cipher so that he could write just as personally as he pleased about what he observed both of himself and of those about him.

A clerk in the Navy office and ultimately a secretary to the Admiralty, Pepys wrote—for the public—*Memoirs of the Navy*, but for himself he wrote intimately of Charles II, whom he served; of London and its plague and fire; of drunken sprees and bribes.

For a century, his diary sat on the shelves here among all his other books. No one thought of it nor knew how to decipher the shorthand. Then in 1818, when John Evelyn's diary was published and received with acclaim, the head of Magdalene College decided to see what could be done with the diary of Pepys.

Tradition has it that Pepys's "indecipherable" code was cracked in a single night. But it took three years to decipher all three thousand pages of the diary.

Mathematical Bridge

This arched wooden bridge that crosses the River Cam into Queen's College was built in 1749 in the Chinese way without nails or pegs. But, over the years, inebriated students so frequently took it apart and then were unable to put it together again that finally it was deemed wisest to affix the present bolts to thwart temptation.

Pembroke College: CHAPEL

Dr. Matthew Wren, Bishop of Ely, had spent seventeen years in the Tower of London. On being released in the 1660s, the joyous prelate wished to thank God for his salvation by erecting a chapel to Him. He asked his young nephew, Christopher Wren, an aspiring architect (*See* London, St. Paul's Cathedral), to design something. A porch on the cathedral at Ely and this college chapel are that great builder's first works.

Peterhouse College

"Playful" fellow students of the poet Thomas Gray ("Elegy in a Country Churchyard") caused him to leave this college for Pembroke. The occupant of second-floor rooms, Gray was terrified of fire and kept a rope tied to a window bar so that, in time of conflagration, he could make a quick escape.

One night, after having set a tubful of water beneath his window, practical jokers set fire to wet straw below Gray's rooms. Smelling the smoke and sliding down the rope, Gray plunged into the tub. As he shook the water off and listened to the gleeful laughter of the jokers, he decided that he belonged in another college.

Queen's College

The Dutch philosopher-theologian Desiderius Erasmus, who came here in 1510 as a teacher of Greek, was not happy at all with his stay. He found that the wine tasted like vinegar, the ale was worse, the cost of living was frightful, and the out-of-doors was frightening because of the prevalence of the plague.

River Cam

Cambridge wags like telling the apocryphal story of how Queen Victoria, visiting here, remarked on the scraps of paper dirtying the water. She was solicitously told that they were students' notes being sent by river to each other when in reality what she was seeing was the Cam being used as a sewer.

Sidney Sussex College

A grisly gift to this college in 1960 was the skull of one of its former students, the seventeenth-century Lord Protector of England, Oliver Cromwell. (*See* London, Westminster Hall.) But it was graciously accepted and properly interred in the chapel here.

Trinity College

The poet George Gordon, Lord Byron, who became a student here in 1805, gained considerable renown because of the pet bear he kept in his rooms and took on daily walks on a chain.

Trinity College: GREAT GATE—STATUE OF HENRY VIII

If this statue were as it should be, Henry VIII, who founded this college, would be holding the orb that is part of the royal regalia in one hand, the scepter of state in the other. But for generations now, Cantabrigians have been climbing up the statue to substitute a chair leg for the scepter.

CANTERBURY

Canterbury Cathedral

Four days after Christmas in 1170, four of King Henry II's knights stormed into this cathedral. Before the altar, they delivered crushing blows to the head of Thomas à Becket, Archbishop of Canterbury, once Henry's chancellor and well-loved friend.

Raised by his king to be the Archbishop of Canterbury, the highest religious office in the land, Thomas had taken his post too seriously, from the king's point of view. Thomas insisted on supporting the Church even when it opposed the Crown. Henry would not have that.

In a fit of pique, he cried out to his barons, "Who will rid me of this turbulent priest?" And four knights did. Later, Henry said he really couldn't remember having wished aloud for Thomas's death, but if he had, he surely never expected anyone to believe him. (*See* Wales, St. David's, St. David's Cathedral.)

◆　◆　◆

When France's Louis VII joined the thousands of pilgrims who visited this cathedral in the twelfth century after the murder of Thomas à Becket, he was wearing, in a ring on his finger, a magnificent diamond known as the Regale of France. Louis prayed fervently, but he did not, voluntarily, leave his valued diamond behind as a donation. Nevertheless, it stayed—mysteriously popping out of his ring, so the story goes, and landing on Thomas à Becket's shrine. There it continued to glitter until Henry VIII took it for himself four centuries later.

Canterbury Cathedral: TOMB OF EDWARD THE BLACK PRINCE

Because he wished to marry Joan, the Fair Maid of Kent, and the Church agreed not to object, though she had been once divorced and once widowed, Edward the Black Prince (so called for the black armor he chose to wear) gave the money to build the chantry here. He left precise instructions as to how he wished to be buried in this cathedral. A warrior above all, he asked that his effigy "be all armed in steel for battle," and so it is.

CHANNEL ISLANDS

Alderney: HANGING ROCK

Legend has it that, at the devil's urging, a boatload of Guernseymen once tied a line to this fifty-foot high rock and tried their best—but failed—to tow the island home with them.

Guernsey: ST. PETER PORT—CASTLE CORNET

It was a miraculous escape with quite extraordinary results. In 1672 when Royalist forces were storing ammunition in the castle, lightning struck, exploding the gunpowder. There seemed no likelihood that anyone inside could have survived.

But the next day, an infant's cry was heard from the rubble, and the castle governor's little daughter was discovered alive and well.

She remained well—becoming the mother of thirty children.

Guernsey: ST. PETER PORT—HAUTEVILLE HOUSE

Though he came here exiled by Napoleon III for opposition to his regime, the nineteenth-century French writer Victor Hugo spent a pleasant fifteen years in this house. He shared it with his wife, but he installed his mistress within seeing distance. He took showers outdoors on the roof, somewhat to the dismay of neighbors, but he also assiduously wrote twenty pages a morning of *Les Miserables.*

◆   ◆   ◆

It didn't matter a bit to Victor Hugo that his predecessor in this house had committed suicide and her ghost was said to be in residence. He was all for spiritualist séances and insisted that, during some of those that he held here, he had conversed with Christ, Muhammed, and William Shakespeare.

Guernsey: ST. PETER'S VALLEY—
GERMAN MILITARY UNDERGROUND HOSPITAL

Some fourteen thousand tons of rock were removed by slave workers and civilian prisoners during World War II when German Occupation forces had this enormous underground hospital built.

Guernsey: VAZON BAY

Residents here had a merry time of it in 1937 when the *SS Briseis* sank off the coast with a cargo of wine. No lives were lost, but much wine was—consumed by Guernsey's delighted citizenry.

Jersey: GOREY—MONT ORGEWIL CASTLE

It is thanks to the preservationist instincts of Sir Walter Raleigh that this handsome thirteenth-century castle still stands. When it was decided that Elizabeth's Castle would be built, plans were under way to demolish this formidable fortress. Governor of the island at the time, Raleigh declared it "a stately fort of great capacity that it were a pity to cast down," and so the fortress was saved.

Jersey: JERSEY ZOO (Les Augres Manor)

The naturalist Gerald Durrell, who had come here to look for a home for his wild animal collection, spent a tiring morning looking everywhere for a suitable site. Then he was invited for lunch at this fifteenth-century manor on its twenty-acre grounds. He knew instantly that he had found the perfect place for his gorillas, monkeys, and orangutans.

Jersey: ST. HELIER—HERMITAGE ROCK

The sixth-century monk Helenius, whose home was once this rock, was determined to bloodlessly end piracy on the neighboring seas.

To do so, he preached his message in a thunderous voice until one pirate, incensed by his powerful words, murdered him in 555. Soon a chapel was built in his honor, and St. Helier itself was named for him.

Jersey: ST. HELIER—ST. SAVIOUR PARISH CHURCH

Young Lillie Langtry, the daughter of the rector, the Reverend Dean William Le Breton, grew up here, attending church with regularity. It didn't "take," they tended to say of her here in later years.

The woman whom fellow-Jerseyite John Everett Millais, the painter, called "the most beautiful woman on earth" enjoyed flaunting her beauty. First, she was an actress on stage; then she was the mistress of Edward VII when he was Prince of Wales; next she was Edward's nephew's mistress. She finally settled down to a life of respectability as a baronet's wife.

Sark

No sooner had VE-Day been declared in 1945 than the late Sibyl Hathaway, the Dame of Sark, its hereditary ruler, sternly ordered the German soldiers who had occupied the island in the war to clean-up duty to straighten up the mess and disorder they had made.

CHESTER

It was in this city where the plague, both in 1517 and in 1647, drastically thinned the population that the nursery rhyme "Ring Around a Rosy, a Pocket Full of Posies" had its beginning. But it was hardly a happy beginning.

In its original, it was no nursery rhyme, but a macabre ditty that began "Ring a ring of roses," to describe the way the plague came out in spots on those afflicted. It continued, "Ktchew, Ktchew, we all fall down," for on the third day, anyone suffering from the plague began to sneeze, then collapsed, and died.

City Walls

The essayist-novelist-lexicographer Dr. Samuel Johnson did not want his good friend Hester Thrale to miss any of the sights to be seen from these two miles of walls. When she, her husband, and her daughter were here visiting him in 1774, he huffed and puffed around the entire circumference of the walls with the Thrale family in tow.

Later, Dr. Johnson expressed his dismay and surprise that Mrs. Thrale, who had been a close acquaintance for more than a decade, was quite out of sorts at their long walk.

City Walls: PHOENIX TOWER

From this tower in 1645 a Civil War–weary Charles I watched his army being defeated by Oliver Cromwell's Republican army on mossy Rowton Moor just three miles away.

God's Providence House: THE ROWS

Though a quarter of this city died in the plague of 1647, the residents of this house were spared—some said because they hung a bunch of onions outside the door. Gratefully, the thankful phrase "God's Providence House" was inscribed above the door.

St. John's Church: THE ANCHORITE'S CELL

It is said that Harold the Saxon did not die on the battlefield at Hastings (*See* Hastings, Battle Abbey) in 1066, as most believe. Instead, he came to this little stone structure where he spent his last days as a hermit beside the River Dee.

St. Olave's Church

When Thomas Crane was the rector of this church from 1772 to 1816, three places were always set at the vicarage dinner table. One was for the rector, one for the sister with whom the rector lived, and the third for the devil, in case he happened by.

St. Werburgh's Cathedral

More than once in history this city has been saved from invaders by the sarcophagus of seventh-century St. Werburgh who is buried here. Whenever it was raised before attacking armies, they took flight. As the story goes, in one instance, a glimpse of the sarcophagus blinded the attackers.

CHICHESTER

Chichester Cathedral

Kindly St. Richard of Chichester, a bishop here in the thirteenth century, had only one notable flaw in his otherwise near-impeccable character. He was, it seems, a slugabed. Distinctly embarrassed by this failing, when he rose late the saint was wont to comment to the birds on their piety, applauding them for being up so early praising God with their song.

◆ ◆ ◆

All through the night of February 20, 1861, workmen desperately tried, fierce winds notwithstanding, to save the tower here from collapse. The previous month, cracks had been noticed in the twelfth-century structure, and timbers had been brought to the site and shoring-up operations begun.

But then the midwinter storm came. Rescue efforts proved to have been of no avail and finally had to be abandoned.

Only an hour later the medieval tower thundered to the ground. Happily, it was rebuilt, and today it and its spire are regarded as among the most graceful of their kind in all England.

COVENTRY

Sir Leofric, the Earl of Mercia, was taxing his people here unmercifully in the Middle Ages. Determined as he was to make Coventry one of the grandest cities in the land, he saw no other way of doing it. Clearly, his poor people were suffering from the taxes that he had imposed to give the city renown.

Word of their misery reached Lady Godiva, Sir Leofric's beauteous, blond wife. Pleading their cause to her husband, she begged him to reduce the taxes.

Leofric's prompt reply was that he could no more have a beautiful city without money to adorn it than she could be a beautiful woman without diamonds and rubies, silks and velvets, to adorn her.

Lady Godiva said that she was not sure that that was so. And then she proposed that, to test Sir Leofric's theory, she ride through the streets covered with nothing but her long golden hair. If she could show that real beauty did not depend on garments and riches, but on nobility, Godiva asked, would he be willing to reduce his taxes? Never believing that she would make such a ride, Leofric said he would. The next noon, to Leofric's dismay, draped only in her long blond hair and mounted on a white palfrey, his wife rode through the streets of Coventry. And no one emerged from his house, and only one looked out his door at her, because all knew that her immodesty was for their sakes.

Tom the Baker could not control his curiosity and opened his shutters a crack to have the slightest glimpse of lovely Godiva. But he never got it. As he peeped, he was blinded, and he has been remembered ever since as Peeping Tom.

Sir Leofric kept his part of the bargain and reduced taxes. Coventry grew without them—as Lady Godiva had predicted—to become one of the four richest cities in England during the Middle Ages.

Legend has it that eleven thousand virgins of Cologne came here in ancient times for a visit. When they returned home, they left behind eleven thousand virtues to be passed on to later generations of Coventry's fair sex.

Coventry Cathedral

On the night of November 14, 1940, the dark skies here grew even darker. For ten hours, German bombers pounded this "city of the three tall spires," depositing thirty thousand incendiaries and five hundred tons of bombs and land mines, leaving 554 dead and 865 injured.

This fourteenth-century cathedral was a smoldering ruin, but, miraculously, its three-hundred-foot spire, renowned as one of the finest in Europe, still proudly soared. And from the rubble of the rest of this cathedral two crosses were fashioned—one of charred roof timbers and one of twisted nails. In this new cathedral built around the lacelike ruins of the old, the crosses remain, a stark reminder of that awful November night.

DEAL

Walmer Castle

Lord Wellington, victor over Napoleon at Waterloo when he was 46, died on a small iron cot in his bed-sitting room here at age 83. Though he might have had any bed that he wanted, the old soldier preferred a simple, narrow army cot, remarking once that its narrowness served as an alarm clock for him. When it was time to turn over, he commented, he knew that it was time to turn out.

DURHAM

Durham Cathedral

With the help of many monks, a cow, and two milkmaids, the bones of St. Cuthbert, after more than seven years of being carried hither and yon, at last safely reached the site of this cathedral.

In 687, Cuthbert had died on the Holy Island of Lindisfarne, where conversion of the English began. Fearful that one day the island might be raided by nonbelievers, the dying saint had begged his followers to take his bones away with them to some Christian place, if indeed the island was invaded and they were forced to flee.

For two centuries, the monastery and St. Cuthbert's bones lay undisturbed. Then Viking raiders swept down from the north, and the monks of Lindisfarne left. Remembering the promise, passed down through the ages, that Cuthbert's bones were not to stay behind, the later monks unearthed the saint's coffin and took it away with them. And one day, after they had wearily laid it down for a while on their journey to a yet unknown destination, they found they could not lift it again, no matter how hard they tried. The befuddled monks camped beside it, waiting for a sign.

The word they received was that the coffin should find a final resting place at "Dunholme." But the men from Lindisfarne had no idea where Dunholme might be. As they considered what to do next, two milkmaids happened by. One had lost a cow and was asking the other if she had seen it. "Certainly," was the reply, "in Dunholme," and off the milkmaids went.

Eager to follow them, the monks tried one more time to raise St. Cuthbert's coffin. This time, they could lift it easily.

Hastening after the young women, they reached this place, formerly called Dunholme, with their burden, and here the predecessor of this church was built.

A carving of a cow on the northeast tower commemorates this event.

EDENBRIDGE

Hever Castle (two miles southwest of Edenbridge)

It was here that love-smitten Henry VIII came courting dark-haired Anne Boleyn. He would arrive for his visits with a cavalry escort, and his approach was announced by the blowing of a horn from a neighboring hill.

ELY

Ely Cathedral

Sailing in the fen waters that surrounded this site in the eleventh century, Canute the Dane heard wondrous music coming from the monastery that predated this cathedral. It was splendid enough, indeed, to make him think that he heard angels singing. Canute ordered his men to put in here where he discovered that the monks of Ely were doing the singing. So taken was he with their music that he endowed the monastery on the spot.

EXETER

Exeter Cathedral

The Germans called it a Baedeker raid, for they used a Baedeker guidebook to pinpoint the cultural targets they planned to strike here in May 1942.

When they were done, forty acres of Exeter were rubble, but miraculously, this fourteenth-century cathedral and its splendid nave with marble pillars had escaped almost intact.

◆ ◆ ◆

Despite the pain of rheumatism and despite sharing the rigors of the battlefield with her husband, Charles I, Queen Henrietta Maria gave birth to a robust girl here in April 1644. She had taken refuge in a house behind the Cathedral Close, and when she arrived none of Oliver Cromwell's Parliamentarian forces were here to frighten her.

But suddenly, word came that Cromwell's forces were arriving, set on besieging Exeter.

Rheumatism and childbed fever notwithstanding, there was nothing Henrietta Maria could do but seek to escape. With her infant, her confessor, and two servants, she fled to a hut some miles outside the city gate. It is said that she stayed hidden there for two days, listening to the tromping feet of the Parliamentarians outside her hideaway who were cursing her for having run away and trying to find her, swearing that they would take her head to London and get a good price for it.

But when they had gone, she gathered her companions together and fled once more, heading for Falmouth in Cornwall. Thence, she took sail for her native land of France.

FALMOUTH

Falmouth Harbor

Honored by the castle that bears his name across the water here, St. Mawes would frequently preach out of doors above the sea. It is said that on one such occasion, a barking seal interrupted his harangue. Picking up a rock, the short-tempered saint hurled it at him. The rock can still be seen where it fell on Black Rocks in the middle of this harbor.

Pendennis Castle

Seventy-year-old Sir John Arundell had no intention of surrendering this castle that Henry VIII had built, Queen Elizabeth had improved, and Charles I's Queen Henrietta Maria had visited. But in 1646 Oliver Cromwell's soldiers wanted it and for five months laid siege to it.

To the first demand that he surrender, Arundell valiantly replied that he would "bury" himself before giving up royal property to enemies of the king. A month later, he refused again to surrender. After that, Pendennis was blockaded even more closely.

Still, it was a long time before the proud Arundell capitulated—and then only for the sake of his starving men. His defense had been so able, his stubbornness so resolute, that the Cromwellians could not help honoring him by allowing him and any others strong enough to march, to come out with their trumpets blowing and their colors flying.

GLASTONBURY

Glastonbury Abbey Ruins

The Holy Grail is the chalice which was used by Christ at the Last Supper and which had caught some of his blood while he was on the Cross. Bearing the Holy Grail, Joseph of Arimathea is said to have found his way here from the Holy Land in 63 A.D.

When he and the eleven companions who traveled with him finally reached this spot, the weary Joseph leaned so hard on his staff that it took root. From it grew the Glastonbury thorn, a white hawthorne that blossomed every year at Christmastime until one of Oliver Cromwell's zealous soldiers cut it down.

Directed by the Archangel Gabriel, Joseph buried the chalice, and a spring gushed forth. He built an abbey on this site—the first Christian church building in England.

◆   ◆   ◆

Legend has it that, desperately wounded in the battle that was to be his last, King Arthur was carried to the sacred spring that bubbled on Glastonbury Tor in hopes of being cured. But he was not, and the great king was buried nearby.

In the twelfth century, however, Henry II had Arthur's enormous skeleton disinterred from the oak tree in which it had been buried sixteen feet deep. At the same time, the remains of Queen Guinevere were brought from Amesbury to lie beside King Arthur's in the abbey church.

But in the sixteenth century, when Henry VIII was wreaking destruction in the abbeys, the tomb of Arthur and Guinevere was among the sites destroyed.

GODSTOW

Godstow Lock
(about two and a half miles from Oxford)

Pretty Rosamund had been sent for her education to the Benedictine nunnery that stood here in the twelfth century. She got more education than her family had bargained for.

Henry II saw her one day, and she so captured his fancy that he built a house for her close to his nearby palace at Woodstock. He built a high maze around it so that Eleanor of Aquitaine, his queen, would be unable to see who was inside.

For years, Eleanor paid the maze no heed, and Rosamund bore Henry two children. Eleanor, however, could not be duped forever.

Not only did she manage to discover who was inside the maze, but, with the help of a silken thread, she found her way to Rosamund's house. As the legend has it, the furious queen poisoned her husband's mistress.

After Rosamund's death, the distraught Henry had a splendid tomb built for his beloved and richly endowed the convent in her memory. Though the convent was largely destroyed by seventeenth-century Puritans, the spirit of Fair Rosamund, as she is called, is said to hover here still.

GRASMERE

Dove Cottage

When William Wordsworth and his sister Dorothy, who moved here in 1799, were not wandering the woods and meadows, they were entertaining friends in this little cottage. It had been an inn, The Dove and Olive Bough, before they bought it.

Always especially welcome was William's best friend, Samuel Taylor Coleridge, whose marriage was faltering. Sometimes, however, the Wordsworth hospitality exceeded the size of the cottage, and guests had to sleep on the floor. Few seemed to mind. Sir Walter Scott, Baronet, who had a longing for grander surroundings (*see* Scotland, Dryburgh, Abbottsford), remarked with some dismay after a visit that he found it unusual that meals were served in the same room in which they were prepared.

◆ ◆ ◆

In the upstairs main room, many an evening was spent with the poet William Wordsworth dictating the verse he wrote in his head to his wife, Mary, or to his sister, Dorothy. After William's marriage in 1802, the threesome dwelt together here with great affection and tranquility.

◆ ◆ ◆

Twice, the shy, young essayist Thomas De Quincey (*Confessions of an Opium Eater*), who had corresponded with William Wordsworth, came here to see him. But both times he went away without having had the courage to knock.

HARROGATE

Ripley Castle (four miles north of Harrogate)

A wounded Oliver Cromwell arrived here demanding shelter in 1644 after the battle of Marston Moor. It was provided, but the staunch Royalist wife of Sir William Ingilby, who owned the castle but was away, sat up all night with two pistols trained on her uninvited guest.

HASTINGS

Battle Abbey: HAROLD'S STONE

As the sun went down here on October 15, 1066, Harold of England, his right eye pierced by an arrow, fell and is generally believed not to have risen again. (*See* Chester, St. John's Church: The Anchorite's Cell.) The Norman, William the Conqueror, was to be king of England.

In conqueror's fashion, he pitched his tent where his Anglo-Saxon foe had fallen and sat down to eat and drink among the enemy dead.

HAWORTH

The Parsonage

Fortunately, no pupils ever applied to the school that Charlotte and Emily Brontë sought to open here in the 1840s. So instead they and their sister Anne used the time they would have spent with their pupils writing novels. Charlotte wrote *Jane Eyre*; Emily, *Wuthering Heights*; and Anne, *Agnes Grey*.

◆ ◆ ◆

For ten years, the Reverend Arthur Bell Nicholls had waited to marry Charlotte Brontë. For his pains in wishing to marry her and making his intentions known, he had been relieved of his post of assistant curate here by her father, Patrick Brontë, who was the curate.

At first, Charlotte really didn't care. She felt sorry for the young man who had fallen in love with her, but she found him narrow-minded. But after he was forgiven by her father and reinstated in his post, he came to be a familiar figure again in her life. Then Charlotte's sentiments toward the young curate warmed, and in 1854 they were married.

Just a year later, weak, ill, and expecting their first child, Charlotte was asking her husband to pray to God to save her life. "He will not separate us. We have been so happy," Charlotte pleaded just before she died.

HELMSLEY

Rievaulx Abbey

In the fourteenth century this remote Cistercian abbey was a gloomy, lonesome place. It is said that one of its monks, who could no longer abide the loneliness of the site and the rigidity of the order, fled from it. He went into the woods, but they soon seemed darker than the abbey he had left. He crossed cold wading streams, he became entangled in thickets, and he had to climb height after height. There was no sign of any human habitation. Suddenly, in the darkness all about him, he heard the

ringing of a bell and, following the sound, found a building.

It turned out that the building was his abbey. Weeping, he begged forgiveness for ever having left and sought
reentry. Clearly, he said, it was the will of God that had
led him back to his starting point.

ISLE OF WIGHT

Cowes: OSBORNE HOUSE

Ordinarily, a stay on the Isle of Wight made the aging
Queen Victoria feel refreshed and bright, but the winter
of 1901, when she was eighty-one, seemed a different
story.

She wasn't seeing and sleeping well. The weather was
cold, wet, and foggy, making her feel even worse. A doc-
tor was sent for. But the queen who had ruled the British
Empire for sixty-four years rallied only once—to ask if
her Pomeranian dog could join her on her bed. Then, on
January 17, as darkness fell, the spirits of the mighty
monarch, Victoria, seemed to darken too. At 6:30 P.M. on
January 17, she died in the arms of her beloved grandson,
Germany's Kaiser Wilhelm II. He would soon be callously bringing the First World War to his grandmother's
land.

Ryde

The proprietor of the York Hotel that September 1870
morning was distinctly startled by the incessant rapping
at the hotel door. It was too late for overnight guests to be
arriving—much too early for a daytime arrival. But the
wind was howling and the rain was pelting. Clearly,
some extraordinary circumstance had brought the two
watersoaked, bedraggled women and the man to the hotel
door.

But little did he know as he took them up to his best
suite of rooms how extraordinary the adventure had been
that had taken them out into the storm. One of the
women was France's Empress Eugénie, wife of Napoleon

III. The night before, with the crowd outside the Tuileries Palace crying for a republic and shouting "Down with the Empire," she and an attendant had managed to escape into the street, hire a taxi to flee the crowd, and find temporary refuge with an American dentist. Then, with the empress playing the role of an insane woman en route to an asylum, the dentist had taken the "patient" to Deauville where they had been accepted aboard an English yacht and brought across the Channel in a raging storm.

Their stay here at the York was brief—just long enough to dry out their wet clothes and sleep a little. Then they were on their way to Hastings to meet the emperor, who had made his own sensational escape.

ISLES OF SCILLY

St. Mary's: PORT HELLICK

Admiral Sir Cloudesley Shovel was drowned, and his body washed up here in 1707, after his flagship and three other ships in his fleet were wrecked on nearby rocks in fog.

Thirty years later, after he had been buried in Westminster Abbey with full naval honors, a woman of St. Mary's admitted to having found Sir Cloudesley while he was still alive. But on his finger gleamed an emerald ring for which she longed, so she had killed him and taken the ring. In corroboration of her story, she produced the ring she had slipped from the admiral's finger.

Tresco

Toward the end of the last century, when maritime interests here were declining and a severe economic depression was setting in, a resident, looking out on his wide expanse of blossoming flowers early one spring, wondered if there might be money in them. He cut some of his narcissus and stock and sent it off to Covent Garden in his wife's hatbox. By return mail, he received not only payment for his flowers but a request for more. And so began the flower exports from this island, where spring comes first to Britain. More than one thousand tons of flowers are shipped annually.

KENILWORTH
Kenilworth Castle

Fireworks and bonfires, jousting, and rafting on the lake were all part of the welcome Robert Dudley, the Earl of Leicester, gave to Queen Elizabeth here in 1575.

For seventeen days, the Virgin Queen remained with her favorite at this castle that she had given him. Gossips of the day whispered about how the earl had "helped" his wife, Amy Robsart, fall down the stairs to her death to free him for Elizabeth.

Even though Elizabeth never found it politic to marry him, no one close to them could help noticing their mutual affection. It was said that when Elizabeth was honoring him with his earldom, she playfully tickled the back of his neck during the ceremony.

KESWICK

The serious-minded nineteenth-century poet Robert Southey, in his years here, worked a long, hard day. He told a visitor once that he rose at 5 A.M., read Spanish from 6 to 8 A.M., then read French and Portuguese for half an hour each. Next, he wrote poetry for two hours and prose for two hours after that. Finally, he would do translating "and so on," he explained.

But he did find time for a little lighthearted tomfoolery when he wrote the story of "Goldilocks and the Three Bears."

KNUTSFORD
Knutsford Chapel

One day a bear ambled into this chapel, climbed into the

pulpit, and placed a paw upon the Scriptures. Learning of this disrespectful event, the horrified bishop is said to have closed the chapel for a year and then had it reconsecrated.

LAND'S END

As legend has it, once upon a time this was not the end of the land. Instead, where the sea thunders today, existed Lyonesse, with 140 villages on it.

But one day the tumultuous sea broke over it, sweeping its houses and people away. Only one man escaped to tell those on the Cornwall mainland his horrific story.

LEICESTER

Bow Bridge

As Richard III crossed Bow Bridge on August 21, 1485 to do battle with the Welsh prince, Henry Tudor, it is said that one spur struck a stone on the bridge's side. An old crone who was watching remarked that when Richard returned, it would be the king's head that would strike on the stone.

And on the next day, after he had been killed in battle (*See* Market Bosworth, Bosworth Field), the king's naked corpse was flung over a horse's back and brought here, striking the stone on the original of this bridge, as the crone had prophesied.

LINCOLN

Lincoln Cathedral: ANGEL CHOIR

To honor the canonized Hugh of Avalon, who served as bishop here in the twelfth century, this Angel Choir with its mischievous imp was carved. The imp, reportedly, was so naughty a child that he was turned into stone to put an end to his pranks.

LONDON

Apsley House (Hyde Park Corner)

Annually, from the time he bought this house in 1817 until his death in 1852, the Duke of Wellington and the generals who had aided him at the battle of Waterloo would celebrate their great victory over Napoleon on June 18, its anniversary, with a sumptuous banquet.

Among the paintings looking grandly down on them as they dined was a Goya painting of Wellington on horseback that had been taken from Napoleon's brother, Joseph. Celebrating as they were, no one ever thought to question how it happened that Joseph Bonaparte had a painting of Wellington in his house. Recently, art historians have discovered that he didn't. Though it is Wellington who appears to the viewer's eye, beneath his likeness is that of Joseph Bonaparte. Overpainting Joseph with Wellington was the politic painter's afterthought.

Apsley House: STATUE OF NAPOLEON

Napoleon hadn't liked it because the Winged Victory carved in his right hand seemed to be flying away from him. But for that very reason this Antonio Canova statue of the French emperor seemed more than appropriate as a royal gift for Lord Wellington, the man who had defeated him. So Britain's Prince Regent, who became George IV, bought it from the Louvre and presented it to the hero of Waterloo.

Banqueting House (Whitehall)

It was through a first-floor window here on January 20, 1649, that Charles I stepped to the scaffold. (Solicitously, the night before, his captors had allowed him to sleep at St. James's Palace so he would not hear the sound of the hammers that were being used to erect the scaffold.)

Before he set out for Whitehall, Charles asked his barber to take pains with his beard clipping, even though his head had such a short time to remain on his shoulders. Next, he asked for three shirts to wear on his walk from the palace to Whitehall. He did not wish onlookers to mistake as cowardice any shivering that he might do from the cold. Then he, his dog, and his guards set out across St. James's Park. Though he had a speech prepared to give, when the king reached the scaffold he discovered that the crowd assembled was too far away to hear his words, so he spoke only to those immediately around him. The only recorded word of those he spoke before the executioner's axe fell was an enigmatic, "Remember."

147 Bond Street

In the house that occupied this site in 1797 a grim, disheartened Lord Horatio Nelson wintered, adjusting to the loss of his right eye in a battle at Corsica and the loss of his right arm fighting in the Canaries. He had gallantly said in Tenerife, as he lay with his shattered arm, that he had "two legs and one arm yet." Here in a dank, dark London winter, he was not so sanguine. He felt, he said then, "dead to his country and the world."

But his greatest victory—his defeat of the French at Trafalgar—was still to come.

Bow Church or St. Mary-Le-Bow

As the legend goes, only those born within the sound of Bow Bells are genuine Cockneys. The bells were shattered in 1941, during World War II (thereby causing a twenty-year hiatus in the birth of true Cockneys). In 1961 they were recast and are again resounding.

◆ ◆ ◆

Though the crowd below looked on in awe that day in 1674 when Sir Christopher Wren's 217-foot-high spire was topped by a dragon weathercock with a live man riding on it, the feat was nothing at all for an acrobat. Stuntman Jacob Hall deemed it the least he could do to honor Wren and his creation.

British Museum: BRITISH LIBRARY—READING ROOM

Unless he had to pawn his own clothes that day for food for his family, the bearded social philosopher Karl Marx, a refugee from Prussia, was certain to be bent over books here in the 1850s. For sixteen hours at a stretch Marx would research and write so that in 1859 the first volume of his *Das Kapital*, the foundation of international Marxism, could appear.

British Museum: DUVEEN GALLERY

Thomas Bruce, the Earl of Elgin, hardly profited by his sale of a dozen statues and fifty-six pieces of frieze from the Acropolis in Athens in the early years of the nineteenth century. He had bought these monumental treasures of antiquity in Greece for £50,000. When the British Parliament finally agreed to purchase them for display, it offered the British diplomat only £35,000.

British Museum: FIRST ROMAN ROOM—
THE PORTLAND VASE

It took almost a century before this first-century blown glass vase with a cameo design could be satisfactorily repaired after a madman smashed it to pieces here in 1845. John Keats had made it famous in his 1819 "Ode on a Grecian Urn."

Buckingham Palace

The Germans said they hadn't intended to strike it in their World War II blitz of the capital. It was a mistake in navigation, they insisted. Nonetheless, six bombs were dropped at Buckingham Palace one day when George VI and Queen Elizabeth, normally outside the city at Windsor, were here. The king kept careful count as the bombs struck the forecourt, the quadrangle, the chapel, and the garden. The doughty queen remarked when it was over, and they both were safe, that she was rather glad it had happened. After that, she said, when she visited devastated neighborhoods of the city, she wouldn't be ashamed to look people in the face.

Cabinet War Rooms (Clive Steps, King Charles Street)

It wasn't easy keeping Prime Minister Winston Churchill inside this underground bastion when the German bombs of World War II were thudding overhead, demolishing buildings of this city, and killing its people. As soon as a bombing raid ended, the prime minister wanted to be out inspecting the damage and extending his own courage to his fellow-Londoners by face-to-face contact.

When his valet tried once to keep him from such an excursion by hiding his shoes, the determined Churchill reportedly exclaimed that when he was a child his nursemaid had never been able to keep him from walking in Green Park when he wanted. Now that he was a man, Adolf Hitler certainly wouldn't keep him out of the park, either.

It is not reported whether his shoes were surrendered, but, cigar in hand, the rotund prime minister was soon out in the streets and parks again.

Carlyle's House (24 Cheyne Row, Chelsea)

One night in the 1830s, there was a light tap on the door here, which historian Thomas Carlyle recognized as that of his close friend, the philosopher John Stuart Mill. A few weeks earlier, the historian had lent the philosopher the only manuscript of the first volume of his *History of the French Revolution*. Carlyle opened the door with enthusiasm, eager to hear Mill's response to his work.

Pale and haggard, Mill stood before Carlyle in the faint light and told him that the manuscript was gone. Taking it for scrap paper, Mill's housekeeper had burned the manuscript in the fire.

16 Cheyne Walk (Chelsea)

Romantic, exotic Dante Gabriel Rossetti, Pre-Raphaelite painter and poet (*See* London Outskirts, Highgate Cemetery—Grave of Elizabeth Rossetti), spent his last days in this handsome house, along with the equally exotic pets he kept in the garden: a kangaroo, a white peacock, a Brahma bull whose soulful eyes reminded Rossetti of a woman he loved, an armadillo, and a wombat said to have inspired the dormouse in Lewis Carroll's *Alice's Adventures in Wonderland*. And here he drank and ate too much (his breakfast of five eggs and congealed bacon was said to have been more than novelist-housemate George Meredith could bear, so they parted company). Finally, in 1882, Rossetti died here of an overdose of the whiskey and chloral he had taken to combat his sleepless and fearful nights.

119 Cheyne Walk (Chelsea)

He was known as Admiral Booth, the rather strange old man who lived here from 1848 to 1851. As the sun rose, early risers in the neighborhood would sometimes see him clad in a dressing gown, standing on the roof, watching dawn streak the sky. They knew he drank too much. What they did not know was that he was Joseph Mallord William Turner, one of the greatest painters England ever produced and whose glowing paintings of sea and sky fill the new Clore Gallery at the Tate.

Cleopatra's Needle (Embankment Gardens)

It took three-quarters of a century for this pink granite obelisk to complete its journey here from Alexandria, Egypt. Six men entrusted with its care died during the journey. For a time, it tossed unattended in the stormy Bay of Biscay.

The adventures of Cleopatra's Needle actually began in 23 B.C. That was when Caesar Augustus ordered that the monument—which then stood in front of the Temple of the Sun God at Heliopolis, where it had been erected in 1450 B.C.—be moved to Alexandria. He wanted it re-erected in front of the palace where Cleopatra had died. There this 68½-foot tall obelisk remained until Britain defeated Napoleon in Egypt in 1798. Eager to have a trophy of their victory, the English knocked the obelisk down, preparing to bring it here. But it proved too heavy to move and was left where it had fallen.

Twenty-two years later, the ruler of Egypt, Mehemet Ali, offered the obelisk as a gift in honor of George IV, newly crowned king of England. But the gift was turned down then and several times later. Not until the land on which it lay was sold, and the purchaser threatened to break the obelisk up, were private funds raised to move it to England.

To transport it, a metal cylinder was constructed that was to be towed from Alexandria.

At last, in 1877, behind the tugboat *Olga*, Cleopatra's Needle was launched in its steel case. Out of Alexandria harbor and into the Bay of Biscay it bobbed. But there, in a heavy storm sea, it yawed uncontrollably, and fears rose that it would capsize the tug, so it was cut loose. When it was abandoned, eight crewmen were on a super-structure attached to it.

In order to save them, a lifeboat was launched—and lost. All six men aboard the lifeboat were drowned.

Still the saga continued. A steamer that was in the neighborhood was alerted to be on the lookout for the men and the cylinder with its historic contents. The steamer did find the cylinder and managed to tow it into a Spanish port. It was delayed there for another three months. Then finally in 1878, it arrived here and was lowered into place. Attached to it was a plaque to the memory of the seamen lost saving the Needle.

The Cross (Charing Cross Station)

In war, Edward I, the Hammer of the Scots, was known for his ferocity and his relentlessness. But in matters of the heart, he was gentle and devoted. When his wife, Eleanor of Castile, died in 1291 in Nottinghamshire, the sorrowing king had crosses erected wherever the funeral procession paused. This one outside the railroad station is an 1860s version of the last of these crosses.

Dickens's House (48 Doughty Street, Holborn)

Charles and Kate Dickens and Kate's seventeen-year-old sister, Mary Hogarth, had just returned from the theater that May night in 1837 when Mary suddenly had a seizure and died in Dickens's arms. For two months, the grief-stricken writer could not work. His "young, beautiful, and good" sister-in-law, as Dickens described her in her epitaph, became the model for Little Nell in *The Old Curiosity Shop*. It is said that Charles's and Kate's marriage never recovered fully from that death. In Dickens's eyes, Kate could not manage to be as pure and as good as her sweet little sister.

Guildhall (King Street)

Mayor Dick Whittington's guests of honor for his grand banquet here were Henry V and Queen Catherine. Eager to please, the merchant-mayor-banker (*See* London Outskirts, Highgate Hill—Whittington Stone) heated the banquet hall with a fire built of rare woods sprinkled with fragrant spices. When the king complimented Whittington on the perfumed fire, remarking on his abilities as a host, Whittington the Banker went one better than Whittington the Host. Over the years he had lent Henry a considerable sum of money. Suddenly the Lord Mayor withdrew from a strongbox the bonds that would ensure the king's repayment. Tearing them into pieces, with great éclat, Whittington tossed them all into the fire, thereby absolving Henry of his debts.

Guildhall: GOG AND MAGOG

Once upon a time, it is said, two giant grandsons of the Roman Emperor Diocletian, after fiercely fighting Trojan invaders to England, were captured and chained here. These nine-foot wooden representations of them, many times made and many times replaced, used to be carried in processions of the Lord Mayor. When St. Paul's bells strike twelve, legend has it, Gog and Magog leave their posts by the Council Chamber door and go into the Guildhall to eat dinner.

Houses of Parliament

One cold night in 1834, a batch of the old wooden tallies that had been used in earlier days to keep track of Parliamentary exchequer accounts were pulled out of their storage place and used to stoke a stove in the House of Lords. The first stoker proved too zealous. Soon the House of Lords was in flames; then the neighboring House of Commons, too, was ablaze.

En route from Brighton to London on the train that evening, a young architect, Charles Barry, exclaimed at the blaze that lit the whole London sky. Arriving in the city, he discovered that the conflagration had engulfed virtually all of England's seat of government. Only Westminster Hall remained. Just then, there was nothing to do but grieve at the loss. But Barry's grief was short-lived.

Obviously there was need for a new Parliament House. He set himself to the task of designing it, and a little more than a year later, it was announced that the young man from Brighton was the winner of the architectural competition instituted to decide who would build the new Houses of Parliament.

For the next twenty-six years, Barry worked on the project, assisted by the talented draughtsman Augustus Welby Pugin. But the two men's work was criticized and monies held back, and neither one was to live to see the great work completed. Eight years before it was done, Pugin died in an insane asylum, driven mad, it was said, by overwork. Barry's son, who completed the task, always said that overwork killed his father, too.

Houses of Parliament: BIG BEN

For fifteen years in the mid-nineteenth century, there was fussing and fuming over which clock maker would have the honor of designing the clock whose bell was to become virtually the symbol of London.

First in 1844, the Queen's clock maker was asked to undertake the task; but he never seemed to get to it. After two years of waiting, an open competition was held for a design.

The competitors set to work. For the next six years they experimented. But still the clock was not put in place. It was not until seven years later that booming Big Ben's voice was first heard.

As the story goes, heaving this thirteen-and-a-half-ton bell into position in the 1850s, the workmen dubbed it Big Ben after Benjamin Count, the champion prize-fighter of his day. The 340-pound Count had caught popular fancy by lasting sixty rounds on his first appearance in the ring. Adulation for him was such that the heaviest of everything was soon being called "Big Ben."

◆   ◆   ◆

Since 1859, when the voice of Big Ben was first heard booming from its clock tower, only the deaths of three kings, World War I, and annual overhauls have, by prearrangement, altered the hourly tolling of this great bell. But now and again, "natural" accidents have stilled it. The most notable were snow that froze on it on New Year's Eve, 1961; a gathering of starlings at dusk in 1949; and a workman whose foot got in the way of the mechanism at some unrecorded time.

Houses of Parliament: THE HOUSE OF COMMONS— CHURCHILL ARCH

On the night of May 10, 1941, during the Battle of Britain, three hundred German bombers swept over London, their bombs thudding with precision on historic targets, including Parliament's House of Commons. When the raid had ended, and the debris was being swept away, Prime Minister Winston Churchill proposed that this archway should remain in its damaged state, to remind future Englishmen of those who had "kept the bridge in the brave days of old."

Kensington Gardens

Here the pink-cheeked, three-year-old Alexandrina Victoria, the future Queen Victoria, enjoyed rides on a much-beribboned pet donkey that was a gift from the Duke of York.

Kensington Gardens: THE SERPENTINE

It was in this pretty artificial waterway, created from a string of ponds by George II's wife, Queen Caroline, that Harriet Westbrook Shelley, an innkeeper's daughter with whom young Percy Bysshe Shelley had eloped five years before, drowned herself in 1816. She was disconsolate over the poet's love for Mary Wollstonecraft Godwin. Her depression was warranted, for Mary soon became Shelley's next wife.

Kensington Palace

Because a gypsy fortuneteller in Gibraltar had told the Duke of Kent, the fourth son of George III, that one day he would have a child who would be a great queen, he hastened here from Germany when he learned that his wife was expecting. It was a long, hard journey with the duke, his duchess, Victoria of Saxe-Coburg, her teenage daughter by an earlier marriage, nurses and maids, and pets all cooped together in one carriage. But they made it in time for the birth here of Alexandrina Victoria on May 24, 1819. As Queen Victoria, she was to be the longest reigning monarch in English history.

◆ ◆ ◆

No servant wished to disturb the slumbering eighteen-year-old Princess Victoria at five o'clock in the morning on June 20, 1837, when the Archbishop of Canterbury and England's Lord Chamberlain came here to tell her that William IV was dead and that she was Queen of England. The bearers of the news pounded first at the palace gate before they could rouse the sentry. Then, once inside, they were forced to ring again and again before they could find anyone willing to awaken the sleeping princess. And when finally she did appear, the young woman who would be England's ruler for nearly seventy-nine years, was still in her white nightdress, her hair tumbling over her shoulders.

Kensington Palace: THE KING'S GALLERY

Afternoon after afternoon, before the fireplace here, William III and his royal guest Peter the Great of Russia, both shy, both scientific, tippled and talked together when Peter came to learn something of the art of British shipbuilding. Nearly as interesting to Peter as were his visits to the shipyards was watching the apparatus installed above the fireplace that allowed William, a sufferer from asthma, to know indoors what the weather was like outdoors and whether it was clement enough for him to leave the palace.

Lincoln's Inn (Chancery Lane)

Oliver Cromwell's visit here on a deadly mission had a happy ending after all.

Cromwell's secretary, James Thurloe, kept rooms here from 1646 to 1659. Cromwell was rising in power but had not yet toppled King Charles I (*See* Banqueting House), and one evening he stopped in for a talk. As the story goes, he was proposing to kidnap the king's children and use them to control their father.

The two men whispered for some time about the plot. Suddenly, Cromwell noticed his secretary's clerk asleep in a corner. Was he *really* asleep, Cromwell wondered, and had he been the whole evening? Thurloe assured him that the clerk was a sound sleeper. Cromwell was not convinced. The news of the plot must not get out. The clerk had best be done away with, Cromwell said. Thurloe pleaded for his friend's life. To assure Cromwell that the clerk was indeed sleeping, Thurloe drew the dagger Cromwell had ready to kill the clerk back and forth over the "sleeping" man's face. The clerk did not stir. Finally, a reassured Cromwell went home, leaving the clerk unharmed.

As it turned out, the stalwart clerk had indeed been wide awake during the discussion. Knowing, however, that death was certain if he had flinched, he had managed not to move a muscle as the dagger was passed across his nose. Word was sent to the king that his children were in danger, and appropriate precautions were taken.

Madame Tussaud's (Marylebone Road)

When she was eighty-one, in 1842, Marie Gresholtz Tussaud modeled the last wax figure for her waxworks exhibition, and it was her own.

In a lifetime of wax modeling, much of it done to stay clear of the guillotine in Paris during the Reign of Terror, she had made death masks of best friends. The fresh-cut heads of royalty were, it is said, among those brought to her. Later, when the tide of revolution turned, Charlotte Corday's and Robespierre's heads were among those that the diminutive woman with the skillful hands was instructed to model.

Though born in Strasbourg, Marie Gresholtz was brought up in Paris by a renowned modeler of wax who taught the little girl his trade. She became so expert that she was sent to the court of Louis XVI to teach her art to the king's youngest sister.

But from there, she went to prison as a royalist and to the ugly business of modeling heads of the executed as propaganda for the Republican cause.

When the Revolution ended, and a marriage she had entered into failed, she brought her two sons and her head collection to England. After touring with them for a while, she established the forerunner of this museum in 1835. Ever since then, Madame Tussaud's Waxwork Exhibition has been one of London's leading tourist attractions.

Marble Arch

Though it stands impressively here today near the Speakers' Corner of Hyde Park, this arch is neither where it was meant to be nor looking as it was supposed to look.

John Nash designed it, after the Arch of Constantine in Rome, to commemorate the victories over Napoleon at Waterloo and Trafalgar and also to be the entrance gate to Buckingham Palace. For its top, proud George IV commissioned an equestrian statue of himself.

The arch proved too tight a squeeze for the state coach to get through, and in 1851, as something of a white elephant, it was moved to this site from the Buckingham Palace grounds. As for the statue, it never got to the top of the arch either, but stands in Trafalgar Square instead.

◆ ◆ ◆

It was on a snowy January 31, 1661, twelve years almost to the day after the execution of Charles I, that what remained of the body of Oliver Cromwell, the man responsible for the king's death, was dug out of its Westminster Abbey grave and hauled near here by sledge to be exhibited. (*See* London, Westminster Hall.) For a day, it dangled from the gallows that stood nearby, and passersby who had heralded the return of the monarchy under Charles II shouted derisively at it. Then it was cut down and tossed into a pit beneath what is now this arch.

The Monument (Fish Street Hill near
Eastcheap and Gracechurch Streets)

The night of September 1, 1666 Thomas Farriner, the king's baker, was weary. He thought, he said later, that he had put out the coal fire in the ovens of his bakeshop in Pudding Lane before he went to bed. It turned out, as virtually all of the City of London was soon to discover, that he hadn't.

About one the following morning, he was roughly roused from his bed by a servant. His room was thick with smoke from the bakeshop below. Heat from the oven had ignited kindling lying nearby. It, in turn, had ignited the grease, oil, and paper that also are part of a bakeshop. Farriner, his wife, his daughter, and the servant fled through a garret window, leaving behind a maid who died in the fire.

It was only minutes before a spark from the bakery roof ignited a pile of hay in a neighboring inn yard. The conflagration had begun. Fanned by a strong wind, fed by the timber houses set close together along the narrow lanes and by the contents of the warehouses on Thames Street edging the river, the flames leapt from building to building. Frantically, householders sought to put out the flames with buckets of water and by tearing down burning timbers with firehooks; but their efforts were useless. Family after family fled their homes for tenders on the river or sought to save household goods by flinging them into the water. The flames swept on.

It was not until a couple of mornings later that the

action which finally stopped the fire was taken. Whole streets were blown up on government orders to make gaps that the flames could not leap over. By September 5 the Great Fire stopped burning, leaving nothing of thirteen thousand houses but charred timbers. One hundred thousand people had lost their homes; eight people were dead; and some four hundred thirty-eight acres had become charred rubble and ash.

To commemorate the terrible event, this 202-foot monument was designed by Sir Christopher Wren in the 1670s. If it were laid flat in the right direction it would stretch to the start of the fire on Pudding Lane.

◆   ◆   ◆

How tempting it has been over the years to have a 202-foot-high monument from which to perform deeds of derring-do in the heart of London town. One evening in 1732, awed bystanders reported that a sailor "flew" with the aid of a rope from the monument's top to a tavern in neighboring Gracechurch Street in less than half a minute. The year before that, a waiter, on a wager from some of his tavern customers, ran up the 311 steps to the top of the monument and down again in two and a half minutes and two seconds.

National Gallery: PEACE AND WAR— SEVENTEENTH-CENTURY FLEMISH ROOM

Peter Paul Rubens's role as a diplomatic representative to the English Court from Antwerp in 1629 involved more than polite conversations. Artist as well as diplomat, he presented this allegory that depicted the joys of peace to Charles I. Art collector Charles accepted it with enthusiasm; but after his execution (*See* London, Banqueting House), it was disposed of for a meager £100. Some years later, however, when Rubens was back in fashion and Charles's excesses were largely forgotten, it was bought back for this national collection for £3,000.

National Gallery: PORTRAIT OF CHRISTINA OF DENMARK—NETHERLANDISH ROOM

Toying with marrying the Duchess Christina of Denmark after the death of Jane Seymour, his third wife, Henry VIII commissioned this portrait by his court painter, Hans Holbein the Younger. As it turned out, Henry never married Christina, ostensibly for political reasons. There is also a tale, however, that the chary duchess, remembering the fate of Anne Boleyn (*See* London, Tower of London: King's House), wrote to the king to say that she had but one head. If she had had two, she said generously, one would happily be at the service of His Majesty.

Nelson's Column (Trafalgar Square)

The fourteen stonemasons who celebrated the erection of this 167-foot-high column surely dined with a view. Perched on its top, they shared either beans or a rump steak (reports of the menu differ). The dinner was served twelve days before the statue of Nelson, victor against the French at the Battle of Trafalgar, was put in place on top in 1841.

The Old Bailey
(Holborn Viaduct and Old Bailey Street)

Prisoners, judges, aldermen—even the Lord Mayor—died from the noisome gaol fever that in 1750 swept through Newgate, the prison that then stood on this spot. For nearly two centuries afterward, to dispel suspected odors, nosegays were carried by judges and sheriffs from May to September, and sweet herbs were sprinkled about.

Piccadilly Circus

Here in the sixteenth century, master tailor Robert Baker specialized in making the shirt frills called pickadills that were popular with Elizabethan gentlemen. So successful was he in his work that, in time, he was able to build an elegant house here. Grateful to the pickadills that had provided the money for it, he called his mansion Piccadilly Hall, hence today's name.

Picadilly Circus: SHAFTESBURY MEMORIAL OR EROS FOUNTAIN

When young Alfred Gilbert, the designer of this fountain, went for a last look at the dawn of its unveiling in 1893, he and the two companions he took with him after a celebratory dinner party were turned away by the workmen who had the fountain hidden under canvas. Three tipsy men in formal dinner attire, insisting, as the sun rose, that they must see the new fountain, since one of them was its sculptor, just weren't to be believed, the workmen said later.

The Royal Hospital (Royal Hospital Road, Chelsea)

Had it not been for the actress Nell Gwynn, mistress of King Charles II, this extensive veterans' hospital that Sir Christopher Wren designed might never have come into being.

Legend has it that Nell's coach was stopped one day by a crippled war veteran begging for money. Tenderhearted Nell could not forget the encounter and did not rest until she had wheedled her royal lover into having this hospital built.

St. Bartholomew the Great (West Smithfield)

Among the merriest of the merrymakers at the court of Henry I was the minstrel, Rahere—a witty conversationalist, a talented musician, a charmer of men and women alike. In that court where the king was the father of twenty illegitimate children by a half-dozen mistresses,

Rahere was right at home. But virtually overnight the atmosphere of the court changed. Henry's only legitimate son was drowned at sea, and the king sank into a deep depression. Those around him, in the fashion of the day, followed suit. Rahere was among them. He laid aside song and gaiety and set off on a pilgrimage to Rome. There he contracted malaria, and, near death, promised that if he recovered he would build a hospital for the poor when he returned to England.

In the throes of his fever, as he later told it, he was grasped in the talons of a winged creature and carried off to be dropped in a bottomless pit. But St. Bartholomew intervened, and, in exchange for saving Rahere's life, asked the minstrel to build a church at Smithfield.

Returned home, Rahere hastened to Henry with St. Bartholomew's request, and Henry gave him a tract of wasteland here—all mud and stagnant water but for a single dry spot that was used for executions. But none of that mattered to Rahere. Off he went throughout the city, seeking others who were devout to help him clean up the land so that a church, a priory, and the hospital could be erected. And in 1123 he began building. The present structure is a nineteenth century restoration. Except for the Chapel of St. John at the Tower of London, this is the oldest church in London.

St. Bride's (Fleet Street)

Although the graceful steeple of St. Bride's Church, Fleet Street, which has been lauded as "a madrigal in stone," didn't start the American Revolution, it might have.

In 1764, it was damaged by lightning and lost eight feet. King George III wished to make certain this would never happen again, so he sought the opinion of experts. Among them was the American Benjamin Franklin, inventor of the lightning rod.

Franklin advised the positioning of pointed lightning rods. Regardless of what Franklin said, the king, who had blunt ones on all his palaces, insisted that blunt rods should be installed. Americans were rebellious and didn't know anything, he appended. To support his own opinion against that of the outrageous American, the king called in an English scientist, Sir John Pringle, the president of the Royal Society.

Pringle tried hard to agree with His Majesty, emphasizing that he always wished to execute the king's wishes, but he affirmed that pointed rods were clearly better. Much as he might like to please the king, he could not alter the laws of Nature.

A disgruntled George III relieved Pringle of his Society post. Had the "rebellious" American, Franklin, held a position of which the king *could* have relieved him, he surely would have.

The records do not say which lightning rods were finally installed.

◆ ◆ ◆

An early nineteenth-century baker named Rich is said to have become rich in fact as well as in name by making tiered wedding cakes designed after the steeple of this masterpiece by Sir Christopher Wren.

St. James's Palace (Pall Mall and St. James Street)

For a week here the Earl of Southampton watched over the embalmed body of Catholic King Charles I, whose downfall and execution in 1649 had been the work of Puritan Oliver Cromwell. One night as he watched, a mysterious visitor came to the coffin, his face hidden under the cloak he wore. His voice was muffled—but not so muffled, the earl reported later, that he did not recognize it. It was Oliver Cromwell himself, the earl always insisted, who stood beside the coffin shaking his head and murmured to the body of the king simply,"Cruel necessity."

◆ ◆ ◆

Here, two-year-old Samuel Johnson was touched by Queen Anne in 1712 in order to be cured of the King's

Evil, scrofula, a disease of the lymph glands. In later years, he could only remember of the event "a lady with diamonds and a long black hood."

St. James's Park

In Charles I's day, in this royal garden browsed the herd of deer he liked to hunt. But when Oliver Cromwell came to power, in a proper plebeian way, it was his wife's cows who grazed these lands, for Mrs. Cromwell liked fresh milk at the dining table.

◆ ◆ ◆

Because he was so fond of dogs, King Charles II was sometimes called the King of Curs. In this palace garden that he opened to his subjects, he walked his beloved spaniels, fed the ducks he had introduced to the ponds, and chatted with his fellow passersby.

Those days when he was feeling especially buoyant, he would stop to play *paille-maille*, a French croquet-like game that gave its name to today's Pall Mall, or to talk with his pretty mistress, the actress Nell Gwynn, to whom he had given a house conveniently set beside this favorite royal strolling place.

St. Margaret's Church (Parliament Square)

Here, in 1656, the blind poet John Milton took Katherine Woodcocke to be his bride and mother to his three motherless daughters. A little more than a year later, he stood here at her funeral. Both Katherine and their child had died in childbirth.

Renowned as a sonneteer, the sorrowing poet went home to write "On His Deceased Wife," his last sonnet.

St. Margaret's Church: THE EAST WINDOW

To celebrate their delight at the marriage of their daughter, Catherine of Aragon, to Arthur, the Prince of Wales, Ferdinand and Isabella of Spain had this window of the

crucifixion—with portraits of the teenage pair on it—
made in Flanders in 1501 for the princess's father-in-law.
But by the time it arrived, the fifteen-year-old bride was
already affianced to Arthur's brother, the future Henry
VIII, whose distaste for her and divorce from her was to
turn all of England topsy-turvy.

St. Margaret's Church: THE HIGH ALTAR

It was in the old Palace Yard that in 1618 a proud Sir
Walter Raleigh, condemned to death by James I for al-
leged conspiracy (*See* Tower of London, Bloody Tower),
asked the executioner if he might feel the axe. Touching
its blade, he smiled and remarked, "This is sharp medicine; but it is a physician for all diseases." The sheriff
asked which way Raleigh would lay his head. "So as the
heart be right, it matters not which way the head lies,"
Raleigh replied. A few minutes later he was dead.

Immediately, his body was hurried here for burial beneath the altar, for he was a popular hero, and prompt
burial was deemed wise to prevent rioting.

His head was taken away in a red leather bag by his
grieving widow, and for the next twenty-nine years—
until she died—she kept it with her. Then Raleigh's son,
Carew, kept it with him until his death. It is believed to
have accompanied him to his grave in this churchyard.

St. Martin-in-the-Fields (Trafalgar Square)

When this church was being grandly rebuilt in the mid-
eighteenth century, King George I's generosity was
hardly repaid in kind.

Thinking that he would be helpful, the king contributed £29,000 toward the James Gibbs design. Pleased,
and thinking that they would be pleasing the king, parishioners made him a church warden. That was hardly,
however, a post fit for a king. George I would have liked
to resign, but resignations from the office were not al-

lowed. In the king's case, it was finally decided to make an exception, but not until poor George had paid a £1,000 fine for failing to fulfill his church warden duties.

St. Marylebone Church (Marylebone Road)

It was a sunny September day in 1846, and the poet Elizabeth Barrett's tyrannical father and the rest of the household were going out for a picnic. Never hardy since a childhood fall from a horse, Elizabeth said she preferred to stay at home.

There was a harangue from her father about taking proper care of herself. Then the family left as they had intended.

Barely was the door closed behind them than Elizabeth and her maid were scurrying about, dressing Elizabeth for her secret wedding day.

They slipped into a cab that brought them here, where the forty-year-old bride was wed to her fellow poet, thirty-six-year-old Robert Browning. It was back home immediately afterward before Elizabeth's father returned. The idea of her marrying was one that he could not abide.

One week later, Elizabeth fled again. This time it was for fifteen years of the happiest of married lives with the man who loved her "for love's sake . . . through loves' eternity," as she had asked him to in one of her poems.

Her father never forgave her for her abandonment.

St. Paul's Cathedral (Ludgate Hill)

In old St. Paul's which occupied this site from 1240 until 1666, Elizabeth I gave thanks for and celebrated the defeat of the Spanish Armada. She made her grand entrance—right into the cathedral—in a carriage drawn by four white horses, with heralds trumpeting.

◆ ◆ ◆

Few tears were shed when old St. Paul's was burned beyond repair in the Great Fire of 1666. (*See* London,

The Monument.) For some two centuries it had been variously used as a public market, a ball park, and a wrestling ground. In 1441, a proclamation had to be issued forbidding wrestling in it. In the Civil War, the cathedral was used as a horse stable; the tombstones were used as gaming tables; and the aisles as nine-pins courts.

◆ ◆ ◆

Time after time, fire has destroyed the cathedral that occupied this site. In the tenth century, conquering Danes torched the church that stood here. In 1087, the structure that took its place was burned again. In 1561, the steeple of the church's replacement was burned to the ground in a lightning storm. The cathedral was largely rebuilt in 1642. Twenty-four years later, in the Great Fire that almost destroyed the City of London, much of it once again was burned. But St. Paul's, it seems, always rose again from the ashes. When, in 1675, Sir Christopher Wren, the architect of this great domed cathedral, was beginning construction, he asked a workman to hand him a flat stone from the rubble to use in his work. When Wren turned over the stone—a grave marker—he found carved on its surface "*Resurgem*," meaning "I shall rise again." To assure that it always will, Wren incorporated the old gravestone into the cathedral.

◆ ◆ ◆

Sir Christopher Wren was thirty-seven when, after having had three of his designs for the construction of this church turned down, he was finally told in 1669 that he had royal approval to proceed. Forty-one years later, at the end of his task, he was too old and feeble to place the last stone, and his son placed it for him. The years when he had been pulled up and down to the 365-foot high dome in a basket several times a week were long over. But he was pleased with his handiwork, and in the time that remained to him (he lived to be ninety-one), Wren often came to sit quietly here to contemplate his masterpiece. In the crypt where he lies is carved in Latin, "If you seek his monument, look around you." Wren would have been pleased.

To assure that his cathedral would be completed according to his design. Sir Christopher Wren constructed it, not section by section but as a whole. That way, no penny-pinching government could decide that one completed part was big and grand enough to be the whole and stop providing funds for the rest. This method of building prolonged construction, however, and twenty-one years after the cathedral was begun, an impatient Parliament reduced Wren's pay for it by half. The docking did not induce perfectionist Wren to hurry, however. It was another twenty years before St. Paul's was completed.

◆ ◆ ◆

One day when James Thornhill, who painted the scenes from the life of St. Paul that are the main decoration here, stepped back on the scaffolding for a better view of what he had done, a student painter noticed there were only inches between Thornhill and the scaffolding's edge. Frantically, the student grabbed a paintbrush wet with black paint and daubed with it at what Thornhill had just finished. Teetering on the scaffolding, the furious artist leaped forward to protect his work and thus was saved.

◆ ◆ ◆

When good Queen Anne, who is said to have weighed more than three hundred pounds in her late years, came for a look at this great cathedral that was completed during her reign, she reportedly had to be hoisted through the roof of her coach to prevent its tipping over and then had to be carried up the steps in a chair. A statue of Anne in her less hefty days marks the west gate of the cathedral. But even there, more than a century and a half after her death, her sizable girth caused a problem.

In 1897, when plans were being made for Queen Victoria's Diamond Jubilee, that statue stood in the way of the prospective service at the west gate. Permission was asked to move it away—at least temporarily. A huffy Victoria denied the request, replying that that would be precedent-setting. If Queen Anne could be moved, so one day could statues of Victoria herself be shifted about. "And that," she said tartly, "I should most dislike."

St. Paul's Cathedral: THE BALL AND CROSS

It was a lovely party that was held in 1820—albeit at a somewhat precarious site—more than 365 feet in the air. The party was to celebrate the replacement of the original ball and cross on the cathedral dome by a new one. A publication of the day reported that the artisans responsible for the new ball and cross were "seated in the clouds like the deities of Mt. Olympus" and drank a merry toast to the crowd applauding below.

St. Paul's Cathedral: JOHN DONNE MONUMENT— SOUTH CHOIR AISLE

Conscience-stricken after a profligate youth and obsessed with death in his later years, the metaphysical poet John Donne, who was dean of this cathedral from 1621 to 1631, not only bought his own coffin and kept it near at hand in his house, but posed, in his shroud, for the drawing that would become the basis of this memorial.

Following a serious illness in 1623, Donne hired a carver to make the urn on which he wished his statue to stand. Next he hired an artist, asked to be wrapped in a winding sheet and, with his hands and feet placed as those of the dead are in their coffins, posed on the urn with his eyes closed, while his picture was drawn. From then on, he kept the drawing by his bed—a solemn sign of what was sure to come. When he died, the drawing was carved in white marble as his monument.

St. Paul's Cathedral: TOMB OF LORD NELSON— THE CRYPT

The remains of Admiral Lord Nelson, who was killed at the Battle of Trafalgar off Spain in 1805, had a rather extraordinary time getting here. During the long sail home, the body was "pickled" in a barrel of the crew's brandy in order to preserve it for a hero's burial. But no one was quite sure which barrel contained the admiral. Thirsty sailors will be thirsty sailors, and when the *Victory*, with Nelson aboard, finally reached port and the barrels were unloaded, every one of them had been tapped dry. Nelson was hurried off as quickly as possible for interment here—in a conqueror's coffin made from the mainmast of the French ship *L'Orient* that he had set afire off Abu Qir, Egypt, in 1798.

The marble sarcophagus in which the coffin is encased had been designed for Henry VIII's Cardinal Wolsey, but Wolsey fell into disfavor (*See* London Outskirts, Hampton Court, Hampton Court Palace—Gardens) and never occupied it. It was next offered to Henry himself, but he declined it. The long-dead Nelson had no choice.

St. Paul's Cathedral: WELLINGTON'S FUNERAL CARRIAGE—THE CRYPT

It was no wonder that on its way here in 1806 this funeral carriage made of captured cannons that support the remains of the Duke of Wellington, vanquisher of Napoleon at Waterloo, bogged down in the mud of Pall Mall. Although the duke was a small man (only five feet tall—three inches shorter than his French antagonist), Wellington's great admirer, Prince Albert, wanted to be sure that the hero was buried in a style befitting his heroic reputation. So his coffin is six feet and nine inches long, while the bronze carriage, twenty-one feet long, weighs eighteen tons and required twelve horses to draw it.

St. Paul's Church (Covent Garden)

When this church was commissioned in the seventeenth century by tightfisted John Russell, the first Earl of Bedford, he announced to Inigo Jones, the architect he had hired, that he could scarcely afford the price of a barn. "Then," Jones reportedly replied, "you shall have the handsomest barn in England."

Statue of Charles I (Trafalgar Square)

In Cromwellian days, when this handsome statue was discovered in the crypt of St. Paul's Cathedral, it was sold as scrap metal. Its purchaser was said to have broken it up and sold the pieces as relics. But that wasn't true. The "relics" that he sold came from other odds and ends of brass, and Charles's statue was left untouched. When the monarchy was restored, the statue was brought to Charles II's attention. He dutifully bought it and hat it erected here.

Statue of Franklin Delano Roosevelt
(Grosvenor Square)

Within twenty-four hours of the time that fund-raising for this £200,000 statue had been announced in 1945, the required money was in hand. The Britons who paid for it, with maximum contributions of 5 pounds each, were pleased to see the World War II American president so honored.

Statue of Wellington Mounted on Copenhagen
(Hyde Park Corner)

Both in life and in bronze, Copenhagen was a powerful creature. He carried the Duke of Wellington on his back for more than sixteen hours at Waterloo. It took forty horses to haul this bronze figure of Copenhagen to this site.

The Temple (Middle Temple Lane off Fleet Street):
MIDDLE TEMPLE HALL

If William Shakespeare was in the cast and Queen Elizabeth I in the audience as tradition has it, then the February 2, 1602, performance of *Twelfth Night* here must have been memorable indeed.

◆ ◆ ◆

Day after day, after the bombing raid of May 10, 1941 that broke the sixteenth-century carved screen here into thousands of pieces, workers searched for them in the rubble. When they were collected, the fitting together began of what some have called "the biggest jigsaw puzzle in the world." It took the patient puzzle-piecers years before their "puzzle" was in place again.

The Tower of London: BLOODY TOWER

In the spring of 1483, a nervous, twelve-year-old Edward arrived here to await his coronation. Though he had arrived in a grand procession, wearing a mantle of purple velvet, and with his people paying him homage, something seemed wrong. He had been hard at his studies in Wales when word came of the death of his father, Edward IV. A band of soldiers had come to escort him to London. When the little group was only part way there, the young king's uncle, Richard of Gloucester, galloped up with more armed men and took the youth away from his soldier-guards, arresting those who had been in charge of the boy.

Edward asked what they had done wrong, but his uncle paid no attention to him.

Nevertheless, it was pleasant to be going to the royal apartments here, to await his coronation. But there was something ominous in the air. Edward's attendants waited on him courteously. He was fitted for his coronation robes, but he had no real companions—no tutors, no friends. There were still more than two months to wait before his coronation day.

Then, happily for him, his younger brother Richard, the Duke of York, arrived. Richard's arrival, however, confirmed that there was something amiss, for Richard talked to Edward of their mother and her fears for them both. He told Edward how she and their five other brothers and sisters were in the well-fortified Sanctuary near Westminster Palace, praying that Edward would be crowned, but doubting the intentions of his uncle.

They were right. Edward was never crowned. Edward and his brother watched their uncle Richard leave the Tower in a purple velvet gown lined with ermine, on his way to Westminster Abbey to be crowned Richard III.

After that, the two boys were kept indoors. They were no longer treated with respect. And suddenly they disappeared.

In the dead of a hot summer night, assassins are said to have crept in and smothered them in their beds. Not until two hundred years later were bones believed to have been theirs found beneath a staircase in the neighboring White Tower.

Who ordered their murder—if indeed they were murdered? No one knows. Was it Richard, who for centuries was considered the perpetrator of the crime, or was it Henry Tudor, who, two years later, took the crown after Richard's death on the battlefield at Bosworth? (*See* Market Bosworth, Bosworth Field.)

◆　◆　◆

His exceptional service to England at home and abroad (*See* Republic of Ireland, Youghal) notwithstanding, Sir Walter Raleigh was imprisoned here for thirteen years. The trumped-up charge against him was plotting to keep James I from the throne. Happily, for much of that time, Raleigh's wife, son, and servants were allowed to join him, coming and going as they pleased. Even Sir Walter had the freedom of the garden at the foot of his tower.

To keep busy during his imprisonment, Raleigh wrote six volumes of his *History of the World*, discussing it as he wrote with learned fellow prisoners, mathematicians and scientists who were also incarcerated for real or imagined political crimes.

For amusement, he turned a henhouse into a still and gleefully produced a cordial whose ingredients included ground pearl. He would walk on his terrace overlooking the river and look longingly out at the Thames that, were he on it, could lead him to the ocean he loved so well.

Tower of London: KING'S HOUSE

Newly wedded to the king of England, Henry VIII, a joyous Anne Boleyn was met by him here with a kiss on May 19, 1533. The happy couple remained here until Anne's coronation on May 31.

Three years later, brought here accused of adultery, Anne stayed again in those rooms where she had been so happy with her bridegroom.

And sixteen days later, three years to the day of her arrival here as an ecstatic bride, the twenty-nine-year-old Anne, somberly clad in black, was led out to the Tower Green to be beheaded. That same king who had kissed her so eagerly such a short time before took a new bride the next day.

❖ ❖ ❖

William Maxwell, Lord Nithsdale, made an escape from the Tower on the eve of his execution in 1715. Lord Nithsdale was a Catholic who had taken sides against George I. George I had refused all entreaties for mercy. Lady Nithsdale, then, had to make other plans.

Accompanied by a carriageful of weeping female friends of various sizes—thin and fat—the golden-haired, twenty-six-year-old wife of the prisoner arrived at the Tower in a black mourning dress. She told the warders that she and her friends had come to say their final farewells. Her distracting loveliness, the few pieces of gold handed out, and the general confusion led the warders to allow the tearful women, sometimes one by one, sometimes in pairs, to bid adieu to Lord Nithsdale. One of the plumper women wore a dress concealed under her outer one. Lady Nithsdale, meanwhile, had concealed beneath her garments makeup to lighten her husband's eyebrows and a wig to match a companion's hair. As each of the ladies left Lord Nithsdale's cell, each carefully held a handkerchief to her eyes.

At last, the moment for the actual escape arrived. The warders had watched so many comings and goings that they were unlikely to take any more notice of them, even if one departing "visitor" did not exactly resemble the "visitor" who had entered Lord Nithsdale's cell.

The plump lady, on her trip in, had removed the hidden dress she wore. Lady Nithsdale had dressed her husband in it, had changed the color of his brows, and had put the wig on his head. The plump lady had gone out, leaving Lord and Lady Nithsdale alone together.

Addressing her disguised husband as "Lady Betty," Lady Nithsdale, in loud tones, had begged him to hurry out after her maid, whom she said she desperately needed. Between her loud voice and her tears, she managed to attract attention to herself rather than to the departing "Lady Betty." No sooner had "Lady Betty" left with handkerchief at her face than Lady Nithsdale returned to the cell to pretend to have a conversation with her husband.

reach a prearranged hiding place, Lady Nithsdale bade the empty cell a loud and tearful farewell, promising her husband that she would return to him on execution morning. Then, going out, she managed to lock the door from the inside and informed the warder that her husband was at his prayers.

By the time Lord Nithsdale was missed, he was already well on his way across the Channel to France, then to Italy, where his courageous and ingenious lady joined him.

◆   ◆   ◆

Germany's Deputy Führer, Rudolf Hess, professing to be on an independent peace mission, flew himself to Scotland and parachuted out in May 1941. His peace proposal was not considered, however, and he was brought here.

For six months he remained a prisoner in the Tower,

but orders were issued that he be treated with the courtesy befitting his rank. Though Hess was subsequently sentenced to life imprisonment in Germany, Sir Winston Churchill called his peace mission "a frantic deed of lunatic benevolence."

Tower of London: THE MARTIN TOWER

The clergyman and his wife who arrived here one spring night in 1671 and asked if they might see the Crown Jewels were a pleasant-appearing couple. Talbot Edwards, the caretaker for the jewels was, as always, pleased to show them off. He would not have been had he known the drama that would ensue.

The clergyman's wife was suddenly taken ill. Kindhearted Mrs. Edwards invited her into the Edwards's own apartment to lie down while the clergyman continued his viewing of the regalia. As suddenly the woman recovered, thanked her benefactor, and she and her husband left—but not before, in idle chatter, she had discovered that the Edwards had a daughter they were hoping would soon find a husband.

A few days later, the clergyman returned here with a thank-you gift for Mrs. Edwards and to suggest that perhaps Miss Edwards would like to meet his nephew who was just about Miss Edwards' age. The evening of May 9 was set for a meeting of the pair.

Mrs. Edwards could not have been more pleased than to think that the young man might prove a suitor for her daughter's hand. But, as it turned out, that was hardly the case. What the clergyman wanted wasn't a bride for his nephew, but the Crown Jewels.

On the appointed May night, the clergyman did return—not with a "nephew," but with three accomplices. All smiles at first, their daggers and pistols under cover, they asked if they could see the jewels while they awaited the arrival of the clergyman's wife. Edwards, who charged all who came to see the regalia, readily agreed. These men were, after all, friends of the clergyman. But no sooner were all in the Crown Jewel room than they set upon Edwards, knocked him down, gagged him, and stabbed him in the stomach. Leaving him for dead, the thieves hastily gathered together the jewels. The clergy-man (in reality, a notorious criminal known as Colonel Thomas Blood), stuffed the crown under his robe while one accomplice began to file the scepter in two and another tucked the orb into his trousers. The thieves readied for their getaway.

Meanwhile, outside the tower, the thieves' "watchman" was having trouble. The Edwards's son had arrived unexpectedly. On an Army leave, he had decided to visit his parents. The "watchman" tried to warn his col-leagues inside the Tower that someone was coming, but by then the thieves were on their way out with the regalia.

Happily, they got no farther than the Byward Tower before Edwards' shouts of "Murder. Help. The Crown is stolen" reached the ears of his son and the yeoman warder at the gate. Shooting and fighting followed. One of the thieves managed to escape, but he, too, was later apprehended, and all the Crown Jewels were recovered.

Tower of London: MIDDLE TOWER

To accommodate the elephant he had received in 1255 as a gift from the King of France, Henry III ordered the construction here of a house "forty feet long and twenty feet deep." A holiday was announced for the day the animal was to go to the Tower so that Londoners could watch it walk through the streets. Keeping company with it were lions, leopards, and a white bear that, while chained and muzzled, was regularly taken out to catch fish in the Thames. The house has since been replaced by this tower.

Tower of London: TOWER GREEN

As legend has it, should the ravens that frequent Tower Green ever depart, England will cease to be. Their wings are clipped, just in case.

◆ ◆ ◆

One of the most bizarre beheadings here was of the seventy-year-old Countess of Salisbury in 1541. The aging countess, a Roman Catholic who had been governess to Henry VIII's eldest—and Roman Catholic—daughter, Mary, remained loyal both to her mistress and to her faith long after both had fallen into disfavor. That was enough to lead her to the block in those bloody days.

But insisting that she was not a traitor and that only traitors laid their heads on the block and lost them, she refused to do so. The executioner sought to lure her into lying down by talking of beheading as being "the fashion," but the countess would not be taken in. As the story goes, it was only by chasing her around the block that the executioner succeeded in lopping off her head with a blow of his axe.

◆ ◆ ◆

Innocent, seventeen-year-old Lady Jane Grey—who found delight in reading Plato in the original; knew Latin, French, and Italian; played several musical instruments; wrote with a fine hand; and did the most delicate of needlework—was beheaded as a traitor in 1554. A devout Protestant, poor Jane was the victim of the ambitions of others who sought to keep Henry VIII's Roman Catholic daughter, Mary, off the throne.

For nine days in 1553, Lady Jane held the title "Queen." Then she became a prisoner here. Though it was December, it is said she found some brief moments of happiness walking in the Tower gardens. Her worries for the fate of her new husband, nineteen-year-old Lord Guilford Dudley, were well founded.

The day before her own execution, she watched her

bridegroom pass under her window on his way to the block here on Tower Green. A little later, she saw his remains pass by.

◆   ◆   ◆

There was a macabre delay in the execution here of Queen Anne Boleyn. She had wished that a French headsman, skilled in the use of a sword rather than the English axe, officiate at her execution. King Henry VIII had agreed to her request. But in his hurry to get here from Calais at the appointed time, the executioner left his costume behind. Anne's death was postponed a day while an appropriate costume for him was stitched together in London.

Tower of London: TOWER HILL

The ghost of Simon Fraser, Lord Lovat, the last person to be beheaded here on April 9, 1747, is said to have walked disconsolately outside the Tower after his execution. Executed for his support of Bonnie Prince Charlie (*See* Scotland, Outer Hebrides, Eriskay: Loch nan Uamh), Scottish Lord Lovat had supplied money and asked that all the bagpipers from John o'Groats to Edinburgh be out piping when his body was carried home.

But they weren't. Indeed, his body never made it home to Scotland. And in stormy weather, the outraged ghost has reportedly been seen with his head beneath his arm.

◆   ◆   ◆

Few went to their deaths here more gallantly than Sir Thomas More, Archbishop of Canterbury. the Archbishop had been condemned by his old friend Henry VIII for refusing to accept the king over Rome as head of the English Church.

As More mounted the rickety five-foot scaffold draped in black, he turned to the officer in charge of the execution and, seeking his help in ascending, said, "I pray you, Mr. Lieutenant, see me safe up, and for my coming down, let me shift for myself."

Tower of London: TRAITORS' GATE

On a gloomy, rainy Palm Sunday in 1554, twenty-year-old Princess Elizabeth was brought by barge to this fearsome gate, through which her mother, Anne Boleyn had gone seventeen years earlier, never to return. Only four weeks earlier, in the yard of this awesome tower, her seventeen-year-old cousin, playmate, and lessons-mate, Lady Jane Grey, had lost her head, too.

Elizabeth was accused of having been party to a plan to usurp her half sister Mary's throne. As she approached this Traitors' Gate, however, she shuddered, denied she was a traitor, and exclaimed that she would not enter the Tower through a gate with such a name. Her warders told her that she had no choice. As the boat pulled up to the Tower stairs and the rain pelted down, one of the attendants, taking pity on the slender young woman, offered her his cloak to protect her from the weather. She refused it. Instead, unassisted, she stepped briskly off the barge, ankle deep in water, exclaiming as she did so, "Here lands as true a subject as ever landed at these stairs. Before Thee, Oh God, do I speak it, having no other friend than Thee alone."

Still, Elizabeth hesitated to enter this tower of doom and sat for a moment on a stone outside. When she was told it was "unwholesome" to sit there in the rain, she murmured, "Better sit here than in a worse place." She only moved inside when one of the attendants who had traveled with her to the Tower burst into tears, crying for her, and she could not bear his tears. Berating him for not supporting her in her hour of need, she, who would become Elizabeth I, rose and grimly entered the Bell Tower.

Tower of London: WAKEFIELD TOWER

When Henry VI was found dead in his oratory here in 1471, his enemies, harking back to a bout he had had with mental illness, insisted that he was mad—dead "of pure displeasure and melancholy." But the truth, it was soon discovered, was otherwise. As he knelt at his prayers, the devout Henry was stabbed to death. His assassins remained unknown. Each year on May 21, the anniversary of his death, Eton College and King's College, Cambridge, both of which he founded, put lilies and roses here to honor him.

William Shakespeare in *Henry VI* echoed the popular thought that it was Richard, Duke of Gloucester, who was his killer, bidden by his brother, Edward IV, to do the deed. But need Henry have been murdered?

Imprisoned here earlier by Edward after a defeat in battle, the gentle Henry had had a dog, a sparrow, his Bible, and his breviary with him during his incarceration. Quite satisfied with these few possessions, he had remarked that as long as he could have them and the Sacrament, he did not worry about holding on to his kingdom here on earth.

Tower of London: WHITE TOWER

One winter night in 1101, Ralph Flambard, the Bishop of Durham, imprisoned here for his unscrupulous selling of bishoprics and taking of Church monies, invited the Norman knights who were his warders to join him for a glass of wine. (Though he was held captive, Flambard, being a bishop, had been given a large apartment and his own servants and could eat and drink whatever he could afford to buy.) Flambard was a roly-poly fellow who enjoyed his drink and victuals, and his captors willingly accepted his invitation. Little did they know that smuggled inside the cask of wine was a coil of rope with which the bishop would make his escape.

After Flambard had plied his guards with sufficient drink so that they fell asleep, the bishop and his servants hauled the rope from the cask, tied one end around Flambard's body, secured the other end inside the Tower, and out the window Flambard went. His portliness hardly aided his descent, and it is said that he swung round and round, striking the tower innumerable times, and injured one arm before he reached the ground sixty feet below. Once there, friends with horses awaited him, and he fled to France. In time, Henry I, who had imprisoned him, pardoned him, and he returned to England and another bishopric.

A second attempt to escape this tower—this time by using knotted bedsheets—failed in the next century when the sheets tore apart and the Welsh prince Llewellyn ap Gruffydd plummeted headfirst to his death.

❖ ❖ ❖

Despite the cruelties being inflicted on prisoners on Tower Hill, Henry III in the twelfth century began the practice of whitewashing the exterior of this particular tower where he sometimes stayed, to give it an aura of pristine "royal domesticity."

Westminster Abbey

Because he had been converted on this site, Sebert, a seventh-century Saxon king, decided that he would build a church here and dedicate it to St. Peter.

As the story goes, the night before its consecration, a ferryman on the River Thames was hailed by a stranger who asked to be taken to the new church. The ferryman agreed, and, curious himself, disembarked with his passenger to see the church that Sebert had built.

As they approached the church, the astounded ferryman saw on its steps angels descending from the skies with candles. Then an angelic choir burst into song while the mysterious visitor sprinkled the church with holy water and touched its walls with holy oil.

When they had returned to the boat, the awestricken ferryman could not keep from asking the stranger his name. "I am Peter, keeper of the keys of Heaven," the traveler reportedly replied, "and I have come here to dedicate my church."

As the centuries passed, Sebert's church fell into ruin, but, knowing the story, the devout Edward the Confessor built this church to take its place on this hallowed ground. Just eight days before the work on it was done in 1065, however, King Edward died—personally invited into Heaven, so his friends and admirers said, by the keeper of its keys, St. Peter.

After twenty-five-year-old Elizabeth I's coronation here in 1559, there were those who said that she showed a lack of decorum in the enthusiasm she exhibited for the job she was about to undertake. The red-haired daughter of Henry VIII, wearing her twenty-three-yard-long mantle of gold and silver threads, also caused displeasure by complaining that the holy oil "stank."

Westminster Abbey: CHAPEL OF ST. EDWARD THE CONFESSOR—CORONATION CHAIR

On only one state occasion since the Stone of Scone beneath this chair was stolen away from Scotland by Edward I in 1296, has it left Westminster Abbey. That was when it was carried out to Westminster Hall in 1653 for the installation of Oliver Cromwell as Lord Protector.

Said to have been where the Hebrew patriarch Jacob laid his head in the desert, this famous stone, legend has it, was carried to Egypt, then to Spain and Ireland, and finally to Scotland (*See* Scotland, Scone, Palace of Scone) where St. Columba, like Jacob, used it as a pillow and died with his head upon it. Because it was so holy, and so prized as their coronation stone by the Scottish kings, Edward I decided he must have it for his own, so he carried it off and had this coronation chair of English oak built around it. Carved on it in Latin, after all, is the prophecy, "If Fates go right, where'er this stone is found/ The Scots shall monarch and that realm be crowned."

Westminster Abbey: CHAPEL OF HENRY VII

Because he had so loved his queen, Elizabeth of York, Henry VII elected to be buried not in a raised tomb, as was customary for kings, but beside her beneath this chapel floor.

Seeking desperately to bear her king more sons after his oldest son, Prince Arthur, had died, Elizabeth, at thirty-eight, had given birth to a daughter in the winter of 1503. But it was a cold winter, and despite furs to keep her warm, and the ministrations of the best physician, Elizabeth had died. After giving directions for her funeral in the resplendent chapel that he had created, Henry went into seclusion.

◆ ◆ ◆

The plan was that Henry VII would create this chapel and dedicate it to his father, Henry VI, and that in conjunction, his father would be canonized. Application for canonization was made to the Pope. The requisite number of miracles was reported to have occurred. The problem was a financial one. The price the papal court asked for canonization was more than tightfisted Henry VII wished to pay, so that project was abandoned, and this chapel was dedicated instead to the Virgin Mary.

Westminster Abbey: CHAPEL OF HENRY VII—
TOMB OF ELIZABETH I

If she did not take him as a lover, surely Elizabeth I loved red-haired Robert, Earl of Essex, as a son. They were friends when he was ten and she invited him to spend Christmas with her. When he grew to be a man, she made him Master of the Horse and Knight of the Garter. At the age of thirty-three, he was Earl Marshal of England. He was tall, gallant, and handsome. But his popularity with the queen—and with the people—went to his head. After fighting successfully against the Spaniards in Portugal, he was heralded by all. When it became known that Phillip II, the Spanish king, was planning to aid the Irish in an invasion of England, Essex went off to punish them at Cadiz. After that he was sent to Ireland to control the rebels. But there he took it upon himself to knight the men in his service, which was strictly a royal prerogative, and it angered the queen. Also, there began to be rumors that he was disloyal to her. Hearing of them, Essex returned to England to clear his name. But despite the kisses with which he is said to have showered her knees when he flung himself into her bedchamber one morning, Elizabeth was not mollified and had him arrested. Though Essex was later released, he never returned to favor.

He tried again and again to see Elizabeth, but she turned down his pleas for an audience. It was said that he was almost driven mad by her refusals. A friend proposed that he force his way into her presence by seizing with armed men first the Tower of London, then the palace, and he agreed to the madcap scheme. It failed. Instead of taking either, Essex was sent to the Tower and was condemned to death.

As the legend goes, years before, Elizabeth had given Essex a ring and told him that if in time of trouble he had need of her, he should send it to her. Up until the very last, proud Essex refused to humble himself by dispatching it. He fully expected her long and deep affection for him, it is said, to stay her hand from signing the order of execution. But when no stay was issued, Essex dispatched the ring. It fell into the hands of the wrong lady-in-waiting, however, and she did not pass it on. Essex was executed.

Not until the lady-in-waiting lay on her deathbed did she admit to having kept the ring. "God may forgive you, but I never can," the heartsick queen is said to have replied. And when Elizabeth was buried here, the ring that she had received too late was put on her tomb. It remained there until this decade, but it is now displayed in the Abbey Undercroft

Westminster Abbey: CHAPTER HOUSE

When the time was right, everything was in readiness for the theft of the king's jewels from behind these thick walls and the seven locks of the crypt below this room. A clump of flax had been painstakingly nurtured in the garden outside so that it was thick and fat enough to be a temporary hiding place for the spoils. Covered baskets had been prepared to carry the loot to the Thames and a getaway boat. And at the end of April 1303, when Edward I was called away to Scotland to fight the rebellious William Wallace, it seemed the perfect time to act.

With the aid of some of the abbey's monks, Richard de Podlicote, the mastermind of the plot, climbed through a chapter-house window and managed to break his way into the treasury. He left, lugging a rich supply of gold, silver, and jewels.

But even the best-laid plans will sometimes go awry, and a nervous Podlicote, or one of his accomplices, dropped four bejeweled crowns on the crypt floor and in their panic left them there. Still, more of the treasure fell into the Thames, but nevertheless, they had a fortune with them when Podlicote and a friend were apprehended across the river. The monks were imprisoned. Podlicote was hanged, and, some say, his skin was tacked to the chapter-house door as a warning to other thieves tempted to own some of the king's riches.

Westminster Abbey: JERUSALEM ROOM

A soothsayer had once said that Henry IV would die in the Holy Land. Over the years, mindful of that prediction, he had prepared for a pilgrimage there. But he had never made it.

Stricken while he was praying in the Chapel of Edward the Confessor, Henry was carried to this room and died here in 1413. The soothsayer had come close. All around the walls hung tapestries of the history of Jerusalem

Westminster Abbey: POETS' CORNER—
GRAVESITE OF ROBERT HAULE

The blue slab with the evangelists' symbols in the corners—the winged lion, the winged man, the winged ox, and the eagle—marks the grave of Robert Haule. It commemorates the dreadful day in 1378 when Haule, a knight in the service of Edward the Black Prince, was murdered during High Mass here.

Fighting in Spain for the Black Prince, Haule and another knight had captured a Spanish count and brought him back to England with them. When the count went home to seek his ransom, he left his young son in his place. Time passed. The father did not return, and his lonely son attracted the attention and the sympathy of the powerful noble, John of Gaunt. John took the young Spaniard's captors captive and sent them to the Tower of London.

One August day, the two knights managed to escape the Tower and fled here to the Abbey. After them, however, stormed the Tower constable and fifty of his men. Round and round they chased Haule and his comrade, paying no heed to the service being said nor to the sanctity of the place where they had drawn their swords. Finally, just before the prior's stall, the pursuers caught up with Haule. With twelve blows of their swords they felled him, his servant, and a monk of the Abbey who had sought to intervene. Not only was the Abbey itself closed for four months for purification, but Parliament, too, was suspended. Its meeting place was in the Abbey Chapter House, and it was feared that the gruesome murder might somehow affect proceedings of the Parliament.

Westminster Abbey: POETS' CORNER—
BEN JONSON'S GRAVE (North Aisle of the Nave)

As the story goes, this gravesite, in just eighteen inches of square ground, was chosen with great care by its occupant. Poet laureate Ben Jonson elected to be standing upright, ready for the resurrection.

Even though his masques and comedies and tragedies were frequently performed and he found royal favor, Jonson always seemed to be short of funds. Conscious of his own spendthrift ways and wishing to assure that he would have a final resting place, the poet asked Charles I for a gift of land. Affably, the king asked how much he would like. "Only eighteen inches of square ground," was Jonson's reply. The mystified king acquiesced. He asked where Jonson would like it and how so little could be sufficient. "Because it will be my gravesite in Westminster Abbey," was the farsighted poet's reply.

Westminster Abbey: POETS' CORNER— SPENSER'S TOMB

The finest poets of the age—Francis Beaumont, John Fletcher, Ben Jonson, and most probably William Shakespeare—sadly assembled here in January 1599 for the interment of "the poet's poet," Edmund Spenser.

One after the other, they read aloud the elegies and poems that they had written honoring him. Then, one after the other, they threw into the poet's grave their elegies and poems and, finally, the pens that they had used in writing them.

Westminster Hall

The year 1236 was a notable one in the history of this hall. At the New Year's feast here some thirty thousand dishes were set out on the tables to feed six thousand poor people. On a less merry but no less colorful occasion that year, the rising Thames flooded the hall and boats were rowed about inside.   ◆ ◆ ◆

Elegantly clad, as was his wont—the handkerchief that he had introduced to England in his hand—Richard II

was forced to abdicate in 1399. It made no difference that
this magnificent great hall was the creation of his reign.
Haughty and stubbornly unwilling to do the bidding of
his barons, Richard was made to leave his throne. A year
later he was dead; no one knew whether it was by accident
or design.

◆　◆　◆

Presiding over the court trying King Charles I in 1649,
Puritan John Bradshaw took the precaution of wearing a
bulletproof hat, but he could not protect himself from
verbal attacks.

He accused the king of bringing all manner of evils
and calamities on England and announced that England
was about to judge him for them. Lady Anna de Lille, a
Scotswoman, the widow of a Frenchman who had served
the king, cried out that it was not the people who were
judging and condemning their monarch, but traitors.

Her angry attack—though hardly her cries—ended
when the court ordered her branded for her interruption,
and guards, armed with hot irons, applied them to her
shoulders and head.

◆　◆　◆

The trial of King Charles I that was held here in mid-
January, 1649, was hardly proper. Of the 135 men summoned to serve as jurors, only sixty-eight appeared.
Among those who declined was Lord Fairfax. Oliver
Cromwell's commander of the army. When his name was
called and he did not reply, his wife responded tartly to
the court that her husband had more "wit" than to appear.

Cloaked in black velvet, the king sat on a crimson
velvet chair. Haughtily, in the presence of the court, he
continued to wear his tall black hat. And throughout the
four days of proceedings Charles refused to testify in his
own behalf, averring that the court before which he sat
was an unlawful body—that he was king through God
and birth, and no tribunal was above him. But he was
condemned all the same as a "traitor, tyrant, murderer,

and a public enemy." When the sentence of death was issued, his guards, on order from their commander, disdainfully blew tobacco smoke into Charles's face and shouted, "Execution! Execution!" "Poor fellows," the king reportedly said of them. "For a sixpence they would say the same of their own commanders."

But in the street outside there were tears and moans when the people heard that a sentence of death had been pronounced upon their king.

◆ ◆ ◆

For twenty-three years the head of Oliver Cromwell, the seventeenth-century Lord Protector of England, remained on a spike on the roof of this ceremonial hall where Charles I, the king he had overthrown, had been condemned to death.

When the monarchy was restored in 1660, Cromwell's body was hauled from its grave and the head was severed. (*See* London, Marble Arch.) Raised to the rooftop, the head withstood sun, wind, and rain until the 1680s. Then it blew down in a storm and fell at the feet of a soldier who, recognizing it and its potential value, carried it home. For more than a century it was passed from hand to hand, sold by speculators, and displayed in museums. Finally, in this century, it found a final resting place at Sidney Sussex College at Cambridge, where the youthful Cromwell had studied. (*See* Cambridge, Sidney Sussex College.)

◆ ◆ ◆

The custom at coronation banquets here was for the King's Champion—the bravest and the best of those who would do battle for the monarch—to attend, in armor, on horseback. He would challenge anyone who questioned the king's right to rule to meet him in singlehanded combat. Then he would throw down his gauntlet.

Only once was the gauntlet picked up. That was in 1689 at the banquet for William III and Mary. Mary's Roman Catholic father, James II, had been forced to leave the throne, and his Protestant son-in-law was brought in from the Netherlands to take it. This time, no sooner was the champion's gauntlet dropped than an old woman on crutches hobbled in, picked it up, and threw down her own worn glove. At the same time, she set an hour the next day when she would meet the Champion at Hyde Park.

Dumbfounded bystanders watching this episode let the woman leave unhindered. The next day, she was at the appointed spot at the appointed time, but the Champion, either being gallant or fearing witchcraft, deemed it best not to meet her for the combat she had suggested.

◆   ◆   ◆

Bold gentlemen could not wince, but ladies could, as the trail of lighted flax, lighting in turn the three thousand candles in the chandeliers at the 1761 coronation of George III and Queen Charlotte, burned so wildly that it seemed to threaten the whole building.

But the banquet proceeded, and not without some amusement. One guest in attendance, entering on horseback, was determined that his horse never have its tail to the king. He had trained the animal so well, it turned out, that it could no longer walk forward at all and was forced—the king's presence notwithstanding—to enter as well as leave the hall rump first.

York Column (Waterloo Place)

To build this 124-foot-high, pink granite monument to the Duke of York, the second son of George III and commander-in-chief of the British Army from 1795 to 1827, every soldier and enlisted man in the British Army lost a day's pay. Understandably, these "contributions" did not please their donors, and unkind critics commented that the monument was built as high as it is so the duke could climb it to escape those to whom he owed money.

LONDON OUTSKIRTS

Brentford: SYON HOUSE

Many are the tears that have been shed on the site of this handsome Robert Adam-designed house.

In earlier days, when a convent stood here, Henry VIII, disenchanted with his "rose without a thorn," Queen Catherine Howard, sent her to it to await her execution. (*See* Hampton Court, Hampton Court Palace.) And in Queen Mary Tudor's day, in the same convent, the Nine Days Queen, seventeen-year-old Lady Jane Grey, awaited her execution. (*See* London, Tower of London, Tower Green.)

In 1646, when the plague was felling Londoners, the children of Charles I were brought, for safety's sake, to the house that had replaced the convent. Visiting thirteen-year-old Princess Elizabeth and eight-year-old Prince Henry before his execution, the solemn Charles dandled Henry on his knee and warned the child never to become king. And then he bade both children farewell forever.

Greenwich: ROYAL NAVAL COLLEGE—PAINTED HALL

The pay was paltry; the result was magnificent. From 1707 to 1727, Sir James Thornhill, for £3 per square yard, painted this 106-foot-long, 51½-foot-wide ceiling depicting William III and Mary II bringing peace to England and Europe.

Hampstead: KEATS HOUSE

A nightingale had nested in the garden that summer of 1819 when the young poet, John Keats, was living here. In love with his eighteen-year-old next-door neighbor, Fanny Brawn (in those days, this house was divided in half), he especially heeded the bird's glorious song. And one day, after listening under the plum tree, he came indoors with his "Ode to a Nightingale" in his hand.

Hampstead Heath: KENWOOD HOUSE

It was the quick thinking of a neighborhood innkeeper that saved this Robert Adam masterpiece from destruction in the eighteenth century.

Riotous marchers, angry at this great house's owner, the Earl of Mansfield, who was also England's unyielding chief justice, wrecked his in-town house in Bloomsbury Square and then set off to do the same to this as well. Thirsty en route, they stopped for a while at The Spaniards Inn nearby. There, as they drank, they loudly proclaimed their intentions of burning Kenwood. And while they drank, the innkeeper, Giles Thomas, had word sent to Kenwood to be prepared, for rioters were on their way. Simultaneously, he sent word, too, to a nearby barracks requesting troops to guard Kenwood. As it turned out, the troops weren't needed. Thomas got the would-be rioters so inebriated that by the time they arrived here they were easily convinced to go away.

Hampton Court: HAMPTON COURT PALACE

The merry time that Henry VIII had here surely contributed to the excessive size that in his last days caused such discomfort to his legs. In 1541, six years before his death, the rotund king's waist measurement was fifty-four inches. Little wonder, then, that the Lord Chamberlain who joined the king at the table in the great Hall was allowed four gallons of ale and a quart and a half of wine at each meal; the king, after all, had to have a companion to keep up with him.

◆ ◆ ◆

It was 1649 and Charles I was dead. (*See* London, Banqueting House.) All his trappings of royalty should go with him, the Puritans said. So, for three years, off and on, the great works of art he had collected—Van Dykes, Titians, Raphaels—and the porcelain, crystal, and ivory that had adorned the banqueting table during the reigns of Henry VIII, Mary Tudor, and Elizabeth I, were auctioned to benefit the Commonwealth. Henry VIII's walking stick was sold for five shillings, and a pair of his gloves was sold for one shilling.

Hampton Court: HAMPTON COURT PALACE—
GARDENS

Whenever she stayed here and the weather was appropriate, Elizabeth I would mount her horse and set off on a hunt, surrounded by her ladies-in-waiting dressed in white satin and riding white palfreys.

On her last visit here, when she was sixty-six, although she did not plan to hunt, Elizabeth prepared to depart on horseback while a storm raged. A solicitous courtier proposed that, in view of her years, taking refuge from the rain in a carriage might be preferable to riding. Insulted as any woman would be, Elizabeth bristled. "My years?" she reportedly snapped, her red wig and missing front teeth notwithstanding. Then she ordered her ladies-in-waiting to their horses and mounted her own. Bent low with age on her mount, she disappeared into the driving rain.

◆ ◆ ◆

Walking in his gardens here, Henry VIII's Cardinal Wolsey did much of the plotting and planning for his own and for England's future. When he was walking, to assure that his train of thought was not interrupted, Wolsey forbade his servants to come any nearer to him than "as far as one might shoot an arrow." And he did plan well for England on these walks. Unfortunately, he did not do as well in planning for himself. Unable to obtain the divorce that Henry wished, Wolsey fell out of favor with Henry. Simultaneously, he found the king coveting his magnificent house and grounds here.

Rather than risk losing his head, he offered his dearly loved lands and home as a gift to Henry, who accepted without hesitation.

Hampton Court: HAMPTON COURT PALACE— THE HAUNTED GALLERY

In his Royal Chapel at the end of this gallery, Henry VIII was hearing Mass. But outside it that day in 1542, Queen Catherine Howard, his fifth wife, was piteously begging him to spare her life.

Accused of adultery, she had been imprisoned, and there was little doubt in the mind of the pretty cousin of Queen Anne Boleyn that her fate would be the same bloody death as that cousin's. (*See* London, Tower of London: King's House.) Having momentarily escaped from her guards, she ran screaming down this corridor. It is said that her cries still echo here.

Hampton Court: HAMPTON COURT PALACE— THE HOME PARK

Though William III was a taciturn man, he loved his gardens and his flowers. Here he planted the box, the yew, and the holly and had them fashioned into their fanciful monster shapes. He had the avenues laid out and had the fountains erected. In the Home Park, he liked to go riding and admire his handiwork. But one day in 1702, a mole from the lovely gardens ran in front of his horse. The horse stumbled. William fell and later died from the injuries he sustained in the fall.

Hampton Court: HAMPTON COURT PALACE— TUDOR TENNIS COURT

As long as his health allowed it (ulcers on a leg and excess weight were problems of his later years), Henry VIII socked tennis balls back and forth across this court he had had built. It is the oldest tennis court in the world still in use.

Highgate: HIGHGATE CEMETERY—
GRAVE OF ELIZABETH ROSSETTI

One night in 1869, by bonfire light, the poet-painter Dante Gabriel Rossetti and a handful of friends watched as the grave and coffin of the poet's beloved wife, Elizabeth, were opened. From the coffin, the tearful Rossetti withdrew a slender volume of poems.

Seven years earlier, as Elizabeth lay dying at the age of twenty-eight, he had written these poems to her. He berated himself afterward for having spent on them the time that he should have spent caring for her. He had put the book of poems into the coffin beside her, since, he said, they belonged to Elizabeth, who had inspired them.

But his friends had insisted that his poetry's place was in the world, not in the grave. They said that his tributes to Elizabeth should be read by all so that she would be remembered by all.

At first Rossetti had demurred, pointing out that she would be remembered in the many paintings he had made of her as his Beatrice. But finally, he had agreed to the disinterment. It is said that, there in the flickering bonfire light, the lovely Elizabeth looked every bit as fair as she had when she was alive.

A year after the disinterment, her husband's love poems to her, *The House of Life*, appeared.

Highgate: HIGHGATE HILL—
THE WHITTINGTON STONE

In the nursery story, here the poor Dick Whittington, weary of drudgery and abuse in the kitchen of London merchant Sir John Fitzwarren, sat tearfully on a stone, deciding to leave London. He was unhappy over mistreatment at work and at having been talked into shipping his pet cat off to faraway lands on a ship of Sir John's.

But as he sat, trying to make up his mind where to go next, he heard the bells of St. Mary-le-Bow in Cheapside (*See* London, Bow Church) ringing and seeming to say, "Turn again, Whittington, Lord Mayor of London Town!" And Dick got up from his stone and went back to his kitchen work, just in time to discover that his cat had won him a fortune.

When the captain of the Fitzwarren ship was trading on North Africa's Barbary Coast, he had found the king's palace overrun with mice and rats and had offered Dick's cat to get rid of them. In exchange for the cat, which quickly set to work devouring all the rodents, the king of the Barbary Coast had offered chests full of treasure. The honest captain had brought them back to Dick. The kitchen boy soon became a merchant himself, and eventually, as Bow Bells had predicted, he served not once, but three times as mayor of London Town.

Though no cat features in the story of the real Dick Whittington, he, like the fictional fellow, worked for Sir John Fitzwarren, was a merchant of note, four times the mayor of London—in 1397, 1398, 1407, and 1420—and a benefactor of renown.

Southwark: SOUTHWARK CATHEDRAL

Miserly John Overs who lived on the Surrey side of the River Thames in the sixth century was singularly unpopular. No bridge crossed the river in those days and Overs was the only ferryman, so he had money aplenty, but never spent it. He certainly was not about to consider giving any of it away as a dowry for his daughter, Mary. She was pretty, but few people knew it, for her penurious father kept her out of sight as much as possible.

Penny-pincher that her father was, he decided on a plan to save even a few more pennies. If he were assumed dead for twenty-four hours, he reasoned, Mary and his servants would have to mourn him. Therefore, they would fast for a while, and the price of the food they would otherwise have eaten would be saved.

Overs, of course, needed someone to help him with his plan, and he talked Mary into wrapping him in a winding sheet and laying him out in a coffin.

As he had expected, his servants gathered round, but, rather than mourning him, they were beside themselves with joy. They raided his cupboards and wine cellar and banqueted royally in celebration of his passing.

Wrapped in his winding sheet and lying in his coffin, John Overs was furious. He tried to unwind himself and jump out to keep them from consuming his stores. But all he managed to do was sit upright and terrify all those who saw him. One, indeed, was so terrified that he struck the figure rising from the coffin with an oar—and, after that, John Overs was genuinely dead. Since he was her father, Mary was unhappy—but not entirely. She sent word to her lover that she was now free to wed. Hurrying to claim her, her lover fell from his galloping horse, and he, too, died.

Mary was heartbroken. After her father's death, she was also rich. Suitor after suitor knocked at her door. But Mary simply wasn't interested. She still mourned her first love, so Mary became a nun and founded a convent on this site. Later, in its place, a church called St. Saviour's was erected (John Harvard was christened in it in 1607). Today that church is this cathedral, born of the miserly ferryman's macabre joke.

Tilbury: TILBURY PORT

It was 1588, and at any moment the Spanish Armada was expected to arrive at this port at the mouth of the River Thames. Hastily, workmen were gathered together to repair this fort that Henry VIII had built to guard the mouth of the river, and soldiers were called up to defend it. An armor-clad Elizabeth I, riding on horseback, reviewed them. She knew armor was not really for her, and remarking on it, Elizabeth stirred her soldiers as she said, "I know that I have the body of a weak, feeble woman, but I have the heart and stomach of a king, and of a king of England, too."

Windsor Castle

As a boy, Edward III had listened, rapt, to stories of King Arthur and his Round Table. When he grew to manhood, Edward determined that he would establish here his own Round Table of the kingdom's most honorable knights.

There were to be three hundred of them, and they would meet in a Round Tower he had constructed here. In it, there was to be a table two hundred feet in diameter, and fifty-two enormous oaks were cut down to build it.

But in the 1340s when Edward was planning his table, the Black Death was sweeping England. The job was never finished. Instead, an incident at a court ball made Windsor famous as the site where Edward instituted England's greatest honor, the Order of the Knights of the Garter.

While the king was dancing one evening, probably with the Countess of Salisbury of whom he was much enamored, the lady's garter fell. The king gallantly retrieved it, remarking to the onlookers who tittered as he returned it, "The time shall shortly come when you shall attribute much honor to such a garter."

It was not long before Edward created the Knights of the Garter whose motto was "Evil to him who thinks evil."

◆   ◆   ◆

James I of Scotland said in later years that his glimpse through a window of Lady Joan of Beaufort, the Englishwoman who became his queen, was worth his eighteen years of captivity here.

Captured by English pirates when he was eleven, the

heir to Scotland's throne was held here until 1424, when he was twenty-nine. By then sufficient money had been raised for his ransom.

James hurried home, but not until arrangements had been made for him to wed his "milk-white English dove," as he called Joan in the loving poetry he wrote about her.

❖ ❖ ❖

On a chill December day in 1648, Charles I was brought here on his way to trial on charges of having made war against his subjects. There had been a plan for his escape en route on horseback in Windsor Forest. But it had failed when his alert Puritan guard saw to it that Charles did not get the fleet-footed horse intended for him.

So Charles spent the last Christmas before his execution here—hollowly celebrating with three new suits of gold, silver lace, and satin. (*See* London, Banqueting House.) He read Shakespeare, took walks, and went to his beloved St. George's Chapel, though the Puritans had stripped it of all its finest ornaments.

❖ ❖ ❖

After the death here of her Prince Consort, Albert, in 1861, a grief-stricken Queen Victoria insisted that his room was to stay just as he had left it.

And so it did, until 1901 when Edward VII became king. Fresh water had been put in the bedside pitcher daily, and beside it was kept the medicine Albert had taken for the typhoid fever to which he had succumbed.

Windsor Castle: ST. GEORGE'S CHAPEL

Though Geoffrey Chaucer's abilities as a poet have never been questioned, he was clerk of the works for a restoration here in 1390 that never seemed to get done. The author of *The Canterbury Tales* was, some speculate, too busy poetizing. He either quit or was fired from his works post after only two years.

MADDINGLY HILL

American Military Cemetery

In this East Anglian countryside at the height of World War II, three million tons of fuel, four thousand tons of bombs, and four and a half million rounds of ammunition were said to have been a daily requirement of the U.S. Eighth Army Air Force that was headquartered here. Today, at this cemetery, 3,811 Americans killed in that war lie buried, and 5,125 men missing in action are remembered.

MALTON

Castle Howard

Over mutton pie at London's Kit Kat Club, where all notable seventeenth-century Whigs met to talk politics, the poet-soldier-playwright John Vanbrugh met the young Earl of Carlisle. As the earl talked of the house he was planning to build here, the playwright doodled a few sketches of a great house. The earl liked what he saw, and even though Vanbrugh had never before designed a house, the Earl of Carlisle hired him to be this building's architect.

MARKET BOSWORTH

Bosworth Field

It took only two hours on August 22, 1485, to change the course of English history. That was when the army of Henry Tudor of Wales defeated that of Richard III.

The king's army was double his opponent's in size. Had it not been for the defection of a supporter, Richard would probably have won the battle, for he fought valiantly. But he made a tactical mistake and joined his men in a headlong attack on enemy lines, crying, "I will not budge a foot. I am the king of England." It was on that charge, as he cried out, that he was unhorsed and struck a fatal blow on the head.

Stripped of its clothes and armor, his body was unceremoniously flung on the back of a horse for its return to Leicester (*See* Leicester, Bow Bridge). The crown that had fallen from his head into a hawthorn bush was put on the head of the twenty-eight-year-old Welshman who would become Henry VII, father of Henry VIII and grandfather of Elizabeth I.

OXFORD

In London, that fall of 1665, thousands of residents were being felled by the plague, so it was deemed wise for Charles II and the royal household to leave the capital for a safer place.

They came here, and until January the revelry of the court overshadowed the scholarship of the colleges. In December the king's mistress, Lady Castlemaine, delivered his child here.

All Souls College

Founder of Eton and of King's College, Cambridge, Henry VI was agreeable enough, in the fifteenth century, to being co-founder of this college with Henry Chichele, Archbishop of Canterbury. He prided himself on his learning. The plan was that prayers were to be said here forever for Henry's father, Henry V, victor against the French at the Battle of Agincourt and for all others killed in the Hundred Years' War. Such paid-for prayers could be of service to Henry's soul, too.

But when spendthrift Edward IV came to the throne, he coveted that royal endowment. Only when he too was promised a share forever in the college's prayers, along with cash in hand, was he willing to let his predecessor's endowment go undisturbed.

Ashmolean Museum

The founding of this remarkable museum is wreathed in mystery.

Sometime in the reign of Queen Elizabeth I, a well-traveled Dutchman named John Tradescant arrived in England from Holland. His varied career had included fighting Algerian pirates and collecting plants in Russia. Though he lacked a sense of smell, he was said to be a fine gardener whose work in time came to the attention of Charles I, who appointed him the Keeper of the Royal Gardens, Vines, and Silkworms. It was Tradescant, with his son, John, who introduced to England lilacs and night-scented stock, among others—plants whose beauty he acclaimed even if their fragrance eluded him.

Not only plants captured the fancy of John Tradescant the Elder and John the Younger. Natural oddities of all sorts were collected and displayed in London as "Tradescant's Ark." Then John the Elder died, and his son inherited the collection, substantially enlarging it when he traveled in America.

Fully conscious of the value of their curiosities, John the Younger and his wife looked for someone suitable to whom to bequeath it. They found him in Elias Ashmole, an antiquarian, scientist, expert in heraldry, and member of Oxford's Brasenose College. For a time, Ashmole had been a lodger with them.

But then they had a change of heart. John Tradescant tried to change his will. The change was upset. He died, and his wife was found dead of drowning in her garden.

Elias Ashmole was the inheritor therefore, even if the Tradescants hadn't wanted that in the end. It was surely a happy inheritance for Oxford, since its loyal son Ashmole said he would give the Ark to the university provided Oxford housed it properly.

The university promptly had the Old Ashmolean, now the Museum of the History of Science, built for it.

That done, per agreement, twelve cartloads of Tradescant's Ark were trundled here from London in 1683 to form the nucleus of the oldest public museum in England.

Ashmolean Museum: ALFRED'S JEWEL

At Athelney near here in 1693, this cloisonné figure of a king bearing two scepters and marked "Alfred had me made" was accidentally discovered.

It gives credence, some say, to the belief held by Oxonians for years that that ninth-century monarch who so loved learning was the founder of this university.

◆   ◆   ◆

When he was a tutor at Oxford in the eighteenth century, Jean Paul Marat, who would be a powerful figure in the French Revolution, stole several links from the gold chain of Elias Ashmole. With the money he made from their sale, he is said to have paid a rooming house bill. Since Marat subsequently died in his bath back in France at the hands of Charlotte Corday, it would seem he should have kept the pieces of chain as an amulet.

Balliol College

To assure that her husband, the Baron John de Balliol, would reach Heaven despite having had an altercation with the Bishop of Durham (*See* Scotland, New Abbey, Sweetheart Abbey), his widow, Devorguilla, had this college that he had started completed.

At the time of his death, as partial penance for an insult to the bishop, he had founded a house for sixteen poor scholars here and provided an allowance for them. Devorguilla saw to that house's considerable expansion.

Balliol College: WOODEN GATES—GARDEN QUAD

In the 1860s when this college was being rebuilt, these old wooden gates that had once hung near the execution

site of Bishops Hugh Latimer, Nicholas Ridley, and
Thomas Cranmer (*See* Oxford, Martyrs' Memorial), were
destined for the flames. The Reverend T. Harling New-
man, however, remarking that it seemed a shame that
gates that had borne witness to so many deaths at the
stake should themselves end in a fire, gained a reprieve
for them. Now they hang on the passage wall.

Bodleian Library

The librarians here have not been willing to break the
rules for either king or lord protector.

When visiting the Bodleian, Charles I asked to borrow
a book. The librarian apologized profusely but explained that the founder did not allow it.

On a similar errand, Oliver Cromwell was also turned
away.

◆   ◆   ◆

Duke Humphrey of Gloucester liked books and presented his collection of them to this university in the
fifteenth century along with a room to house them.

The reforming commissioners of Protestant Edward
VI's brief reign (he ruled from the age of nine until he
died of consumption at sixteen) felt differently about
them. Though Duke Humphrey's collection was rich in
the works of Dante and Petrarch and Boccaccio rather
than religious tracts, they were nervous about it. Since
Duke Humphrey had been Catholic, they feared there
might be popish propaganda in the collection, so they
rid the university of it.

A century later, however, young Thomas Bodley began his studies at Magdalene College, and, though there
were house libraries here, he quickly saw the need for the
lost central one. It was to be some years, however, before
Bodley was able to do anything about it. That was when
he married a wealthy widow, hired a London bookseller
to tour the Continent to choose books for the library,
talked his friends into giving their libraries to the univer-

sity, and the university itself into accepting what he gave.

❖   ❖   ❖

Sir Walter Raleigh, who had attended Oriel College, was sent by Queen Elizabeth I to destroy Faro, Portugal, when it was in Spanish hands. He sacked the city as was expected, but sailed away with the remarkable library—largely of books in Arabic—that had belonged to the bishop there. They were Raleigh's gift to the Bodleian.

❖   ❖   ❖

In 1605 when James I came on a visit here, he quipped that clearly Sir Thomas Bodley had been misnamed—for his good works, he should have been Sir Thomas Godley. And furthermore, the king announced, were he ever to be a captive and have any choice of where his prison might be, he would choose the Bodleian and willingly be weighted down with the two thousand pounds of chains that held the books in place.

Clearly, the Bodleian had come into its own.

The Cathedral: ST. FRIDESWIDE'S SHRINE

Eighth-century Princess Frideswide, the daughter of King Didan who ruled here then, had only one wish: to become a nun. So her father built her her own church where Christ Church now stands, and she took the veil.

But Frideswide was one of the loveliest women in the land. Her vows notwithstanding, a neighboring king, Algar of Leicester, wanted her as his bride.

First he sent ambassadors to plead his cause. To the horror of all, they turned blind when they sought to abduct her.

But Algar was not deterred and came here himself after Frideswide. Frideswide fled to the woods, hiding at a swineherd's. And there as he searched for her, Algar was blinded, too. The conscience-stricken Frideswide, taking pity on him, prayed to St. Margaret to return his sight (*See* Binsey, St. Margaret's Churchyard: The Treacle Well). She stayed with him until her prayers were answered.

Then she returned to Oxford, to the church her father had built and of which this shrine is believed to have been a part. Her power was said to be so great that no enemies dared come here. Even as late as 1285, fearful of the saint, Edward I declined to enter this city.

Christ Church College

Magdalene College, where Thomas Wolsey had studied, was a beautiful college. When he became a cardinal, powerful and proud, Wolsey wanted an even grander college to be remembered by. Though he had money of his own, he needed even more for his grand scheme, so he got papal permission to close down some twenty monasteries and expropriate the funds to build a college without equal. To it he lured the best of scholars from all over England and Europe, and he called the college he was building Cardinal's College.

But then Wolsey failed to get the annulment Henry VIII sought of his marriage with Catherine of Aragon. Wolsey's power and prestige were gone, his land and property confiscated (*See* London Outskirts, Hampton Court: Hampton Court Palace—Gardens). He took much of his disgrace stoically, but he could not be a stoic about this college that meant so much to him. He wrote of sleepless nights and days of weeping, thinking of what would become of it and its scholars. In any action Henry took that might destroy the college, he begged the king to consider "those poor innocents" who studied there.

And when, finally, the college itself petitioned to be saved from dissolution, Henry replied that he would save it, but it would not be of the magnificence that Wolsey had envisioned. Henry's greedy advisers continually urged him to dissolve all colleges and take their lands and money as he had done with monasteries and convents. The wise Henry always replied that he "judged no land in England better bestowed than that which is given to our universities, for by their maintenance our realm shall be well governed when we be dead and rotten."

Dead himself by then, Wolsey need not have feared for his "poor innocents."

◆ ◆ ◆

The shy and stammering Charles Dodgson, who wrote under the pseudonym Lewis Carroll, studying and later lecturing in mathematics here, found it hard to make friends because of his stammer. But little Alice Liddell, the daughter of H. G. Liddell, the dean of Christ Church in his day, seemed never to have trouble understanding him and the tales that he told her.

So it was that she became the heroine of Dodgson's *Alice's Adventures in Wonderland* and *Through the Looking Glass*, which began with a rabbit hole in the garden of Christ Church Deanery. (*See* Binsey, St. Margaret's Churchyard: The Treacle Well.)

Martyrs' Memorial

It was near this spot in 1555 that the Protestant martyrs, Nicholas Ridley, Bishop of London, Hugh Latimer, Bishop of Worcester, and Thomas Cranmer, Archbishop of Canterbury, all perished at the stake on order of Queen Mary Tudor.

All had been friends and advisers of her father, Henry VIII, disavowing their Catholic faith and endorsing Protestantism for him. The zealously Catholic Mary saw nothing to be done but make a grisly example of them. (*See* Oxford, St. Mary the Virgin.)

Merton College: SUMMER HOUSE

Day after day, rain, snow, or shine, William Merle, a fellow of Merton in the fourteenth century, recorded the weather here for seven years. He achieved the distinction of being the first monitor of the weather in the western world.

New College: STATUE OF LAZARUS

The morning after viewing this 1951 Jacob Epstein statue of Lazarus rising from his grave, Soviet leader Nikita Khrushchev remarked that he was so haunted by its melancholy spirit that he had spent a sleepless night.

Oxford University

In the early days of this university, it was hardly a peaceful place. If, indeed, it had been, Cambridge University might never have been founded. When in 1209 a prostitute was discovered murdered in student lodgings, three of the students who lived in the same house were hauled from their rooms and hanged by enraged townspeople. As one story has it, in the wake of the hanging some three thousand students and masters then fled Oxford, terrified that they might suffer the same fate.

Some went to Cambridge, where they founded that university. Others established the university at Reading.

But that was hardly the end of untoward events between Oxford town and gown. A melee began at a tavern here one afternoon in 1355. Under the influence of drink and unhappy at the quality of what they were being served, two students tossed wine at the tavernkeeper. A fight began between the students' supporters and the tavernkeeper's friends. One of the latter ran to summon help by ringing the bells of the city's Church of St. Mary's. One of the student's friends went to get university aid by ringing the bells of the university's St. Mary's Church.

Fearful that the rioting would spread beyond the tavern, town bailiffs hurried to the university chancellor and demanded that he have the wine-throwing students arrested. When he declined to arrest them, the bailiffs went to complain to the king.

The rioting continued. Before it had ended, several students had been killed, and relations between town and gown were severely strained. The town was fined, the mayor sent to prison, and, when released, ordered to attend a Mass said annually for the souls of the dead students.

Queen's College

For centuries, at Christmastide, a boar's head was served in the dining room here. It was to commemorate the Queen's College member who, walking in a neighboring forest one day and reading Aristotle, was set upon by a wild boar. He had the presence of mind to save himself by thrusting his book into the charging animal's mouth.

St. Mary the Virgin

The elderly Archbishop of Canterbury, Thomas Cranmer, holding himself erect with the help of a white staff, faced a papal legate sent in September 1555 to examine him on his religious tenets. He heard himself accused of blasphemy and heresy because he refused to recognize the pope's law above all else. In the days of Roman Catholic Mary Tudor, that was not to be tolerated.

The following March Cranmer was here again. Old, tired, weary of long imprisonment, with his execution day already set, Cranmer had finally signed a recantation of Protestantism in his prison cell. But he remained condemned to death and was brought here to hear his funeral sermon preached. He was applauded by his accusers for having changed his mind and told that, while he was burning at the stake, they would be praying for him and a funeral dirge would be sung for him in every church in Oxford.

Then he was asked to publicly repeat his recantation.

He had a change of heart. Instead of recanting as had been expected, he cried out that his recantation had been a mistake. The hand that had written it, therefore, should be the first part of him to feel the pain of the execution fire.

The horrified Roman Catholics pulled him down

from where he stood and took him forthwith to the stake. Cranmer approached calmly and valiantly and thrust his "offending" hand into the fire. (*See* Oxford, Martyrs Memorial.)

University College: STATUE OF SHELLEY—
FRONT QUAD

This life-size nude statue showing Percy Bysshe Shelley being tossed about by a wave was meant originally for the Protestant Cemetery in Rome where the poet was buried after drowning off Viareggio in 1822. But cemetery commissioners in Rome found the Edward Onslow Ford monument too large and turned it down, so it came here where Shelley had studied.

The poet's career here, however, was a short one. Less than a year after arriving, he published a pamphlet on "The Necessity of Atheism" that did not sit well with the authorities. And so young Shelley was asked to leave the room that he had filled with books, papers, boots, pistols, and bags, and was told to write his diatribes—and his poetry—elsewhere.

PENZANCE

Union Hotel: DINING ROOM

England's first word of Admiral Lord Nelson's victory and death at the Battle of Trafalgar came from the gallery above this dining room in 1805.

A Penzance fisherman had been hailed with the news by a vessel headed toward neighboring Falmouth.

PERRANZABULOE

As the story goes, two saints who were building a fire to distill whiskey discovered the tin that for centuries provided livelihood for Cornishmen.

One day St. Piran came over from Ireland to Cornwall for a visit, bringing with him some good Irish whiskey. Here in Cornwall, he found a hermit saint, Chigwidden, who—hermit or not—was quite agreeably surprised by his Irish visitor and welcomed him and his whiskey into his little dwelling.

The Irishman talked and talked in the best Irish tradition. Chigwidden listened and drank in good Cornish tradition.

When morning came, of course, the whiskey bottle had been drained dry, and both saints still wished for more. No easier said than done, St. Piran announced. Piling up some stones, he built a fire, planning to show his new Cornish friend the art of distilling. A silver liquid squirted out from the black stones he had laid on the fire.

And so it was that tin was discovered.

PETERBOROUGH

Peterborough Cathedral

Sexton and gravedigger here for much of the sixteenth century, Roger Scarlett died in 1594 when he was just under a century old. He was still sorrowfully reminiscing about the two queens whom he had buried here: Henry VIII's Catherine of Aragon in 1536 and Mary, Queen of Scots after her execution in 1587.

Scarlett did not live to participate in the disinterment of Mary by her son, James I, when James had his mother's remains moved to Westminster Abbey.

◆ ◆ ◆

It was just a day or two before her death that Catherine of Aragon, for twenty-four years the wife of Henry VIII, wrote him a tender, loving note. For the love of younger, gayer Anne Boleyn, Henry had had his marriage to Catherine annulled and had left the Roman Catholic Church. It did not seem to matter to the dying former queen. She ended her letter of forgiveness with the longing phrase, "Mine eyes desire you above all things."

Perhaps even the hard heart of Henry was touched, for he saw to it that her funeral and burial here was a grand affair with all the local gentry summoned to pay their respects. (In issuing the order, though, those twenty-four years of marriage that he and Catherine had shared were ostensibly forgotten, for he called her only "our dearest sister.")

PLYMOUTH

The banquet aboard Francis Drake's *Golden Hind* here to celebrate his circumnavigation of the globe was one of the most splendid banquets since the days of Henry VIII.

Knighting the sea captain at the gala celebration in 1580, playful Queen Elizabeth remarked that she could, of course, just as easily cut off the good captain's head with the sword in her hand. Drake didn't flinch.

Barbican: MAYFLOWER STONE

The little band of emigrants seeking religious freedom had hoped that they could reach America in time to plant for a fall harvest. But there had been many delays (*See* Boston, Guildhall), and it was not until September 16, 1620, that the determined party of 102 aboard the cargo ship *Mayflower* finally sailed out of Plymouth harbor.

America's Pilgrim Fathers were on their way.

Plymouth Hoe

Even though a Spanish fleet of sixty-two ships was reported just down the coast, Sir Francis Drake really saw no need to hurry the game of bowls he was playing on this hill on July 19, 1588.

"Play out the game; there's time for that and to beat the Spanish after," he is reported to have lackadaisically told the messenger who hurried to him with the news of the approaching Armada.

PORTSMOUTH

Tinkering in his cobbler shop here in the eighteenth century at those times when he had no shoes to mend, John Pounds is said to have invented the umbrella.

Royal Dockyard: HMS *VICTORY*

Perhaps he had a premonition. On October 9, 1805, Admiral Lord Horatio Nelson fell to his knees in his cabin on this ship when it was at the Battle of Trafalgar, off Spain. He prayed for victory over Napoleon. He did not pray for safety for himself. Then he arose and sitting at the cabin desk wrote a codicil to his will requesting that England look after his beloved mistress, Lady Hamilton, and his daughter, Horatia, in the style to which they were accustomed. That same day as he stood on the deck he was struck by French musket fire. Three hours later he died.

Southwick House

It was D-day, June 6, 1944. There was no hesitation in the voice of General Dwight D. Eisenhower, Supreme Allied Commander, when he said, "All right. We'll go." Whereupon the largest invading army in the history of the world, aboard 4,266 barges, landing craft, and warships left Britain for France's Normandy.

RICHMOND

Richmond Castle

There are those who say that King Arthur sleeps in a tunnel here.

As the story goes, in the sixteenth century, a Richmond man who was exploring this Yorkshire castle's Gold Hole Tower found a tunnel leading out of it. He followed it, and at the end, in a room that was filled with gold, he saw King Arthur and his knights sleeping.

Just as the intruder was considering stealthily stealing a little treasure, King Arthur awoke, the man reported, and asked in a sleepy voice if it was time yet to rise.

The terrified intruder fled back up the tunnel. No one else has ever found the tunnel or King Arthur's treasure.

RIPON

Fountains Abbey

The outlaw Robin Hood had learned in his Sherwood Forest hideaway of a remarkable friar who dwelt at this twelfth-century Cistercian abbey. It was said that the friar was an archer of great renown, so Robin Hood set off to find him. As he neared here, he told his men that he would go alone after the friar. Should he need their help for any reason, he would, as always, blow his horn to call them.

Not far outside the abbey, near one of its many ponds and rivulets, the outlaw noticed a portly friar, his gown hiked up about his knees, gamboling in a somewhat unseemly way for a man of God. Wondering if this might be the friar he sought, Robin Hood accosted him. Then Robin demanded in a peremptory way that since the friar had his gown hiked up he come over the stream that lay between them and carry him across.

Without complaining, the friar did just that. But once he had done it, he made the same request of Robin Hood: tit for tat. Robin Hood picked up the friar and carried him back to his side of the stream. But then the outlaw asked to be carried back across again.

Tired of the game and halfway across, the man of God dumped Robin Hood into the water and, smiling merrily, suggested that he either sink or swim.

Robin Hood swam, but there followed a ferocious daylong fight between the two men. It did not end until dusk, when Robin Hood, lying exhausted in the grass at the friar's feet, admitted that he was the loser but asked permission of the victor to blow the horn he carried.

Strange though the request was, the friar granted it. Suddenly from out of the woods with bows drawn sprang all of Robin Hood's Merry Men.

The annoyed friar then asked if he could whistle three times. Robin Hood allowed it. From behind the abbey came a pack of dogs with teeth bared. Snarling at the outlaw chief, two of them attacked Robin and tore his jerkin of Lincoln green from him.

Robin Hood's outlaws let fly their arrows, and several dogs were felled before the friar and Robin Hood reached an agreement. Clearly, Friar Tuck was the caliber of man Robin Hood liked in his band. As attractive as this abbey is, the friar found life in it too confining for his high spirits and so it was that Friar Tuck joined Robin Hood and his Merry Men.

ROCHESTER

Rochester Cathedral: SHRINE OF WILLIAM OF PERTH

A generous and devout Scottish baker, William of Perth always gave one in ten loaves of the bread he baked to the poor. For many years he had longed to make a pilgrimage to the Holy Land, and at last in 1201 he left his bakery in other hands and set off to the south.

He reached Rochester one fine May day, sought and was given shelter for the night, and the next day started toward Canterbury.

But poor William had barely left the town before he was set upon and stabbed to death. His body was returned for burial here, and it is said that soon miracles began to occur. This shrine became so popular that contributions to it were sufficient to enlarge the cathedral.

ROSTHERNE (North of Knutsford)

Church of Rostherne

It is said that a playful mermaid who inhabits the mere below this church sometimes rings one of its old bells underwater.

As the story goes, when the bells were being put in place, one of them fell and was roundly cursed by the workmen hanging it. So defiled, the bell was not, of course, fit for a church any longer and was rolled into the mere, where the mermaid has enjoyed it ever since.

RYDAL

Rydal Mount

Living here with his family from 1813 to his death in 1850, William Wordsworth was busy writing, and there was no disturbing him. The call for dinner would go unheeded when he was most immersed in his work. In desperation, servants would sometimes drop old crockery or glassware outside his door to rouse him from his creativity. Since Wordsworth was a careful man, he tended to be disturbed enough when he heard dishes breaking to respond to the dinner call.

ST. MICHAEL'S MOUNT

It is said that the fierce giant, Cormoran, built this mount of white rock to be his home. Since the mainland was barely a giant's step away, he would make frequent journeys to it to steal cattle for his meals.

Young Jack the Giant Killer, a farmer's son who became the hero of the nursery story of that name, learned of Cormoran's depredations and sought to end them by digging a deep pit at the foot of this mount, covering it with straw, then blowing his horn loudly to disturb the sleeping giant.

Cormoran did just what was expected. Rising from

sleep in a rage, he raced down the mount and fell into Jack's pit. Jack did him in with his pickaxe and filled up the hole.

◆   ◆   ◆

In ancient days Joseph of Arimathea prospered carrying tin between Cornwall and Phoenicia. On one of his journeys he brought with him here on an outing Mary and the infant Jesus.

SALISBURY

Recently returned in 1618 from his unsuccessful journey to Guyana, Sir Walter Raleigh was en route to death in the Tower of London (*See* London, Tower of London: Bloody Tower). He had not returned with silver for James I, and, clearly, he was to be punished for his failure with the supreme penalty.

But if he could explain to James how illness had forced abandonment of the expedition, Raleigh thought there might yet be some hope of pardon.

He found a bizarre way to make his captors halt with him here while he wrote a letter to the king. Raleigh painted himself to look like a leper and said that he felt ill and needed time to rest. His horrified captors willingly gave him the time he asked and kept their distance.

Unfortunately Raleigh's plea to the king went unheeded. His "leprosy" faded, and his journey to the Tower continued.

Salisbury Cathedral

According to local legend, the siting of this cathedral, notable above all for its majestic spire, was very simply done. The bishop of Old Sarum, an ancient Roman town that sat on the hill above this present city, simply proposed that an arrow be shot to the plain below. The site where it fell was where this cathedral was built.

SAWREY

Hill Top Farm

With the help of "Peter Rabbit's" royalties, Beatrix Potter bought this farm, "as nearly perfect a place" as she had ever lived, she said. Then she settled down to write *Tom Kitten, Jemima Puddle-Duck,* and *The Roly-Poly Pudding* in this house that still seems inhabited by them.

In 1913 when she married and moved across the field and gave up writing to be a wife, sheep farmer, and conservationist, she gave this farm and the lands around it to the National Trust so the land would be preserved forever for the kittens, rabbits, puddle-ducks, squirrels, and titmice that had inspired her.

SHOTTERY

Anne Hathaway's Cottage

In 1582, eighteen-year-old William Shakespeare made regular pilgrimages from neighboring Stratford Town to this pretty, half-timbered cottage to woo twenty-six-year-old Anne Hathaway. It was in November that year under somewhat questionable circumstances (the marriage bans were published only once, not twice) that the young couple wed. Anne gave birth to their first child just six months later.

STONEHENGE

There are some who say that it was Merlin the Magician who brought these stones from Ireland and, with his magic, arranged them this way and that.

STRATFORD-UPON-AVON

Because so many eighteenth-century callers came to see the mulberry tree in the yard of the house where William Shakespeare had died, its peevish owner chopped the tree down and had souvenirs made from it

When sightseers continued to gawk at the house, the irascible owner simply had the house torn down, its Shakespeare connections notwithstanding.

Charlecote House

Since poaching was a practice of his day, legend has it that young William Shakespeare thought little of illegally taking a deer or two on this great Stratford estate, but he was caught and forced to flee Stratford for a time.

TINTAGEL

As the Arthurian legend goes, Uthur Pendragon, King of Britain, disguised with the help of Merlin the enchanter, was able to enter this castle where Igerne, wife of the Duke of Cornwall, was hidden. Having once caught sight of Igerne, the British king was smitten with love and was determined that she would be his.

And so she was—after Uther Pendragon had killed the duke. Arthur was born of their union. In Arthur's infancy Merlin carried him away from the castle that stood where these ruins are now. He was given over to the care of a good and kindly knight, Sir Ector, who reared him secretly until Uther Pendragon died. Then Ector brought him forth and presented the "kidnapped" boy to his astounded mother, and Arthur was proclaimed king.

TONG

Boscobel House: ROYAL OAK

After losing the Battle of Worcester in 1651, with his face stained dark and his hair cut short, twenty-one-year-old Charles II took refuge in a hollow oak tree here as the soldiers of Oliver Cromwell searched for him all about. The tree that now rises in this garden is said to be a descendant of that royal oak.

ULLSWATER

Gowbarrow Park

Walking by this lake one spring day, William and Dorothy Wordsworth happened upon that "host of golden daffodils" that William so unforgettably described in "I Wandered Lonely as a Cloud." Dorothy wrote equally evocatively of them in her journal, describing some resting their heads on the mossy stones of the water's bank; others that "tossed and reeled and danced and seemed as if they verily laughed with the wind that blew upon them."

WARWICK

Warwick Castle

In 1312 within these gloomy walls, Piers Gaveston, Edward II's witty, handsome best friend and confidant, was put on trial by the King's barons, led by Guy of Warwick. Gaveston had gaily nicknamed Warwick "the Black Dog of Arden." Having promised that Gaveston would feel his bite, the Black Dog took him to neighboring Blacklow Hill and had him beheaded.

WELLS

Wells Cathedral

The soldiers of the Duke of Monmouth, one of Charles II's illegitimate sons, did not want Roman Catholic James II on the throne. Though their effort in 1685 to oust him and put the duke in his place was short-lived, it lasted long enough to damage and desecrate this cathedral.

The lead from the cathedral roof was melted down to make bullets for Monmouth's men. They sacrilegiously served beer from a barrel they put on the altar, and they stabled their horses in the nave.

WINCHESTER

Winchester Castle: THE GREAT HALL AND KING ARTHUR'S ROUND TABLE

Entertaining his guest Charles V of the Holy Roman Empire in 1552, Henry VIII brought him here to see this historic round table, seventeen feet in diameter. It was said that King Arthur and his twenty-four noble knights had sat around it.

Because Henry himself found this to be one of the most thrilling sights in his kingdom, he wanted Charles to admire it too. To make certain the emperor would, Henry had the table repainted in his royal guest's honor.

Winchester Cathedral: THE LADY CHAPEL

On July 25, 1554, attended by sixty grandees, dressed in a robe of brocade adorned with diamonds and pearls, and wearing a collar of beaten gold, Philip II of Spain took thirty-eight-year-old Queen Mary Tudor to be his bride.

Queen Mary's attire was as resplendent as her bride-groom's. But the queen's personal touch of donning scarlet shoes was deemed unseemly by many of those in attendance.

◆ ◆ ◆

In 1642 down this nave, the longest in the world except for that of St. Peter's in Rome, thundered the hooves of the horses of Oliver Cromwell's men. When they reached the altar, the horse-borne soldiers dismounted, struck the heads from statues, scattered the bones of the buried, and destroyed the organ before they remounted and thundered out again.

Winchester Cathedral: JANE AUSTEN'S GRAVESTONE

It was some fifty years after the author Jane Austen died here in Winchester in 1817 before any mention was made in this burial place of her attributes as a writer. When this gravestone was set in place, it was deemed more seemly to recognize England's greatest woman writer for the good life she had led, rather than for the great works she had produced.

Winchester Cathedral: ST. SWITHUN'S SHRINE

St. Swithun, Bishop of Winchester, was a self-effacing man. On his deathbed in 862 he said that he was not worthy to be buried within the cathedral. But a century later it was felt more appropriate, no matter what he had said, to have his bones resting inside.

The reburial day was set for July 15, but it rained and the transfer could not be made. And for forty days thereafter it rained, and St. Swithun could not be removed from the churchyard.

It was this storm that gave rise to the still-quoted saying that if it rains on St. Swithun's Day, it will rain for forty days more.

Winchester Cathedral: TOMB OF WILLIAM II

After much-detested William II (known as William Rufus for his red hair) was killed while hunting in the New Forest, he was brought here for burial. Those given the task of burying him shivered at the prospect of his being interred in so holy a place as a cathedral, for he was such an evil man, they said.

As befitted his station, however, he was laid to rest here, but in a virtually unmarked tomb.

God is said to have taken umbrage even at that and struck the tower of this cathedral in 1107 so that it collapsed and had to be rebuilt.

WINDERMERE LAKE

Though his cries are little heard nowadays, legend has it that there was a time when the Crier of Claife Heights would call and moan intermittently here. His cries boded no good. Almost always afterwards, there would be some untoward occurrence on this lake.

One notable seventeenth-century tragedy said to have been Crier-caused was the drowning of a wedding party of forty-seven, returning from the festivities at Hawkshead by ferry. It was said that the Crier had moaned and taken them off their course.

WOODSTOCK

Blenheim Palace (seven miles northwest of Oxford)

In 1704 the conquering hero, John Churchill, Duke of Marlborough, had just come home from victory over the French at the Battle of Blenheim in Bavaria in the War of the Spanish Succession. Queen Anne wished to reward him. She gave the duke her manor here and the two-thousand-five-hundred acres that surround it and told him the nation would build him the palace of his choice on it.

On June 18, 1705, the cornerstone was laid. Buckets, bowls, and pans of wine and punch and ale were served, and there was Morris dancing in celebration. Marlborough had chosen the poet-playwright-soldier-architect John Vanbrugh (*See* Malton, Castle Howard) to design his palace for him. For so great a military man as Churchill, Vanbrugh fashioned a monumental structure with gateways weighing seventeen tons and a courtyard that seemed a mound of stones.

But it was all extremely costly, and though Churchill continued winning battles for England, this great gift-monument for him fell out of favor with the nation. His wife, a confidante of the queen, also fell out of favor with Her Majesty. Parliament stopped paying for Blenheim's construction, and in 1722 when the hero-duke died, much of his dream palace was still a dream.

◆　◆　◆

The architect for this enormous palace, John Vanbrugh, brought his wife here to see his handiwork. But

Sarah, Duchess of Marlborough, whose home it was and who had never liked either Vanbrugh or his design, ordered her servants to turn away the couple.

◆ ◆ ◆

"I took two very important decisions here—to be born and to marry," Winston Churchill said of this great house that his ancestor, John Churchill, Duke of Marlborough, had built. (It was in a summer house beside the ornamental lake that the young Churchill asked Clementine Hozler to be his bride.)

"I am happily content with the decisions I took on both these occasions," Sir Winston concluded.

YORK

Castle Museum: CONDEMNED CELL

It was in this cell that highwayman Dick Turpin spent his last months. Then he gaily and gallantly went to his execution in 1739. When his right foot trembled as he mounted the execution ladder, he stamped on it. He grandly left money, hatbands, and gloves to the five men he had hired to be his mourners.

Though much embellished in novelist William Harrison Ainsworth's *Rockwood*, Dick Turpin's real life story was a colorful one, too. He liked to retell it to his guards here in those months as he awaited execution.

While working as an apprentice butcher in his youth, Dick began stealing cattle to provide good meat for the shop. When he was found out, he took to the road, joining a band of highwaymen terrorizing the Essex countryside. Its other members were caught, but Dick managed to escape, joining forces this time with just one highwayman.

Turpin and his accomplice did well for some years, attacking coaches and single travelers in lonely places. Then once when they were cornered by armed men, Dick mistakenly killed his accomplice, but escaped himself.

For some years he seemed to have disappeared. The

roads in Essex and Epping, where he had tended to prey, were again safe to travel. About this time, a horse dealer named John Palmer moved into the town of Welton near here, where he became noted for his fine marksmanship and expert riding.

One evening when he was sitting outside a tavern, a gamecock flew by. Palmer raised his musket and shot it dead. Its furious owner demanded retribution. In reply, Palmer raised his musket again and threatened the man's life.

Before he knew it, Palmer had been arrested both for shooting the bird and for his threat against its owner. It was while Palmer was in prison that he was unmasked and found to be the notorious highwayman Turpin (not the gallant one of stories). In court, among other ignominious acts, he was not-so-fondly remembered for having threatened to hold an elderly widow over her fireplace fire until she revealed to him the whereabouts of her life savings.

Clifford's Tower

In the twelfth century, in a flurry of anti-Semitism, the Jews of York feared for their lives and took refuge in this tower. A white-robed monk was inciting townspeople to attack this castle and drive out the refugees.

In terror, the Jewish families staying here met and discussed their future. It was not a happy one. Clearly, they would soon be prisoners of the larger, more powerful Christian population.

And so, as their forebears had done at Masada centuries earlier when faced with capture by the Romans, the Jews of York took their own lives. Those few who didn't, died, as they had feared, at the hands of the Christians.

Jorvik Viking Center (Coppergate)

In 1967 digging began for the Coppergate Shopping

Center, and the diggers found more than they were bargaining for. Under the site that they had selected they unearthed four rows of ancient Viking structures, dating from those ninth-century days when this was the capital of a Viking kingdom. The dampness here had so preserved the contents left behind that it was possible to reconstruct the Viking structures of long ago.

Micklegate Bar

At first Margaret of Anjou, wife of Henry VI, paled when she was offered the head of her enemy, Richard, the Duke of York, on the end of a lance after she had defeated him in the Wars of the Roses. But she soon recovered. He had sought to take the throne from her husband and son, and in death, as in life, he would pay for his presumption. She ordered that, crowned with a coronet of grass since he claimed to be a king, his head should be spiked above this gate. William Shakespeare had her exclaim gleefully in *King Henry VI, Part III* that that way "York may overlook the town of York."

◆ ◆ ◆

Though in 1541 York's citizens were not sure they looked forward to his visit, Henry VIII was expected here. Town fathers accordingly decorated this entry gate to welcome him. Henry had been closing down the monasteries, which was a practice that did not meet with local approval. But he was the king.

At the last minute there had to be a change of plans. Town fathers learned that Henry was coming not in friendship but in wrath. Hastily the decorations were taken down, and festive events were cancelled. A somber delegation of town fathers, all dressed in their drabbest garb, knelt abjectly and subserviently by the roadside as the king came in through the lesser Walmgate, not through this impressive gate.

St. Michael's Church: SPURRIERGATE

In those days in the Middle Ages when wolves howled at night in the forest around this city, many a traveler lost his way. One of those who lost his way but then found it again rewarded this church for his deliverance. As the story goes, it was the 8 P.M. curfew ringing here that led him to safety. Ever grateful, he left monies to continue forever the ringing of St. Michael's curfew.

The Shambles:
MARGARET CLITHEROW'S HOUSE (No. 35)

In the 1580s few women of York were more highly regarded for their kindliness and generosity than Margaret Clitherow, the butcher's wife. But Margaret was a Catholic, and Catholicism was not to be tolerated in those days after the atrocities of Catholic Mary Tudor. That the butcher's wife had hidden Jesuit priests in her attic was unacceptable.

So Margaret Clitherow was brought to trial and sentenced to death for harboring the priests. Death was imposed by laying a door on her chest and piling it with stones until she was crushed. In 1970 she was canonized as St. Margaret of York.

Sheriff Hutton Castle Ruin (near Flaxton)

Joyously, eighteen-year-old Elizabeth of York learned in August 1483 that her imprisonment in this now-ruined castle had ended. Instead of prisoner, she would be Queen of England.

The daughter of Edward IV and Elizabeth Woodville had not had a tranquil life. Two of her young brothers had disappeared from sight and had presumably been murdered. (*See* London, Tower of London: Bloody Tower.) With her mother and other brothers and sisters, she had lived fearfully for a while in the fortified sanctuary at Westminster. She had been affianced to the Dauphin of France and was gaily dressing in the prettiest of French fashions so she would please him when Louis XI suddenly called off the engagement. Then her father had died. Determined to make her Queen of England, her mother had arranged for her to marry Henry of Richmond, destined to become Henry VII.

But while she was waiting, her uncle, Richard III, came to the throne and she was dispatched to court as a companion for his ailing wife, Anne. Rumor had it that the pretty niece had caught the king's eye, too. There was even a rumor that he had helped "dispatch" his wife so that he could marry Elizabeth.

But when Elizabeth made it clear she had no interest in him, she was sent here under guard. And here she was when Richard died in battle at Bosworth Field. (*See* Market Bosworth, Bosworth Field.) Then Henry of Richmond, now Henry VII, sent for his delicate blonde fiancée, and at last her troubles were finished.

Treasurer's House

In the 1950s, when archaeological digging was going on in this area, a young apprentice installing plumbing beneath this house thought—or imagined—he heard the sound of a trumpet. It seemed odd to him that if there were a band in the street, he should hear its music so clearly. Nonetheless he kept on with his work.

But suddenly there was the clatter of hooves and arms in the cellar, and a man in Roman dress riding a horse appeared. Behind him more men in Roman garb passed on foot. The apprentice fell from his ladder. The Romans disappeared and the shaking boy hurried upstairs to describe what he had seen.

But he didn't have to. One look at his pale face, and the curator nodded knowingly. He said that he too had seen the ghostly Romans who once had inhabited this city

York Minster

In 625 to secure more land for his kingdom, pagan King Edwin of Northumbria asked for the hand of Christian Ethelburga of Kent. She was given to him on the condition that her priest come with her. Though Edwin declined to change his faith, he did agree when his first child was born that she might be christened by her mother's priest.

Among the visitors at that day's christening was a servant of the king of West Saxony, there ostensibly to offer congratulations on the birth—but in actuality, to murder Edwin.

He tried, drawing a dagger as the king raised his horn to his lips to drink his new daughter's health. But one of Edwin's men, seeing the glint of the dagger, stepped between it and his lord and saved the king.

Immediately, Edwin readied for war against the king of West Saxony, and he prepared to ask his pagan gods for help in his endeavor.

The queen's Catholic priest, Paulinus, gambled. He proposed to the king that he pray this time, instead, to his wife's and daughter's Christian God. And if his prayers were answered, Paulinus proposed that perhaps the king would choose to be a Christian, too.

That was precisely what happened. In 627 a victorious Edwin returned here to be baptized on Easter Eve. For the ceremony, he had constructed on this site a little wooden church that was the first real home of Christianity here.

Kindly Archbishop William, great-grandson of William the Conqueror, had just drunk from the Communion chalice here when, writhing, he dropped dead.

Though he was gentle and thoughtful, the monks he oversaw had never liked his being of royal blood. Once they had had him ousted from his post by Rome, but townspeople got him back. But this time there would be no coming back. The monk serving him his Communion wine had seen to that.

◆ ◆ ◆

Roger, the Archbishop of York, couldn't have looked any sillier, perched as he was on the knee of Richard, the Archbishop of Canterbury.

It all began in 1177 when Roger was late to a gathering here that the cardinal was attending. Roger found the Archbishop of Canterbury seated at the cardinal's right hand. As he saw it, that was the most important seat in the minster after the cardinal's. York Minster was, after all, *his* minster. What was the Archbishop of Canterbury doing sitting in *his* seat?

In a fury, he plunked himself down on Richard's knee. Richard objected. So did visitors from Canterbury in attendance, who pulled the York archbishop off Richard's knee. They treated him roughly enough to tear his embroidered cope, and they flung him down on the dusty floor.

More enraged than ever, the archbishop stormed off. He was on his way, he said, to see Henry II to find out which archbishop the king felt was more important. When Roger found him and presented his case, the king could barely control his laughter and said that he could take no stand. The matter of precedence was up to the two archbishops.

In time, word of his archbishops' unseemly conduct reached the pope. He solved the matter once and for all by making the Archbishop of York the primate of England, but the Archbishop of Canterbury primate of *all* England.

◆ ◆ ◆

Though he should have held his tongue, Richard Scrope, Archbishop of York, preached vehemently against Henry IV from this pulpit. He was accused of treason, tried, sentenced to death, and, his face to its tail, sent out on an old nag to his execution place near York

Castle. It is said that as he rode out he prayed unceasingly
for the souls of his executioners. Whether he also prayed
for His Majesty, however, remains a matter of conjecture.

Soon after the execution, Henry IV began to suffer
from leprosy-like lesions. Many thought they were in
retribution for his execution of England's second-highest
prelate.

◆ ◆ ◆

Oliver Cromwell's Puritan soldiers were smashing the
statues and windows of England's great churches everywhere, deeming such decoration frivolous and idolatrous.
The stained glass windows of this great cathedral were to
suffer the fate of all the others. But among the Puritan
generals was a Yorkshireman, Sir Thomas Fairfax.
Knowing how much the splendid stained glass here
meant to his fellow Yorkshiremen, Fairfax convinced his
comrades to leave the windows unharmed.

◆ ◆ ◆

Three times fires have devastated this fifteenth-century
Gothic cathedral.

One winter morning in 1829 a chorister on his way to
sing here slipped on the ice and, falling on his back,
looked up to see smoke coming from the lantern tower. It
turned out that a madman whom voices had told to destroy the minster had set fire to the organ the night before. By the time the chorister saw the smoke, virtually
all of the choir had been destroyed.

Eleven years later a workman left a candle burning in
the southwest tower. The tower went up in flames, and as
it was consumed, the tower bells fell.

Most recently, one July night in 1984, lightning set the
south transept on fire, cracking the 8,000-piece fifteenth-
century Lancaster and York Rose Window into forty-
thousand pieces.

Happily, contributions poured in from all over the
nation to repair the great window that joined the red rose
of Lancastrian Henry VII with the white rose of Eliza-

beth of York, that had been created in 1485 to celebrate
the marriage of that pair and the end of the thirty-two-
year-long Wars of the Roses.

York Minster: THE FIVE SISTERS WINDOW

It was just after the disastrous Battle of Gallipoli in
World War I. Helen Dragge Little, the widow of a military man, was watching the wounded being brought
back and admired the gentleness and devotion with
which their nurses tended them. She thought as she
watched that when the war was done a memorial should
be erected somewhere to those brave women.

And then one night in 1922 she woke, startled, from a
dream in which she saw her two long-dead sisters standing in white before this window, pointing to it. Beyond
it, she could view a group of women dressed in the gray-
green clothes of military nurses.

In the morning, Mrs. Little came here to the minster
and saw that this window was in need of repair. She
started a campaign to raise money for it, as her memorial
to those nurses of Gallipoli. Within nine weeks, some
thirty-two-thousand donors had contributed to the fund,
and more than enough money was raised for the restoration.

2
SCOTLAND

ALLOWAY

Alloway Kirk

It was a terrifying scene. The stray Highland bullock had found its way into the walled churchyard here and could not get out. Without food and water, it began to bellow and race from end to end of the churchyard enclosure. An old woman passing by, hearing the bellow and seeing horns peeking out over the wall, was sure that the devil was in residence.

Bellowing herself, she fled to the nearest house and panted out her tale. Though her fears were calmed after a party of bold souls investigated and found the bullock, the story of the devil in residence spread. Nine-year-old Robert Burns is said to have listened open-mouthed as it was recounted.

Years later Burns remembered the old woman's tale and told it in his own way in "Tam o' Shanter." (*See* Dumfries, Ellisland Farm.)

Brig o'Doon

As poet Robert Burns imagined it, it was halfway across this bridge that Tam o' Shanter, in the poem of that name, was pursued by a witch and his horse's tail pulled off by the pursuer.

Burns Cottage

The week of January 25, 1759, the wind howled and the snow swirled here with such fury that the roof of this little cottage was swept away. Newborn Robert Burns and his mother had to be carried to shelter in a neighbor's house. Later when he was a poet renowned for his verse but notorious for his love affairs, Burns remarked that it was not surprising that one who entered life in such a storm should be the victim of stormy passions.

ARBROATH

Arbroath Abbey

It was affection for the dying King George VI that led the patriotic Scots who stole the Stone of Scone away from Westminster Abbey in 1950 to inform officials that they had left it on the altar here.

For 109 days the Stone of Destiny that England's Edward I had taken from Scotland in 1296 (*See* England, London, Westminster Abbey) was gone from its place beneath the Coronation Chair in Westminster Abbey. On Christmas Day of 1950, two Scottish students from Glasgow broke into the Abbey and dislodged the ninety-pound stone on which the kings of Scotland have always been crowned. Wrapping it in a blanket, they hauled it out to the street where other students waited to carry it in a car back to Scotland.

Soon word was out all over Scotland and England that the Stone was gone. The students chose to hide it in a hedge in the country until the heat of the hunt for it was past. There, as it turned out, the Stone stayed longer than they had expected, for gypsies chose the land around it as a camping place.

All the same, within a matter of weeks the Stone was secretly brought to this hallowed site, where in 1320 the Scottish Parliament first declared Scotland's freedom from English rule.

But terminally ill King George put out an appeal for the return of the Stone of Scone. He feared, it is said, that if he died before it was found and Elizabeth was crowned, Scotland (which joined the United Kingdom in 1707) would be lost forever to the British crown.

So King George could die with peace of mind, the students grudgingly let it be known that the Stone of Scone was here in Arbroath.

BANNOCKBURN

The ten-foot tall statue of Robert the Bruce that honors his 1314 victory here was made by five-foot-tall R. C. Pilkington Jackson. The difference in size between the sculptor and the statue posed a problem. But the sculptor solved it by setting Robert and his horse on an automobile lift so that he could raise and lower them to the appropriate height for working on them in his Edinburgh studio.

BEMERSYDE

Scott's View

When the funeral carriage bearing the remains of the poet-novelist Sir Walter Scott reached this spot above the Tweed and the Eildon Hills where, in his lifetime, Scott had always stopped to contemplate the view, his horses drew to their accustomed halt. It was half an hour—Scott's usual contemplation time—before they stirred again and the funeral cortege could move on.

BORTHWICK

Borthwick Castle (not open to the public)

The wedding of Mary, Queen of Scots to the Earl of Bothwell in May 1567 was a somewhat hasty affair (*See* Edinburgh, Holyrood House: Great Hall), but a quiet honeymoon in the country here was in prospect. It turned out to be hardly quiet, however.

Barely had the couple arrived when some one thousand Scottish lords opposed to Bothwell and the queen's marriage to him arrived to storm the castle. Realizing the castle was not easily defensible, Bothwell climbed out a window and escaped through a postern gate. Remaining behind, Mary sought to remonstrate with the lords outside, but their demand was that she abandon her new husband and return with them to Edinburgh. Mary declined. The lords sent for more soldiers, and when night had fallen, dressed in the costume of a page, Mary fled to be reunited nearby with Bothwell. The honeymoon had proved a sorry one indeed.

CAWDOR

Cawdor Castle

Shakespearean legend has it that an ambitious Macbeth, after graciously welcoming his kinsman, King Duncan, to the castle that stood near this site in the eleventh century, foully murdered him in the night.

Macbeth was influenced by the prophesy of three witches he had met on the heath near Forres who had promised him the kingdom, and by his scheming, unscrupulous wife. Macbeth took the knives of the king's bodyguards as they slept a drug-induced sleep. Then, with the knives, he murdered the king, putting the bloody daggers back in the bodyguards' sheaths to throw suspicion on them.

When the guards awoke to find their master dead, Macbeth murdered them, too, before they could raise an alarm. He explained afterward that he had killed them in a blind rage after seeing Duncan foully killed and finding bloody daggers on the guards.

And the kingdom did, indeed—historically—become his for seventeen years. Then Malcolm, one of Duncan's sons, killed Macbeth in battle.

◆ ◆ ◆

Happily in the end, it turned out all right for red-haired Muriella of Cawdor, but her adventures were considerable in her childhood.

Born in 1408, five months after the untimely death of her young father, Thane John of Cawdor, the red-haired infant was to inherit his castle. But she had three uncles who wanted it, too. Foreseeing that, in his final illness, her father had made her a ward of the Crown. The king, in turn, had appointed guardians to look after her affairs until she was old enough to wed and would have a husband to look after them for her. Like little Muriella's uncles, the guardians coveted the property that was hers.

One of them, the Earl of Argyll, thought longingly of the possibility of making her in time the wife of his son, John, and thereby having a claim on the castle.

It took him a while to put his thought into action, but by the time Muriella was four, the earl had decided he would kidnap her.

In issuing the orders for the kidnapping, the hard-hearted earl was heard to say that if the child should prove too delicate to survive the one hundred mile journey to his castle at Inveraray (*See* Inveraray, Inveraray Castle), it didn't really matter. Any red-haired four-year-old girl could easily be substituted for her and, when she grew up, be married to his John. And the horsemen rode off to do the earl's bidding.

The day that they reached the grounds here, Muriella was out playing with her nurse. The child's mother was at home in the castle and her uncles were away on a journey. Suddenly, horsemen appeared through the trees.

The leader told the nursemaid that he had been sent by the Earl of Argyll, head of the Campbell clan and one of the king's appointed guardians, to take Muriella back with him to Inveraray for safekeeping.

The nurse protested, but alone there was nothing that she could do to protect her little charge. She, too, however, had heard it said that it did not matter to the earl what red-haired child he got so long as she was believed to be Muriella. So feigning the need to wrap the little girl more warmly, the nursemaid covered Muriella from head to toe with her own tartan shawl. While doing so, out of sight of the Campbell kidnappers, she bit off the tip of one of Muriella's little fingers so she would forever be different from other little redheaded girls.

It was not until the Campbells were well on their way with their charge that they discovered what had been done. Kindlier than the earl who had sent them, they bandaged the little finger, stopping the flow of blood. Muriella, in due course, arrived at Inveraray.

There she grew to adulthood, nurtured by the earl's wife, a gentle soul who reared her lovingly. And, as the earl had planned, when she came of age he married her to John.

Cawdor Castle: CENTRAL TOWER

It is said that a donkey selected the site for the imposing castle of which this tower was a part. When the Thane of Cawdor was trying to decide where he would build his castle, he had a dream that directed him to set free a donkey laden with gold and to build where the donkey lay down to rest.

Doing as he was bid, the thane hung a sack of gold around the animal's neck and followed its wanderings across his moorland as it nibbled for hours at thistles. Tired of the unaccustomed weight of the gold, the donkey lay down in the shade of a hawthorn tree and where it rested the thane built his castle

COMRIE

The Museum of Scottish Tartans

Hanging here is a portrait of John Brown, the Highland servant and confidant of Queen Victoria. In 1883, the last year of his life, Brown, whose power over the then-widowed queen was considerable, had this portrait done by the court painter and hung in Balmoral Castle.

After the queen had died, her son Edward VII, who had never approved of Brown's role in his mother's life, one day attacked the painting with a stick (repairs can be seen in one leg and a shoulder). He then sent the portrait off to Brown's family. The painting disappeared for years, but in 1963 it was found in an old shed by the Tartan Society and salvaged for this museum of Highland memorabilia.

CULLODEN

On April 15, 1746, the night before the Battle of Culloden, the soldiers of the Duke of Cumberland had celebrated the twenty-fifth birthday of their leader with brandy toasts. The next day they presented him with victory over Prince Charles Edward Stuart and his Highlanders as a birthday present. (*See* Outer Hebrides, Eriskay.) Later there was still another gift. The composer Handel wrote "See, the Conquering Hero Comes" about him.

CULROSS

Princess Thenew, the Christian daughter of the King of Lothian, had vowed to remain a virgin, but she saw nothing wrong in sharing her bed with a neighbor girl. But the "girl" turned out to be the prince of a neighboring tribe.

When the princess discovered that she was expecting, her irate father sent her out across the Firth of Forth in an open boat with no provisions. With the help of wind and tide, however, the boat was carried here. Thenew and the baby boy she bore as soon as she had landed were both cared for by the monks of St. Serf, who in the sixth century had a settlement here. Indeed, her little boy, whom the monks named Mungo, was brought up by St. Serf himself. When grown to manhood, Mungo went away to found a monastery of his own where Glasgow is today and to become St. Mungo. (*See* Glasgow, St. Mungo's Cathedral.)

DRUMNADROCHIT

Loch Ness

One gloomy day in 565 A.D., the missionary St. Columba, crossing the River Ness near here, saw the much-mutilated body of a man being dragged out of the water. Inquiring as to what had happened, the distressed saint was told that while the man was swimming, a huge monster had surfaced and viciously attacked him. Concerned that there might be another such occurrence, Columba directed one of his followers to swim out into the loch to try to rouse the beast again.

Dutifully, though without great enthusiasm, the follower plunged into the dark waters. Suddenly the smooth surface erupted, and with a great roar and open mouth, so the story goes, a monster hurtled toward the swimmer. But Columba, making the sign of the cross, commanded the huge beast to return to the loch's depths. Miraculously, the cowed monster retreated to his dark, dank home. From time to time since, a strange, enormous creature, variously described as humpbacked or camel-headed, is said to have been seen in Loch Ness. It has never, since then, been known to have attacked a man.

DRYBURGH

Abbotsford

In the beginning, Sir Walter Scott envisioned Abbotsford

simply as a summer dwelling. But the more he built, the more enchanted he became with this dwelling on the gray, windy moors. He added turrets to the outside, and he filled the inside with memorabilia that delighted his romantic heart—Napoleon's cloak-clasp, a lock of Bonnie Prince Charlie's hair, a macabre painting of the head of Mary, Queen of Scots made the day after her execution, a glass that had been Robert Burns's. And here he entertained guests with enthusiasm, rambled the moors with Washington Irving, and talked books and poetry with Thomas Moore and William Wordsworth.

◆ ◆ ◆

All day and late into the night for the last six years of his life, Sir Walter Scott wrote in his small, dark study here to pay off a £160,000 debt of his publisher. Two decades earlier, when an old schoolchum, James Ballantyne, had fallen on hard times and approached him for a loan, Scott had instead invested as a "silent partner" in his friend's printing business. In time the printing company became a publishing concern, largely printing Scott's works. But no one involved in it was good at business. It began to flounder. Unfailingly honorable, Scott took it upon himself to save it and clear the names of all those concerned.

And so, night after night, Scott labored at his desk, and in the six years between 1826 and 1831 he produced four novels, a nine-volume life of Napoleon, part of a history of Scotland, and *Tales of a Grandfather*.

But the endless work finally affected both his mind and his body. Although it was not so, he began to believe that at last all the debts had been paid. It was with that happy notion that he died on a bed set up for him in the dining room on a warm, still September day in 1832, where the River Tweed that he loved so much could be heard rippling over its pebbles through the open window.

DUMBARTON

Dumbarton Castle

Of course in 1548 it was quite an adventure for five-year-old Mary, Queen of Scots to board a sailing ship sent here from France. As playmates she had the four Marys who were to be her companions for the next thirteen years, and three older half-brothers. All the same, it was hard parting from her mother, Mary of Guise. Both the pretty little girl with the silky hair and her mother wept copiously as they said goodbye to each other. Mary was going off to become the bride of the four-year-old dauphin, Francis (she actually married him in 1558), who became, briefly, Francis II of France, while she became his queen.

DUMFRIES

Poor Kirkpatrick Macmillan. For years in the early nineteenth century, he had been feverishly experimenting—spinning wheels and turning pedals of a new machine at the smithy in nearby Weir. At last, his work seemed done. The first bicycle had been invented, and its proud inventor took it for a ride. He rode it here, wobbling a little on his way. As it turned out, Macmillan's new machine wobbled into a market girl, knocking her down, and bicycle inventor Kirkpatrick Macmillan was summarily arrested.

Drumlanrig Castle (11 miles northwest of Dumfries)

For forty-three years, from 1645 to 1688, builders worked on this magnificent red sandstone castle for the first Duke of Queensberry. But when it was finished, despite its splendor, the duke was so horrified at the price it had cost that he stayed in it only one night.

Ellisland Farm (6 miles north of Dumfries)

One afternoon, walking along the river here with his wife and children, the poet Robert Burns began to croon. Sensing that a poem was in the making, his wife let him wander off while she entertained the children. Suddenly Burns began to wave his arms to her, and, as she drew closer, she could see tears of joy rolling down his cheeks and heard him reciting the poem that was to be "Tam o' Shanter."

DUNDEE

Dundee Law

One day in the eighteenth century a storm-driven ship full of Seville oranges took refuge in this port. The storm had been bad enough so that the ship, bound for Edinburgh, had been driven off course, and the oranges were well past their prime.

But that didn't matter to thrifty Janet Keiller, whose husband, John, kept a grocery store. It was true enough that the oranges were too ripe to sell in his store as they were, but there certainly was something one could do with them. Marmalade was her answer.

Ordinarily, in those days, marmalade recipes called for pounding the oranges with a mortar and pestle, adding plenty of sugar, and boiling the mixture like jelly. But a whole shipload of oranges was just too much to pound tediously to a pulp. It was easier to chip the peels with a knife after squeezing out the juice.

And that was what Janet Keiller did—adding pound sack after pound sack of sugar from her husband's shop to the oranges in the traditional way. Janet's untraditional method of chipping rather than pounding the orange skins helped to make her descendants prosperous and this city notable for its marmalade. That's what makes James Keiller and Son Ltd. marmalade different and what makes Dundee an unforgettable name among marmalade lovers.

DUNFERMLINE

The Abbey Church (East End)

Clearing away the ruins of the abbey built here by Malcolm III and St. Margaret (*see* Edinburgh Castle, St. Margaret's Chapel), workmen of 1818 unearthed, beneath a pile of shattered stones, a broken marble monument and the remains of a coffin of oak and lead. In it, in a shroud interwoven with threads of gold, was the pitch-preserved skeleton of Robert the Bruce. Even if it had not been for the richly woven shroud that the men unwound, they would have known the skeleton was his, for the ribs above the heart had been cut away.

When he lay dying, the Bruce had made one last request. His life long, he had been so busy fighting for Scotland that he had been unable to go on the Crusades. He asked his best friend and comrade in arms, Lord James Douglas, to take his heart on that journey for him. Douglas had tried, but died in the attempt.

En route to Palestine, Douglas had paused in Spain, where he was persuaded to try to stop the Saracens invading from Granada. After that helpful Christian act, he was told he could be on his way to the Holy Land.

At the start of the battle with the Saracens, it looked as if Douglas would be the victor. The Saracens began to retreat, and the Scots went after them. Suddenly the Saracens turned and charged their pursuers. The Scots tried to counterattack, and Douglas, who carried the Bruce's embalmed heart in a silver casket around his neck, flung it before him into the fray. He shouted as he would have done had the Bruce been alive with him on the battlefield, "Pass first in fight, as thou wast wont to do, and Douglas will follow thee, or die."

That was what happened. When Douglas's friends lifted his body, they found the heart of the Bruce beneath him. It never did reach Jerusalem; it never joined his body here. It was buried, instead, at the abbey at Melrose. (*See* Melrose, Melrose Abbey.)

Pittencrieff Park

When Andrew Carnegie was a child longing for a pretty place to play outdoors, he would look wistfully out onto this green land from the cottage where his father wove tablecloths. A private estate, Pittencrieff was open to the public for only one day each May. But even then, because of a feud between the Hunt family that owned it and Andrew's forebears, the Carnegies were forbidden entry.

When Carnegie became a millionaire industrialist, he bought this land and presented it as a gift to the town so later generations of children would be more fortunate than he.

Pittencrieff Park: MALCOLM'S TOWER

Malcolm III gave sanctuary in the tower here to the shipwrecked young Edgar Athelstan, the Saxon who was heir to the English throne, and his mother and sisters. Malcolm fell in love with the golden-haired sister, Margaret. (*See* Edinburgh, Edinburgh Castle: St. Margaret's Chapel.) Malcolm could not read but loved her so, it is said, that he would take the missals she gave him and kiss them tenderly because they meant so much to her. Here he asked her to be his bride, and though the thoughtful, deeply devout Margaret had planned to be a nun, she accepted the King's offer. In the course of time, she gave him five children. She gave to Scotland the enthusiasm for learning that has remained a characteristic of the Scots from her eleventh-century day to this.

DUNKELD

On holidays here, a lonely little Beatrix Potter, who grew up to write *The Tale of Peter Rabbit*, made friends with the rabbits and the hedgehogs, carrying them back to London with her on the train. A rabbit hutch, she later wrote, was exceptionally useful for carrying books, galoshes, and the seashells gathered on a summer holiday.

The rabbit itself could be nicely cuddled under an arm. (*See* England, Sawrey, Hilltop Farm.)

EDINBURGH

Arthur's Seat

One day in 1846, five Edinburgh boys went rabbit-hunting and were led by their dog into a little cave. Inside, to the boys' horror, were what looked like seventeen miniature coffins. All were four inches long and, but for their lids that were affixed with brass pins, were made of single pieces of wood.

After overcoming their initial fright, the boys began to play among the tiny coffins, tossing them back and forth to each other. In doing so, several broke. Then, thinking more seriously of what they had found, the boys reported their discovery to their schoolmaster.

To this day no one knows the history or significance of the little coffins, though they are now on display in the National Museum of Antiquities here. Some surmise that they might have been a witch's way of cursing those she wished to die.

Brodie's Close

By day Deacon William Brodie, for whose family this close is named, was the most respectable of citizens. He was a burgess and a member of the town council. When his father, who had been prosperous and equally highly respected, died in 1782, the younger Brodie inherited both property and a considerable sum. He was also a cabinetmaker of skill.

But by night, it was quite a different story.

At first, Brodie simply gambled at a social club to which he belonged. But cockfighting began to appeal to him particularly, and more and more he bet on the fights and lost. Although he continued to do well at his cabinet-making, he needed money for betting. To get it, he became a nighttime burglar.

During the day, as Brodie went from house to house and shop to shop, doing his work and visiting friends, he carried wax with him and would make impressions of the keys that in those eighteenth-century days were hung behind the doors. Then, when night fell, he would return to his flat here, disguise himself with a change of clothes, attach his pistols, and be off about the ugly business of thievery.

In his town councillor role, Brodie might have dined out at the home of a fellow councillor. But that in no way would prevent his returning stealthily after midnight to the house where he had been a guest and rifling it.

At first, he did his burglaries alone. But as his gambling debts increased, he found he needed more money than single-handed thievery was bringing him. He hired accomplices, and that was his undoing.

There was money aplenty to be had, Brodie knew, at the Canongate Excise Office, and he and his henchmen decided to go after it. All would have gone well if an excise office employee had not gone back to work the night the burglars struck.

There was a bit of a comedy of errors: the employee thought the form that he saw in the shadows was a fellow employee who, like him, had forgotten something and come back to work, and the burglars misidentified the employee as one of theirs.

In any case, it was a frightening experience for all. The take was not so large as expected, and one of the disgruntled, nervous hirelings turned informer. But somehow Brodie managed to escape—for a while, at least. He took a boat to Holland. But when he sent love letters home to Edinburgh, he was traced and returned to Scotland, where he was duly tried and hanged.

As a cabinetmaker Brodie had helped "perfect" the gallows on which he was hanged, and he has always been admired for the courageous way in which he faced his execution. The night before it, he gaily whistled from "The Merry Widow" and wrote a will bequeathing both his good and bad qualities to friends. His life is said to have inspired Robert Louis Stevenson's *Dr. Jekyll and Mr. Hyde.*

Church of St. Giles (High Street)

The market woman Jenny Geddes was not to be crossed, as Dean Hannay, the minister here, found out one July Sunday in 1637.

Charles I had just decreed that a new order of service would be instituted in all of Scotland's churches as it had been in England's. And following orders, the dean began to read from this new liturgy.

To Jenny Geddes, carrying the portable stool she brought with her to sit on during church services, the new readings smacked too much of popery.

"Do you dare to say Mass in my ear?" the irate woman cried, hurling her stool at the poor dean, who only escaped a crack in the head by skillful ducking.

Edinburgh Castle

Lovely Jane Douglas, Lady Glamis (*See* Glamis, Glamis Castle), pleaded in vain here in 1537 that she bore James V, King of Scots, no ill will. The king had exiled her brother, and she had corresponded with him. She, her husband, son, and chaplain were all imprisoned, and she was charged with having plotted to poison the king. She asked her judges to find out where she had bought the poison, and, since she had no access to the king, how she could have used it if she had it. Her judges were moved by her beauty and her denial and sought clemency of the king. But James was adamant. An informer he trusted had told him of her dire plotting, and she would be burned at the stake for it.

And while her horrified husband was made to watch through his prison window, she was burned. Indeed, so horrified and so terrified was he by the sight that that very night he sought to escape from this castle and fell to his death from Castle Rock.

Edinburgh Castle: BANQUETING HALL

What a jolly time the three boys—ten-year-old James II, King of Scots; William, the sixteen-year-old Earl of Douglas; and his younger brother, David—seemed to be having that November afternoon in 1440 when the two Douglas boys accepted the invitation of the king to come to play and stay for dinner. But the dinner hardly turned out to be as hospitable an event as the Douglases had expected.

The royal feast was elegantly laid out in the Banqueting Hall. Weary of romping and hungry for a good repast, the tired boys took their places. But suddenly a servant entered from the kitchen carrying a black bull's head on a platter and placed it directly in front of the older Douglas. The boy blanched. The symbolism of such a dish was known by all—it meant death to him before whom it was set.

William of Douglas jumped to his feet. His brother rose beside him, and both sought to leave the great Banqueting Hall. But that was not to be. Fearful of the power of young William, James II's regents had decided that William and his brother must die. Though the boys fought valiantly, guards overcame them, bound them, and hauled them before the boy-king who minutes before had been their friend and still would have liked to be.

But the regents would not have it. Though the king sobbed and cried out against the regents who had forced him to be part of their plan, he was forced, too, to condemn his playmates to death. The regents told him that the kingdom of Scotland did not have room enough for both Douglases and a Stuart, and since the young king was a Stuart, it was he who must live. His two young guests were led out to the courtyard and beheaded.

Edinburgh Castle: BIRTHING CHAMBER
OFF QUEEN MARY'S ROOM

In the little chamber here, on June 19, 1566, Mary, Queen of Scots, gave birth after a long and arduous labor to the infant who was to become James I of England, James VI of Scotland. Or was he?

In 1830, workmen doing repairs here unearthed an oaken coffin with a baby's bones inside wrapped in rich cloth, embroidered with the letter "J." Did James live, or did he die? Was a substitute princeling put in his place so that his royal mother would never know?

◆ ◆ ◆

For a long time, Mary, Queen of Scots's husband, Lord Darnley had been casting aspersions on the queen's character, suggesting that his royal wife had been having liaisons with other men. To lay all that to rest, no sooner had her son, James, been born than Mary, Queen of Scots summoned her husband to this room. Thrusting the baby into his arms, she exclaimed to Darnley loudly in the company of all those gathered round that the child he held was his and no other man's.

"He is so much your own son," the queen, long out of love with Darnley, sorrowfully added, "that I fear it will be the worse for him hereafter."

Edinburgh Castle: DUNGEON OF ARGYLL'S TOWER

It did not matter to Charles II of England in 1660 that, nine years earlier, it had been Archibald Campbell, Marquis and 8th Earl of Argyll, who had placed the crown on his head at his coronation at Scone Palace. Rumored to be a traitor, the marquis was taken into custody and condemned to death. Hearing the sentence, Argyll commented placidly and without rancor that he had had the honor to set the crown on the King's head. "And now," he said, "he hastens me to a better crown than his own."

But Argyll's wife was not so placid. She determined to

rescue him from this tower that has borne his name ever since. After arriving one afternoon for a visit in her sedan chair, she convinced Archibald that, dressed in her clothes and wearing her veil, he could escape in that same sedan chair. Indeed, she got as far as clothing him in her gown before he had a change of heart. He feared that he might be discovered, and then it would not go well for her. He would go to his execution as scheduled.

But twenty-one years later when his son awaited execution in this same dungeon for his outspoken support of Presbyterianism, the younger Argyll, the 9th Earl, did not hesitate to escape.

His daughter-in-law, Lady Sophia Lindsay, came for a last farewell the night before his execution. Accompanying her was her page. An hour later on that stormy December night, she left the dungeon while a "page" held her train high to keep it out of the mud, but held his own head low.

All went well until they neared the last gate. A guard halted them there and laid his arms on the arm of her servant. The nervous "page" dropped the train. Only the quick-wittedness of Lady Sophia saved the day.

"Thou loon!" she reportedly cried, flinging her skirts in the page's face so it was splattered with mud beyond recognition. Approving of her rebuke to her awkward servant, the guard let both pass.

Outside the gates, once safe with friends, the earl took off his page's garb and ultimately fled to Holland.

Edinburgh Castle: ST. MARGARET'S CHAPEL

Although she did not know that her husband, Malcolm III, and her eldest son, Edward, had been killed in battle on November 13, 1393, Queen Margaret must have sensed it and known that her own end, too, was near. For some time she had been increasingly exhausted but had refused, devout Catholic that she was, to give up fasting and long night vigils. Feeling wearier than ever and restive three days after the battle, she asked to be carried to this little chapel that she had had built so she could take Communion here. Then, much refreshed, she returned to her chambers. There Margaret learned that both her son and the husband she had met when she was a Saxon child-princess and he already a king, who had rescued her and her family when they had been shipwrecked fleeing William the Conqueror, was dead. (*See* Dunfermline, Malcolm's Tower.) It was more than she could bear to know that both her husband and eldest son were gone. Margaret died.

It had been her wish to be buried in the abbey at Dunfermline that she and her husband had founded. But while preparations were under way for the body's removal, her husband's brother, seeking the throne, began besieging the castle.

Nonetheless, with the help of the welcome mist that Scots still call a mysterious gift, the queen's sons managed in the dark of night to lower their mother's body from this castle's craggy rock so it could be carried away for proper burial at Dunfermline.

Firth of Forth

It was hardly the sort of conduct one would have expected from a native son, but privateer John Paul Jones, now serving America, was bobbing in the Firth of Forth in his vessel, *Bonne Homme Richard*, and it looked as if he was about to attack this city. Without a protective naval force on hand, the only thing Edinburgh could do was pray.

And that was exactly what the Bishop did. He asked for a chair, had it carried down to the shore of the Firth, and placed in the sand when the water was at low tide. And there he reminded God of his service to Him for forty years and asked that, in return, God send a westerly gale to drive the privateer away. "Or I will sit here until I drown," the bishop reportedly said.

Happily, he didn't have to. Though the water rose around his ankles, then his knees, then up to his chest, the wind increased and moved into the west as he had asked. For a day and a night Jones remained in the Firth, hoping the wind would change so he could sail down it for his attack here. Though he had returned from the shore, the bishop had never stopped praying, and the wind did not abate. Finally, Jones deemed it unwise to wait any longer. British ships were likely to be on their way, so he sailed away leaving Edinburgh intact.

Greyfriars Churchyard (Candlemaker Row)

For fourteen years the devoted Skye terrier Bobby kept vigil at his shepherd-master's grave here, and his loyalty is commemorated by the statue of him outside Greyfriars Bobby Inn.

Bobby's master, Jock Gray, had been a weekly visitor to the city for years to sell his sheep at the outdoor market. After the market the pair would go together to Traills Cafe (now Greyfriars Bobby Inn) nearby. There, Jock would eat his lunch while Bobby would gnaw happily on a bone.

But then Jock died and was buried here. At Traills, after the funeral, patrons talked of the companionship between the man and the dog which clearly had been a close one. And they spoke of how they would miss the pair.

But they didn't miss Bobby for long. Only a few days after his master had been buried, Bobby was at Traills seeking a bone. Sorry for him, the owner provided one. Bobby came again the next day, and the day after that, and the one after that. But he never stayed on as he had when Jock had been alive. He simply accepted the bone that was offered with a grateful wag of his tail and left, carrying it, always headed in the same direction.

After a while, the curious proprietor of Traills followed him and discovered that Bobby had created a job for himself and was guarding his master's grave.

Holyrood Abbey

In the twelfth century when forests grew here, devout King David I, son of St. Margaret (*See* Edinburgh Castle: St. Margaret's Chapel), pursuing a stag, fell from his horse. In danger of being gored by the stag that he was hunting, he reached for its horns to fend it off. Miraculously, the stag pulled back, and in place of the horns he had been grasping, the king found a crucifix. In gratitude, he founded this Abbey of the Holyrood, or Holy Cross.

◆ ◆ ◆

It was Catholic Mary, Queen of Scots's first Sunday back in her native land after widowhood in France, and she was looking forward to hearing her first Mass in her private chapel here. But, instigated by staunch Presbyterian John Knox, pastor of St. Giles, a crowd opposed to Roman Catholic worship stood at the chapel doors and tore the candles for the altar from the almoner's hands. The young queen was so saddened by the attack that all festivities celebrating her return were ended.

Holyrood House: GREAT HALL

The marriage here of Mary, Queen of Scots to the Earl of Bothwell was hardly a much-heralded event. There were no extravagant entertainments, no exchange of grand gifts, no applauding crowds. There had been all three when, as the young widow of the King of France, she had become the bride of the dashing Lord Darnley, the great-grandson of England's Henry VII. That had been a day of merrymaking in Edinburgh—pageants, masques, and feasting—and the queen was clearly radiantly in love.

But for her marriage to Bothwell, believed to be Darnley's murderer (*See* Holyrood House: Royal Apartments—Turret Chamber), there were few celebrants. The service was not Roman Catholic as the queen was, and the care of her soul was virtually abandoned by her confessor. Like much of Scotland, he was aghast that only three weeks after Darnley's death Mary would be marrying the man all believed to be his murderer.

Mary had no new wedding finery; only old clothes relined. Gold had been scattered to the crowds outside the palace when she married Darnley, and love gifts of all sorts had been presented by her to him. Her wedding gift to Bothwell was simply a hand-me-down bit of fur that had been attached to her mother's dressing gown.

And all day long on her wedding day the queen seemed doleful, reporting, so her friend the French ambassador said, that she never expected to be happy again.

Holyrood House: NORTHWEST TOWER

The marriage in 1503 of thirteen-year-old Margaret Tudor, daughter of Henry VII of England, to James IV, King of Scots, was the grandest wedding Scotland had ever seen. The premarital festivities began when the thirty-two-year-old king, clad in crimson velvet edged with cloth of gold, traveled the six miles to Newbattle Abbey to meet his young intended. Before that, work had gotten under way on this castle tower in her honor.

To show his English bride that Scotland was a wealthy land, the king saw to it that, on her entry into Edinburgh, the houses were covered with tapestry. Duels, tilts, and tournaments were provided to entertain the princess along the arrival route.

For her wedding in the chapel here at Holyrood, the princess wore white damask and a collar of gold and pearls and had her hair trailing down to her feet.

Escorting her on this happy marital journey into Scotland was her father's friend, the Earl of Surrey.

A decade later, the merriment all gone, it was Surrey who led the English to the Battle of Flodden Field in which Margaret's James was killed.

Holyrood House: THE PICTURE GALLERY

All 110 Scottish kings depicted here—some real, some imagined—were painted in just two years from 1684 to 1686 by a Flemish painter, Jacob de Wet. He got for his labors only a few shillings a painting (and had to provide his own paint and canvas). But Charles II wanted them. Feverishly executed, the paintings were done at the rate of more than one a week.

Holyrood House: ROYAL APARTMENTS—
TURRET CHAMBER

Mary, Queen of Scots was dining happily here the night of March 9, 1566, with her half sister, several nobles, and the young Italian David Rizzio, her secretary, whose fine singing voice and abilities as a musician made him a special favorite. There was laughter and gaiety and the promise of songs after dinner. Suddenly the tapestry over the private staircase to the tower was thrust aside and the queen's husband, Lord Darnley, entered.

Throwing an arm around the queen, he seemed in amorous spirits, though it was known that recently their relationship had not been the warmest.

But scarcely was Darnley seated than the tapestry opened again, revealing Patrick, Lord Ruthven, a friend of Darnley's. It was strange enough that he had entered by the private staircase. But stranger still was the suit of armor he was wearing—hardly appropriate dress for a dinner party, especially for an uninvited guest.

The queen asked what he was doing in her private chamber. Lord Ruthven assured Mary that he meant no harm to her. As for her secretary, who was impugning her honor by being with her so frequently, that was another story. Hearing this, the stunned Rizzio shrank away. The queen's attendants sought to surround Lord Ruthven. But by then more armed men had entered the dining chamber.

Mary turned beseechingly toward her husband. He protested that he had had no foreknowledge of what was happening, but he did not stop the armed intruders.

Begging the queen's help, Rizzio hid behind her, clinging to her skirts. Pursuing him, one of the intruders cocked a pistol at Mary's throat, threatening to kill her if she gave the alarm.

Only then did Darnley enter the fray—grasping the queen's arms and holding her to him, so that she was torn away from poor Rizzio. While he screamed for her to intercede, Rizzio was hauled out of this room to the main staircase landing. There daggers were plunged into him until fifty-six stab wounds assured his attackers he would never rise again. After that, the band of murderers hastily fled out a window, with Mary crying that there would be revenge.

And there was! Her husband's protestations of innocence in the murderous affair were not heeded. Mary knew of Darnley's jealousy of Rizzio and held him responsible for the secretary's death.

To help her wreak her vengeance, Mary sought James Hepburn, Earl of Bothwell, who was handsome, strong, and manly. Eleven months later, it was he who hatched the plot, so it is said, that blew up Darnley when gunpowder was placed beneath his bed.

John Knox House (High Street)

With panoply hardly befitting an austere Protestant man of God, fifty-eight-year-old John Knox rode home to this house in 1563 with his new young bride. According to accounts of the day a great cortege accompanied him. He rode a trim gelding and was decked out in taffeta fastened with gold rings and precious stones. Born of Lowland peasant farmer stock, Knox was marrying Margaret Stuart, a seventeen-year-old with royal blood in her veins. Knox's Roman Catholic enemies insisted it could only have been by sorcery that he had obtained so buxom a prize.

◆   ◆   ◆

As he lay in a coma on his deathbed here, devout Presbyterian John Knox was asked if he could hear the prayers being offered for him. Suddenly, the fiery theologian who was so instrumental in the downfall of Roman Catholic Mary, Queen of Scots (*See* Edinburgh, Holyrood Abbey), was roused for the last time.

"I would to God," those assembled heard him say, "that you and all men heard them as I have heard them." Then raising a hand toward Heaven, John Knox died.

Lady Stair's House (High Street)

In this house that now contains memorabilia of the Scottish writers Sir Walter Scott, Robert Burns, and Robert Louis Stevenson, there were in the seventeenth century strange goings-on indeed. Then it was the home of Lady Eleanor Campbell and James, Viscount Primrose, a dissipated, choleric man to whom she had been married when very young.

On the most notable occasion that is recorded, her ladyship looked into her mirror one morning to see her husband creeping up behind her, sword drawn. Jumping up from her dressing table, Lady Eleanor fled out an open window into the street.

With his wife gone, the dissolute viscount went off to Europe on a binge. The story goes that while he was there, a fortune-teller came to Edinburgh. The unhappy Lady Eleanor paid a visit to him. She said she sought information about someone who had gone abroad. The fortune-teller led her to a mirror in which she saw a foreign church, and at the altar with the bride stood her husband!

But suddenly a wedding guest appeared who looked astonishingly like Lady Eleanor's brother who was on a trip abroad. Clearly enraged, the "guest" approached the bridegroom and drew his sword. The bridegroom sought to defend himself. Then the soothsayer's mirror clouded over. Shaking, the distraught Lady Eleanor left the fortune-teller's.

Some months later, when her brother returned home from his travels, she asked him if he could possibly have seen her husband while he was away. At first, he hesitated. Then he told the tale of what she had already seen in the fortune-teller's mirror.

In Amsterdam, her brother said, he had met a merchant who told him his daughter was about to marry a Scot and had issued an invitation to the wedding.

When the brother arrived, a single glance showed him that it was his brother-in-law at the altar. As he had done in the mirror, he stopped the ceremony, though he had not, as Lady Eleanor had surmised, killed her husband in his rage.

It was not long, however, before Primrose's dissolute behavior led the viscount to the grave. Still young and now free, his pretty widow had suitors aplenty but had little interest in entering into another marriage. But there was one suitor, the Earl of Stair, who persisted. His efforts seemed hopeless until he bribed a servant to let him into the room above High Street, where each morning Lady Eleanor said her prayers.

Arriving well before she did, the earl appeared at the window in enough of a state of undress to embarrass the lady he was wooing. Lady Eleanor had no choice, as the earl had hoped she wouldn't. For propriety's sake Eleanor agreed at last to become Lady Stair.

Princes Street

Down Long Gait, today this bustling commercial street, nineteen-year-old Mary, Queen of Scots, on August 19, 1561, rode on the first side-saddle with a pommel ever seen in Scotland.

Widow of Francis II of France, she was making a state entry into her capital after thirteen happy years abroad.

To protect her from inclement weather, a purple velvet canopy with a red taffeta lining was carried above her head by sixteen members of the town council. To warm the cockles of celebrants' hearts, red wine in Mary's honor bubbled from the city fountain, and townspeople by the hundreds drank to her health in it.

FALKLAND

Falkland Palace

Supervising the use of a new cannon at Roxburghe Castle in 1460, James II was struck by a flying fragment from it and died. (*See* Kelso, Floors Park: Yew Tree.) His bereaved widow, Mary of Gueldres, left with five small children and having been named regent for the eldest, nine-year-old James III, came here where she found peace in her private garden. She had a new room added to the palace with a door to the garden. Out of it Mary would go to forget the affairs of state among her flowers and the trees of Falkland Woods.

◆　◆　◆

It was curious that in adulthood James V retained affection for this palace and chose to die here. For it was here, as a youth, that he was kept a prisoner for four years in the sixteenth century by his stepfather, the Earl of Angus.

Perhaps his affection for Falkland came from the indulgences of his stepfather who, to sweeten the "imprisonment," gave James horses, hawks, and hounds, the finest of clothes and jewels, and lute-playing lessons, though other studies offered were minimal.

Or perhaps James was pleased that, ultimately, when he was sixteen, he made use of his ingenuity and gathered together the courage to flee his captors.

On a pleasant spring evening in 1528 he commented that it seemed good hunting weather, so he would retire early and, accordingly, be up early for the hunt. He advised his "guard" to go to bed early too, so he would be ready to join him

Once all were slumbering, James crept out of bed. Dressing himself in clothes he had borrowed from a stableman, James galloped off toward Stirling Castle.

When morning came and he was found to be missing, those in the household who knew he was trying to escape wished him well and chuckled when his captors nervously looked for him. They said slyly that he had probably gone to town to share some woman's bed. Since women were among the indulgences his stepfather allowed, worries about his whereabouts were quieted for a time—long enough to allow him to reach Stirling, where he had his own soldiers to protect him.

◆ ◆ ◆

Appropriately, carvings of the heroes and heroines of mythology belonged in the round medallions over the courtyard here. When the French master-mason sent by James V's father-in-law arrived to make them, James had a different idea. Gay blade that he had been in his youth, he wanted instead carvings of three mistresses of his younger days. Only afterward, as a sop to his family and friends, did he agree that more proper portraits could also be put there.

◆ ◆ ◆

In happy times, James V embellished this palace with Renaissance ornamentation to welcome the bride he hoped to have, Magdalene, daughter of Francis I of France.

In a less happy time, a heartsick James came here after the death of two infant sons, a defeat in war, and a feverish nightmare in which a man he had had put to death was cutting off his arms and threatening to return to take his head.

The weary, distraught king, who had shut himself inside, took the dream to mean that he, like his little sons, would soon be dead. Joylessly he received the news that his second wife, Mary of Guise, had borne him a daughter, Mary, who became Mary, Queen of Scots.

The news brought an anguished sigh and the remark that the Scottish Crown had come to the Stuarts via a "lass" when Marjorie, Robert the Bruce's daughter, had wed a Stuart. It would go with another lass—James's newborn daughter, Mary. With that, the thirty-year-old king turned to the wall and died.

FORRES

Brodie Castle (8 miles west of Forres)

It was a cold February night in 1776. Before bidding his wife, Lady Margaret, good night, James Brodie made sure the fire in her bedroom fireplace was a good one. Then he retired to his own bedchamber. He had had a busy day with friends and quickly fell asleep. He had no idea how soon afterward it was that he heard her crying out and, running to her room, found it enveloped in flames.

The fire notwithstanding, Brodie, who had loved Margaret enough to elope with her, carried her out all aflame.

But it was too late. His Margaret was dead. It is said that her spirit still walks this castle's halls.

FORTINGALL

Churchyard

There was, of course, no way that the young woman whose newborn son lay with her beneath the yew tree here could know that he would grow up to be one of the world's most infamous men. He was a likely-looking enough infant, and surely he came from good stock. His father was an envoy from Rome to King Metallanus of the Caledonian tribe that inhabited this region. The young mother was of that tribe. With a Roman father, it was appropriate that the child be given a Roman name. The Caledonian mother called her little son Pontius Pilate.

GLAMIS

Glamis Castle

Had it not been for the fairy folk who lived on the nearby hill, legend has it that this castle would have occupied that site. Indeed, construction of it began there. But every night the stones that were put up by day would be knocked down by the hill's inhabitants. Finally the dream of a hilltop castle was abandoned and this was built below.

◆ ◆ ◆

Malcolm II, grandfather of Macbeth, is said to have been murdered here in 1034. On the anniversary of his death, to this day, boards in the castle are said to creak. And the ghost of lovely Lady Glamis, who was burned at the stake (*See* Edinburgh, Edinburgh Castle), walks here, too.

GLASGOW

The Burrell Collection (outskirts)

It was almost forty years after the great and varied works of art collected by shipbuilding tycoon Sir William Burrell had been bequeathed to this city that this red sandstone and glass building became their home. From the end of World War I until his death in 1958 when the family shipbuilding firm was sold, Sir William collected art that he loved. In his lifetime, it filled his Glasgow mansion. On his death, he wished it to belong to the people of the city—but only if it would be properly cared for. It must, he said, "be housed in a rural setting far removed from the atmospheric pollution of urban conurbations, not less than sixteen miles from the Royal Exchange." In Glasgow, those were difficult requirements to fulfill. Not until 1983 was such a setting found and this building completed.

George Square

Apocryphal as the tale may be, it is said that arriving in Glasgow by train and stepping out of the Queen Street Station toward this square filled with statues of Scotland's notables, England's Edward VII inquired what graveyard he was looking at.

Glasgow Green

Dressed up in what they could wear of the twelve thousand cloth shirts, six thousand cloth coats, six thousand pairs of shoes and stockings, waistcoats, and bonnets which their supporters in Glasgow had given them, the Highland Army of Bonnie Prince Charlie marched in stylish review in this city park in December 1745.

Among the onlookers was pretty Clementina Walkinshaw. She found the pale, fair prince who had come to Scotland from France to reclaim the throne for the deposed Stuarts much to her liking. The feeling was reciprocal, and when, after the prince's disastrous defeat at Culloden (See Culloden), he fled back to France, Clementina joined him, bore him a son, and stayed with him the rest of his life.

◆ ◆ ◆

Sometimes, after a hard week of work at his father's butter and egg shop, young Thomas Lipton would walk here along the River Clyde dreaming of sailing and faraway places. In 1861, when he was eleven, his dreaming led the precocious boy to start a yacht club on the river for those who built their own boats.

When he was an adult, and a millionaire with tea plantations in Ceylon, a thriving grocery business in Scotland, a print and paper works, and a bacon-curing house in Chicago, Lipton was still dreaming of boats and boat-building. Sir Thomas, knighted in 1898, competed five times for the America's Cup in one vessel after another that he hopefully called Shamrock. Five times he lost, but after his last defeat in 1930, the eighty-year-old grand old man was given a gold cup for his fine sportsmanship.

The Necropolis

Treasure taken from the back of a captured runaway elephant is said to have paid for the enormous Romanesque mausoleum with the leering heads that stands on the brow of the hill here.

As the story goes, Major Archibald Douglas Monteith had captured the elephant and thereby obtained the fortune when he was an officer for the East India Company. When he retired to Glasgow in 1842, he arranged for a sizeable portion of his money to be used for an imposing mausoleum to remember him by.

Provand's Lordship (Castle Street)

It was January 1567, and Mary, Queen of Scots had come here to visit her sick husband, Darnley, ill of smallpox, and to take him home to Edinburgh and to death by murder.

It is said that, torn between her eagerness to do the bidding of her new lover, the Earl of Bothwell—even if murder was part of it—and her conscience, Mary wrote to Bothwell. Mary wrote passionately, distractedly, anxiously. The letters and poems that she wrote (if they were, indeed, hers) were found in a silver casket after the queen's capture by enemies and after Bothwell's flight to avoid capture. At her trial in England, those same enemies, producing the letters, sought to prove that Mary had been an accessory to her husband's death.

Glasgow Cathedral

St. Mungo (*See* Culross), whom legend says was the founder of this city in 543, was an ascetic, indeed. In his day, the Molendinar, a pretty stream, bubbled here. In good weather and bad the saint would sit in it each evening until he had recited all 150 of the Psalms of David. Then understandably exhausted, he would lie down on a rock to dry off and sleep.

◆ ◆ ◆

All across Scotland in the sixteenth century the churches and cathedrals were being destroyed by the reforming Presbyterians, and the time had come for the attack on this Gothic structure. But word of the plot got out to the Incorporated Trades of Glasgow. They would have none of it. The Hammermen, Weavers, Gardeners, and all the rest encircled the cathedral and, when the reformers arrived, forbade them entry. Ranting and railing, the reformers cried out against the trappings of Catholicism inside and warned the tradesmen that they would be damned for their stand.

A compromise was finally reached. The tradesmen let the reformers go inside the cathedral and do their smashing of saints and altars—but only on the condition that they did not damage the structure of the building itself, on which the tradesmen had worked so hard. Thanks to the tradesmen, this is the only pre-Reformation Gothic church still standing on the Scottish mainland.

◆ ◆ ◆

When Oliver Cromwell was campaigning in Glasgow, he stopped one Sunday for a service here. It was distinctly not to his liking since the preacher, Zachary Boyd, harangued against him for two hours in his sermon.

The service finally ended. Proposing that bygones be bygones, the "magnanimous" Cromwell invited the offending clergyman to dinner. But that was hardly the end of the matter. With characteristic subtlety, Cromwell retaliated by subjecting his long-winded critic, after dinner, to three full hours of prayers!

GLENCOE

February 13, 1692 was an infamous day, when, after twelve days of jollity together in this mountain glen, men of the Campbell clan turned on the MacDonald clan that had offered them hospitality and murdered their hosts. And it is said that, even now, in remembering that harrowing event, a MacDonald will not knowingly sit down to eat with a Campbell.

The story begins in 1688 when the Catholic James VII of Scotland (James II of England) was deposed and his Protestant daughter, Mary, and her Dutch husband, William of Orange, were invited to take the throne while James fled in exile to France. Many a Highland clan, however—the MacDonalds of Glencoe among them— longed for the return of James.

William demanded that by January 1, 1692, all swear an oath of allegiance to him. Loyal supporters of James were reluctant to do so without his approval, so messengers were sent across the sea to ask him.

James dilly-dallied in sending them a reply, and it was not until December 12, 1691, that he finally freed his supporters of their obligation to him, and the Highlanders' messengers set sail home to Scotland.

It was December 21 before they were back in Edinburgh, and sending word from clan to clan was not an easily accomplished task. Four days after Christmas, MacIan, chief of the MacDonalds of Glencoe, heard that he was free to swear allegiance to the new king.

As quickly as he could, he set out to see the sheriff to whom he had been directed to give his pledge. Because of a multitude of delays, including a blinding blizzard, the pledge could not be given by the required date.

That was all the impetus the government needed to destroy the clan. A complement of soldiers led by Campbell of Glenlyon was sent to accomplish the deed. To do a thorough job, all men and women under age seventy would be massacred, and all children. The plan was to billet the soldiers with the MacDonalds for a while and then make the attack one early morning when the MacDonalds would be unsuspecting.

And that was exactly what occurred.

In the hospitable tradition of Highlanders, the Mac-
Donalds provided the accommodation requested by the
120 soldiers, even though they were a trifle suspicious
since most of them were of the Campbell clan with
which they were not friendly. But, in the course of the
twelve days that the soldiers stayed, they passed pleasant
times together—wrestling, playing hockey, dancing, and
singing together in the evening, and enjoying bottles of
army whiskey.

But at 5:00 A.M. on February 13 all that changed. The
MacDonalds were murdered in their beds; their homes
burned; their cattle and sheep driven away.

Little wonder that, even today, a MacDonald will not
knowingly eat with a Campbell.

GLENFINNAN

Nowadays they say the figure atop this monument to the
five thousand clansmen who rallied round Prince
Charles Edward Stuart (*See* Outer Hebrides, Eriskay:
Loch nan Uamh) when he arrived in Scotland in 1745,
simply represents a clansman. It does. But it wasn't
meant to.

When the monument was being constructed, a statue
of the prince himself was commissioned for its top. John
Greenshields, the sculptor, learned of a portrait of the
prince at Lee Castle in Lanarkshire and went to take a
look at it. As it turned out, on the day he arrived, only
servants were at home. They willingly let the sculptor in,
however, and he went to the wall where he had been told
the prince's picture hung to make a sketch of it.

But full-length portraits of two young men hung
there—one in a kilt; the other in tartan trousers. Having
to choose between the two, Greenshields decided the
young man in the kilt was more likely to be Prince
Charles. Accordingly, he based his statue on that painting. Not until his work was finished did he learn that the
figure he had chosen was not Charles but one of the
young clansmen who had joined with him. By then, it

was too late to correct the error, so it is George Lockhart of Carnworth whose statue stands here.

HAWICK

Hermitage Castle

It is said that the original owner of this castle was so wicked that his neighbors took him captive, wrapped him in lead, and boiled him to death in a cauldron. But that hardly undid all his horrid excesses. So great were they, the legend continues, that the castle itself has been sinking ever since beneath the weight of the heinous deeds performed within its walls.

◆ ◆ ◆

To this gloomy brown sandstone castle, twenty-three-year-old Mary, Queen of Scots made a fifty-mile round trip from Jedburgh in a single day for a two-hour glimpse of her beloved Earl of Bothwell who lay here, wounded, after a foray with the English.

Under normal circumstances the ride itself would be enough to have been tiring, but, as it turned out, the weather was abominable that October day. Still married to Lord Darnley but longing for her new love, Mary was anxious and distraught, and when she returned to Jedburgh, she came down with convulsions and a high fever. There were even moments of unconsciousness and her doctors feared for her life. (*See* Jedburgh.)

INNER HEBRIDES

Iona

A homesick St. Columba landed here with twelve companions in 563, driven by a religious feud from the Ireland he loved. He had already stopped once en route, on the little island of Oronsay. From there, when he looked out, he could still see his Irish homeland on a clear day, and he did not wish to. So he and his disciples set sail again. They landed here, where Ireland was out of sight.

Immediately they set to work and built a missionary church from which Columba and his disciples set out to make conversions.

But sometimes Columba stayed at home, too. When he did it was to illumine manuscripts—more than three hundred of them. And there are some who say the Book of Kells (*See* Republic of Ireland, Kells), an eighth-century illuminated copy of the Four Gospels often called the most beautiful book in the world, was illumined here by one of his followers. It was sent to Kells in Ireland for safekeeping when Viking raiders in the ninth century began burning and pillaging here.

Mull: TOBERMORY

Time and again, treasure hunters have tried to salvage the Spanish Armada galleon *Florencia* blown up three hundred yards off this shore in 1588. In it, some say, was the gold to pay the Armada crews.

But only in 1688, on the very first attempt, did treasure hunters meet with any success. As time has passed, the vessel has sunk deeper and deeper into the hard silt.

There are many tales of how the *Florencia* came to be blown up on the eve of her departure for home. After the defeat of the Armada, she had set sail for Spain, but a storm forced her captain to seek shelter in this quiet harbor. Carrying fifty-six cannons, highly decorated, and richly painted, she was a sight to behold. Many an island resident rowed out for a look at her while she lay here. Among those who did so, and who, indeed, went aboard her, was Sir Lachlan MacLean, the 13th Earl of Duart, owner of and resident in this island's largest castle.

To his amazement he discovered a Spanish princess on the *Florencia*. Dark-eyed, dark-haired, she was very different from any Scottish lady. One story says that Mac-Lean fell in love with her on the spot and was ready to leave his castle and follow her to Spain.

Learning of his love, his jealous wife sought the help of a witch in destroying her rival. The witch sent an army of fairy cats to sink the galleon by setting off an explosion with the sparks from their fur.

The less fanciful say that when the *Florencia* was forced to stay here longer than had been foreseen, her commander asked MacLean to supply him with sufficient provisions for the journey home. MacLean agreed, but only with the understanding that he would be paid for the goods he provided. When word reached him that the galleon was setting sail without the bill's being paid, he sent a debt collector after it. When payment was not made, the collector set fire to the powder magazine. The *Florencia* and her crew and all their gold went to their watery grave.

Skye: DUNVEGAN CASTLE

It is said that one evening, in this ancestral home of the MacLeods, a nursemaid left the MacLeod infant-heir in his tower room for a while to join the adults in the main part of the castle. Visitors came, and the maid was sent after the infant-heir so he could be shown to the guests.

It was a warm night and the baby had been left uncovered. When the maid returned to his room, she found a curious cloth of oatmeal-colored silk, darned here and there, with a few dots of red embroidery on it, over him.

Not taking time to remove it, she carried the baby downstairs. As the legend goes, she heard voices chanting that the flag was a gift from the fairies and that, if waved three times, it would save the clan three times when it was in danger. It was never, however, to be waved except in dangerous times, or woe betide the clan.

Twice now, when the clan has been imperiled, the flag has been waved, and the clan saved. And once, the strong box in which the flag was kept was broken open. The flag was waved just to see what might happen, and the son of the clan's chief was lost at sea.

Skye: CHAPEL OF TRUMPAN

Two times before her actual burial in the churchyard here, Lady Grange, the wife of James Erskine of Orange, the Lord Justice Clerk of Edinburgh, had burial services said for her, and coffins, supposedly with her remains, were interred.

It all came about because Lady Grange was both a curious and a gossipy sort and did not approve of her husband's politics. Once when he and friends were discussing the restoration of the ousted Stuart family to the throne, she hid under the sofa to hear what was going on and then jumped out to announce that she would tell on all of them.

Clearly, it wasn't safe to keep her in Edinburgh, so she was secretly brought here to Skye while a funeral was held for her in the capital. Later she was taken to the island of Haskeir off North Uist, then to St. Kilda's. In the course of her exile, Lady Grange, who had few island friends because of her aristocratic airs, whiled away the time learning to spin. One day she managed to smuggle out a note in a ball of yarn, telling of her whereabouts.

Alerted relatives went to the government, and a naval vessel was sent for her. Learning of it, her captors shipped her off again.

Finally, Lady Grange died here in 1746. This time, afraid that her exhumed body might be used against them in some way, the kidnappers filled a second coffin with sand and buried that one in Duirinish.

Staffa: FINGAL'S CAVE

The singing of the wind and the roar of the ocean echoing here inspired the German Romantic composer Felix Mendelssohn, after a visit in 1829, to write his "Hebrides Overture," duplicating the sounds.

INVERARAY

Inveraray Castle

One night in 1523, at the castle that then stood on this site, a tearful, water-soaked Lady Catherine Campbell, sister of Colin, the Earl of Argyll and the owner of this castle, arrived at her brother's door with a wild tale.

Her husband, Sir Lachlan MacLean, the second Earl of Duart and owner of Duart Castle (*See* Mull, Tobermory), had tired of her, for she had borne him no son. He had abandoned her offshore on the rock known as Lady's Rock. When the tide came in, he expected her to be swept out to sea.

But it was not to be so, for Catherine's cries reached fishermen who rescued her and brought her here to her brother's castle.

Angrily, Colin listened. Then a new visitor—his brother-in-law—was announced. Lady Catherine was quickly hidden. This time, a tearful MacLean recounted how he had lost his beloved wife by drowning. Colin commiserated and asked his bereaved brother-in-law to stay on for dinner.

When they all sat down at the dining table, a veiled woman was among the guests. She said nothing, but listened intently as MacLean again told of his wife's death that afternoon by drowning. Suddenly, Catherine raised her veil. Certain that he was seeing a ghost, the disbelieving MacLean fled.

But that was not entirely the end of the matter. MacLean was found murdered on a trip to Edinburgh a short time later—presumably by a member of his wife's family.

INVERNESS

Tomnahurich Cemetery (Hill of the Fairies)

Long before this cypress-clad height became a cemetery site, it was renowned as the Hill of the Fairies, and children were warned to stay away for fear the fairies would kidnap them and make them their own. That was not exactly what they had done with the fiddlers Farquahar Grant and Thomas Cumming of Strathspey, but almost.

Legend has it that the two wandering musicians came one day to play in Inverness and were stopped by a bearded man as they crossed the River Ness seeking lodging. He needed some fiddlers, the old man said, and would willingly pay a good price to them if they would follow him.

Having no other engagement, the visiting pair readily acquiesced and went along with the elderly gentleman, his curious garb of a long cloak and a peaked red cap notwithstanding. Halfway to the top of Tomnahurich the old gentleman stopped and stamped on the ground, and a door into the hillside opened. Inside, to the musicians' amazement, was a brightly lit hall full of dinner guests.

But they were not ordinary dinner guests. All of them were small. All were clad in green. Though taken aback a bit, the two musicians played merry dancing tunes as they had been bid, and the little people danced with delight for hours. Then the old man reappeared, informed the fiddlers that morning had come, and the dancing ended. He thanked them, paid them, opened the door to the subterranean room, and bade them be back on their way to Inverness.

Chatting enthusiastically about their pleasant and well-paid night, the pair started back across the bridge they had crossed on their way up the hill. Could they be mistaken? The night before it had been wood. Now it was stone. The night before it had been a simple span. Now it was supported by arches. And as they entered the town, the pair perceived that the clothes of those they passed were quite different from the clothes they wore, and the buildings were not as they remembered them.

More than a little dismayed, they headed home to Strathspey. Passing through the cemetery on their way to

their respective homes, they found it aclutter with tombstones they did not remember. Dumbfounded, they discovered their own. They hurried into the church to find
out what had happened on their brief journey to Inverness. There, the story goes, the two musicians and their
pocketfuls of fairy gold crumbled to dust. It was not just
a single night that they had been fiddling on Inverness's
Fairy Hill, but an entire century.

JEDBURGH

Mary, Queen of Scots House

For days in 1566, even though she was young and strong,
doctors feared for the life of twenty-three-year-old Mary,
Queen of Scots as she lay here, fever-wracked. The love-
smitten queen returned here cold and wet after her fifty-
mile ride in a storm to spend two hours at the bedside of
her beloved Bothwell at Hermitage Castle. (*See* Hawick,
Hermitage Castle.)

KELSO

Floors Park: YEW TREE

James II was delighted when Philip the Good of Bur-
gundy sent him two splendid cannons. The finest sup-
plier of artillery and ammunition of the 1460s, Jehan
Cambier of Mons, had designed them. James had a fondness for weapons. Meanwhile Scotland's old enemy, the
English, had captured Roxburghe Castle. The new cannon was the perfect weapon to dislodge them so James
went to assist.

But, too interested, he stood too close to the mighty
cannon. As it was fired it burst, and James was killed.
This tree marks where he fell.

Mellerstain House

In 1714 the Christmas dinner that was served by Lady
Grisell Baillie and her husband, George, to family and

friends in this elegant Robert Adam–designed house was surely a sumptuous feast. Plum pudding and plum soup, mince pies, fricassee of chicken, and roast beef were the first course. It was followed by roast goose and roast waterfowl, tongue, and oysters served in rolls.

For dessert there were stewed pears and peach cream, jellies, apples, walnuts, almonds, and chestnuts, and finally butter and cheese.

But whatever joy the Baillies had was surely well deserved.

Grisell and George had met each other when she was only twelve. She was smuggling notes from her father to George's father, who was in prison in Edinburgh for his support of Presbyterianism at a time when the Anglican Church was the church of the land.

George's father was hanged for his beliefs—with his young son looking on. To escape capture, Grisell's father was forced into hiding in a dank, dark church vault.

There, for a month, Grisell took him food each night. So no one begrudged Grisell and George these better times in middle age.

Smailholm Tower (7 miles west of Kelso)

As a child staying with his grandparents at nearby Sandyknowe, Walter Scott loved to come to this sixteenth-century watchtower to play. He could climb to the top and look out over the Borderlands and make up stories about who had been kept prisoner in the dungeon above the cattle cellar. He could relive the exciting battles of the Border ballads his grandmother read to him.

And so, as an adult, in 1799 when he learned that the tower was to be knocked down, he tried to see what could be done to save it. He was told perhaps it could be preserved if he would write a ballad immortalizing it. He did, in the ballad of love, murder, and ghosts that he called the "Ballad of the Eve of St. John."

KINROSS

Loch Leven Castle

For eleven months in 1567–68, Mary, Queen of Scots was kept prisoner in this island castle, accused of complicity in the murder of her second husband, Lord Darnley. Here she miscarried the twins of her third husband, Bothwell. Barely recoverd from her miscarriage, she was forced to abdicate in favor of her infant son, James. Then, gradually recovering her health, charm, and beauty, she stirred the sympathy and the devotion of George Douglas, the half-brother of her jailer, Sir William Douglas, and of sixteen-year-old Willie Douglas, another resident of the castle. Together, they hatched a plot to help her escape.

Banished to the mainland by Sir William after an argument, George Douglas asked permission to return home to bid farewell to his mother. He said that he planned to move to France. This visit gave him a chance to talk a boatman into assisting in the escape.

On the morning of May 2 young Willie visited the tower where the queen was incarcerated and whispered the news to her that freedom was in prospect. She should await the arrival of a pearl earring as a signal that all was going well, and at eight that evening he would return for her. Meanwhile, George Douglas, his mission accomplished with the boatman and his farewells said to his mother, left the castle and returned to the shore of the loch where he had horses and supporters ready to carry away the queen.

Toward evening the queen feigned illness. She explained that she would retire to her bed. While she play-acted her sick role, Willie was removing the drainage plugs from all but one of the castle boats to ensure that there could be no pursuit once he and his royal charge had fled. That done, he plied Sir William with sufficient wine at the dinner table so that he became drowsy and dropped the keys to the queen's tower on the floor. Willie scooped them up in a napkin and sent one of the queen's maids to her with the pearl earring—the signal that all was well. By prearrangement that morning, once she had received the pearl she was to dress herself in a serving maid's cloak and await his opening of her prison door.

Moments later the disguised queen and a ten-year-old servant girl were crossing the castle courtyard to the one boat that had not been tampered with. Willie came hot behind them, flinging the prison key into the water as soon as he had made sure the prison door was locked.

The queen and servant climbed into the boat. Young Douglas pushed the boat out and leaped in himself. The oarsman rowed away as fast as he was able, but legend has it that that was not fast enough for Mary, who had been so long confined. Halfway to the shore when she saw horses and her rescuers waiting, she grabbed an oar herself.

Once landed and mounted, Mary and her retinue galloped off to the Firth of Forth. There another boat was waiting to carry them to overnight safety at Niddry. Then, in the morning, they were on their way again to a still safer spot.

KIRKCUDBRIGHT

Dundrennan Abbey

Dressed in borrowed clothes and wrapped in a hooded cloak, her red-gold hair shorn to help in her disguise, an exhausted twenty-five-year-old Mary, Queen of Scots arrived at this Cistercian abbey on May 16, 1568. She had been abandoned by her husband the Earl of Bothwell and lost a battle for her kingdom. On the last night of her life on Scottish soil, sitting here she wrote her cousin, Queen Elizabeth of England, and sought the sanctuary that would end twenty-five years later with her execution.

LADYKIRK (7 miles northeast of Coldstream)

Kirk o'Steil

To assure that it would stand forever, James IV in 1500 had this church built entirely of stone. It was his thanks to God for having saved him from drowning in the River Tweed near here.

LINLITHGOW

Linlithgow Palace: QUEEN MARGARET'S BOWER

In August 1513 in this little octagonal tower, Margaret of Scotland kept her sorrowful vigil when her husband, James IV of Scotland, went off to England to wage war against her brother, Henry VIII. James never returned from the Battle of Flodden.

St. Michael's Church: SOUTH TRANSEPT CHAPEL

As tradition has it, James IV was at his prayers here when he was interrupted by a curious figure in an azure-colored robe with sandals on his feet and long blond hair. James was readying to set off for war in England. Sternly, the figure said that the Virgin Mary warned that neither he nor any who went to England with him would do well in the undertaking. Further, the figure told the king (enamored at that time of Anne, Queen of France) to "avoid the counsel of women."

Even if James was shaken by the apparition, he laid all fear aside. Wearing the turquoise ring that the French queen had sent him, he followed her bidding to invade England, the land of her enemies. And as the apparition had warned, neither James nor many of his men ever returned. (*See* Linlithgow Palace: Queen Margaret's Bower.)

LOCH AWE

Kilchurn Castle

It had been a long, hard foreign war in which Sir Colin Campbell had been fighting. Many men had not returned from it, and Sir Colin seemed to be among them. That being the case, his wife took the rents from his estates and built this castle with the money. Though everyone urged her, she would not marry another man until she was sure that Colin was dead.

She waited and waited. The last of the stragglers seemed to have come home. There was still no sign of her Colin, so she accepted the proposal of another man.

The wedding feast was just ending when a servant drew the bride aside to say there was a surly beggar at the door. He would not leave, the servant said, nor raise a toast to the newlyweds, until the bride herself had filled his cup. And so the bride agreed and did. But when the beggar handed back his emptied cup, inside it lay Sir Colin's ring. The beggar on the doorstep was, of course, Sir Colin, returning just in the nick of time.

LOWER LARGO

As a young man, the cantankerous Alexander Selkirk (whom Daniel Defoe transformed into the hero of *Robinson Crusoe*) was publicly reprimanded in this village where he was born for his "unseemly attitude toward the church." In something of a fit of pique, he went off to sea on a privateer. His temper got him into trouble again. Angry at the captain, he asked to be put ashore in the Juan Fernández Islands in the South Pacific.

After he was picked up six years later, he returned here where he built himself a grotto like the cave he had inhabited in the Pacific. He lived as a recluse and hermit just as he had been forced to live when put ashore in the South Pacific. Hardly a favorite native son in his lifetime, he is fondly remembered now by the statue near the harbor.

MAUCHLINE

In order to try out the dancing lessons he had been taking, young Robert Burns went off one evening in 1784 to a dance being held in this village. But the evening was not a success. Walking home, the youth wistfully remarked to his collie dog that he wished he could find a woman to take dancing who would be as faithful as his dog. His comment was overheard by the local mason's daughter, Jean Armour. A few days later when Burns was back in the village, she saw him again and asked if he had found the woman he was looking for.

That was the start of a long and star-crossed life of love for the pair. They were betrothed, but Burns was too impatient to wait for the wedding day to consummate their love. Jean became pregnant. Her father broke the engagement. On the rebound, the heartbroken Burns asked Mary Campbell, the Highland Mary of the poem of that name, to marry him. But Mary died before they could wed.

A melancholy Burns tried life in Edinburgh. But city life was not for him, and he returned here. Ultimately, he was forgiven by Jean Armour's family, and he and she were married at last.

MELROSE

Melrose Abbey

Again and again this twelfth-century Cistercian abbey where the heart of Robert the Bruce is said to lie (*See* Dunfermline, The Abbey Church) had been under attack but it, seemingly, will not be destroyed. Bearing witness to that is the statue of the Virgin Mary with a child that has lost its head.

It is said that in Reformation days, a Presbyterian seeking to smash the church's graven images tried to batter the figure. The infant's head fell on the man's arm, and he was never again able to use it.

NEW ABBEY (near Dumfries)

Sweetheart Abbey

The love affair of Devorguilla of Scotland and her husband, English nobleman John de Balliol, never ended. But sometimes in his relations with others Sir John's temper got the better of him. That was the case in a conflict with the equally irascible Bishop of Durham.

When Sir John insulted him in a confrontation over who owned which parcel of land, the bishop exacted as penance not only a public scourging of the nobleman on the steps of Durham Cathedral, but acts of charity. (*See* England, Oxford, Balliol College.) And when de Balliol died, to make certain that there would be no conflicts with the hierarchy in Heaven, Devorguilla had this Cistercian monastery erected in 1273 in his memory.

Her deep devotion to him led her to carry her husband's embalmed heart, encased in a casket of ivory and silver, with her wherever she went until her own death twenty-one years later. At that time, according to her directions, it was buried beside her here. Hence the abbey name.

OUTER HEBRIDES

Eriskay: LOCH NAN UAMH

The French ship that sailed into this loch on July 25, 1745, came as a complete surprise. Even more of a surprise was its handsome, twenty-five-year-old passenger, Prince Charles Edward Stuart, grandson of James VII of Scotland who had fled to England in 1688 after the revolution that left his daughter, Mary, and Dutch son-in-law, William of Orange, the rulers of Britain.

This "Bonnie Prince Charlie" of legend and song had landed here to try to raise an army to win back Britain for the Stuarts. He came up empty-handed except for seven friends and the pink flower seeds that fell from his pocket and began to grow. (These still produce pink, bell-shaped "Prince's" flowers on this island.)

Nonetheless, the gallant, optimistic, energetic, and charismatic young prince was in the best of spirits. The Highland chieftains whose support he sought were convinced of the folly of the enterprise that he was proposing. They tried to convince him to go back to France, but when he said he wouldn't, they rallied round, rousing their fellow clansmen to join his cause. (*See* Glenfinnan.)

But it was doomed. On September 20, 1746, a little more than a year after his arrival, exhausted, heartsick, and leaving many noble Scotsmen dead (*See* Culloden), Prince Charles boarded another ship from France and sadly stole away.

PEEBLES

Traquair House (16 miles southeast of Peebles)

In later years when he was a homeless beggar, given a place to die by a charitable Edinburgh cobbler, the Earl of Traquair remembered how callously he had turned his old friend James Graham, Marquis of Montrose, away from his door after the Battle of Philiphaugh.

Once a staunch supporter of the Presbyterian cause, Montrose had changed his allegiance from it to the cause of Charles I. He would try, he said, to win Scotland for the king. And with an army of fierce Highlanders and Irishmen he was doing remarkably well until Philiphaugh.

But there it was a sorry and bloody defeat. When it seemed that there was no hope, Montrose, and those of his men who could, fled the field. Galloping the sixteen miles to this great gray house of his erstwhile friend, the earl, he sought refuge here. The earl told his servants to say that neither he nor his son was at home.

From then on, the fortunes of the Earl of Traquair seemed to fail, until at the end, living from hand to mouth on the streets of Edinburgh, hungry and sick, he found a cobbler who granted him the hospitality he had denied Montrose.

Traquair House: THE BEAR GATES

Not since 1745 when Bonnie Prince Charlie (*See* Culloden) left through these gates have they been opened. Tradition has it that they never will be until a Stuart sits again on the throne of Great Britain.

PERTH

Church of St. John

Preaching here on May 11, 1559, fiery John Knox condemned the Catholic Mass and called upon those who gathered near him to destroy all graven images. When Knox's service ended and a Roman Catholic service began in this parish church that served three separate congregations, a boy who had heeded Knox cried out against the Catholic Mass. The priest boxed his ears. The boy responded by hurling a stone at him. It missed the priest but struck the altar. A melee broke out. Those of Knox's congregation just filing out turned around and, following the boy's example, ripped saints and angels, figures of the Virgin and of Christ from their niches and smashed them on the floor. Then down the road they went to the Blackfriars Monastery and to all the Catholic structures here, hauling the statues out, breaking them, and setting fires that soon destroyed all but this one small church.

Huntington Castle (3 miles northwest of Perth)

Though today a seventeenth-century building stands between the two towers of this castle, in medieval days they were no more than nine feet apart, and that space became known as the Maiden's Leap.

One of the occupants of the castle then was a pretty young woman who fell in love with a man her parents did not like. All the same, from time to time, he would visit the castle and occupy one of the tower rooms. When he did, the daughter of the house would go to visit with him.

But one night as she shared his bed, she heard her mother's footsteps. Desperately she looked for a place to hide and, finding no accessible alcove but seeing a window open in the tower opposite, leapt out one window across the space into the other. It was a successful leap.

North Inch

In this park along the River Tay the noblest members of two Highland clans—Clan Chattan and Clan Kay—fought to the death in 1396. When the battle was done, only two of the sixty who had fought were still alive. With the king, queen, and members of the nobility looking on, such battles were the customary way to settle feuds between two clans in ancient days.

In this instance, however, the combat was somewhat unusual. Just as the fighting was about to start, the leader of the Chattan Clan found that, face to face with the swords and axes and daggers of Clan Kay, one of his thirty fighters had fled. There could be no combat unless each side had the same number of men. So a call was put out for a fighter-to-hire. Only one respondent, a bow-legged blacksmith, offered his services with the understanding that if he lived through the fight he would be supported for the rest of his life.

As it turned out, he was one of the two survivors.

PITLOCHRY

Queen's View

Pausing to admire the view here Mary, Queen of Scots is said to have been so entranced by it that she ordered one of her harpists to compose music about it. Similarly entranced some three hundred years later in 1886 was Queen Victoria, who exclaimed, too, at the beauty of this spot.

POOLEWE

Inverewe Gardens

His neighbors all said that the ground he owned was useless. Nothing could possibly be grown on it. All Osgood Mackenzie had to do to know they were right was look at the single three-foot willow that was struggling to survive on his peaty land.

A son of the twelfth chieftain of the Gairloch Clan, Osgood Mackenzie was not a man who was easily discouraged.

He drained his peat bogs, excavated the rocks, and planted trees and a woodland garden. By 1922, sixty years after he had made his first planting, he had created a sub-tropical garden that was among the finest in Northern Europe. Today, more than one hundred thousand visitors come annually to see the eucalyptus, hydrangeas, and magnolias that thrive on that "useless" ground of 1862.

PORT OF MENTEITH

Inchmahome Island: INCHMAHOME PRIORY RUINS

The army of Henry VIII of England was invading Scotland. At the Battle of Pinkie in 1547, ten thousand Scots had died. Henry VIII was demanding the five-year-old Scottish queen Mary so that she could be the bride of his son Edward.

But neither her Catholic mother, Mary of Guise, nor the rest of Scotland wanted the marriage. Late one night the little queen was taken away from Stirling Castle where she had been staying, hustled into a rowboat, and rowed out to this island in the Lake of Menteith. And here she stayed briefly among the black-robed monks of the abbey, while Henry VIII and his spies looked in vain for her on the mainland.

It is said that while she was here, the little queen planted a garden and a boxwood bower to play in. Though skeptics scoff at the thought that she had either the time or the inclination for such a pursuit, Queen Mary's Bower, bearing the name of Mary, who became the Queen of Scots, grows here.

ROSSLYN

Rosslyn Chapel: APPRENTICE'S PILLAR

While his master was away on a journey, a skilled apprentice carved the delicate flowers and leaves that decorate this pillar. Legend has it that when he returned and saw it, the less skilled master killed the carver in a fit of jealous rage.

ST. ANDREWS

The Castle

In the sixteenth century it would have been difficult to find a Scottish preacher more beloved than George Wishart. When the plague had broken out in Dundee, he had hurried to the city to offer prayers for the sick and dying. It was because of his popularity, of course, that the Catholic cardinal of St. Andrews, David Beaton, wanted him destroyed. Beaton had him arrested, convicted of heresy, and burned at the stake outside this castle while the cardinal unconcernedly looked on.

But the executioner felt differently. Kneeling before Wishart before he bound him to the stake, he sought his forgiveness for the deed he was about to perform. Gently kissing him on the cheek as a token of that forgiveness, Wishart told him to do his duty and proceed.

It was quite different just three months later when the cardinal himself was about to be slain.

Supporters of Wishart came to do justice to the cardinal who had condemned him. Entering the castle while

Beaton was still in bed, they headed for his door, and though he barricaded it and fearfully shouted that he was a priest and therefore should not be slain, they broke the door down, murdered him, and hung his body from the castle walls.

But that was not the end of the story. The Catholic Mary of Guise, mother of the child-queen, Mary, Queen of Scots, and her daughter's regent, laid siege to this castle where the cardinal's killers and those who sided with them had taken refuge.

They managed to hold out for a year, until a fleet from France sent in support of the French-born queen mother sailed into St. Andrews Bay. The French landed their mighty guns and, firing them from the neighboring cathedral walls, forced a surrender.

Among those captured on that summer day in 1547 and condemned to two years as a galley slave was Wishart's bodyguard, the budding theologian John Knox. (*See* Edinburgh, Holyrood Abbey.)

St. Andrews Golf Links

The wind was blowing here on the morning of the golf championship in 1860. All the same, Maitland Dougall was readying to play when a frantic call came that a ship was foundering off shore. The strongest man was needed to stroke the local lifeboat to the rescue.

For the next five hours, Dougall bobbed about with fellow rescuers in the little lifeboat and rowed the ship's crew to the safety of shore. Then he came back, put buckshot in his golf ball to steady it and keep it low in the fierce wind, and won the championship with a score of 112.

St. Regulus Church

One night in the fourth century the monk who became St. Regulus (or Rule) was awakened by a vision in his cell in Patras in western Greece. It told him to take with him, for safety's sake, what remained of the bones of St. Andrew, martyred in Patras, and sail west until he received a sign from God.

As the legend goes, Regulus took with him for company a priest, two deacons, eight hermits, and three "devout virgins."

They sailed around the coast of Spain and France and headed north, with still no sign from God. Then a fierce storm arose as they neared here. Their ship was wrecked, and all that they carried with them was lost except for the precious box that held St. Andrew's bones.

From a height above the beach, the King of Picts had seen their vessel overturn and had hurried down to the shore to plunder it. The water-soaked Greek missionaries were just stumbling ashore when the king arrived. But as he prepared to kill the shipwrecked missionaries, a bright light seared the sky—a white cross against the sky of blue. Without further ado, it is said that here, below the searing cross, the King of Picts turned Christian. Here, too, the flag of Scotland—a white cross on a field of blue—was created.

As for the bones of St. Andrew, the patron saint of Scotland, they are believed to have been buried beneath the western tower of this church.

SCONE

Palace of Scone

When in the ninth century the Pictish tribes inhabited most of Scotland, their king ruled from this site until the day that Kenneth Macalpine, son of a Pictish princess and a Scottish father, came for a visit from the southwest with some of his men.

Graciously—or so it seemed—he gave a banquet for his hosts, plying them well with food and drink. But when they were at the height of their merriment, his men drew the bolts that held up the seats of the diners' benches. The Picts tumbled this way and that and were quickly set upon by their Scottish guests. All the Picts were killed and Kenneth Macalpine became the first king of the Scots.

With him from his land in the southwest he had brought the Stone of Scone. For the next five hundred years, this precious Stone of Destiny stayed here. Until James I, all of Scotland's kings were crowned on it. (*See* England, London, Westminster Abbey: Chapel of St. Edward the Confessor.)

◆ ◆ ◆

It was understandable that eight-year-old Alexander III grew restless during his coronation on this site in the thirteenth century. It had all started out entertainingly enough with his being seated on the big flat stone that had been grandly draped with a silken cloth woven with gold. Then he was consecrated by the Bishop of St. Andrews. It was even fun for the child when all the nobles present took off their cloaks and laid them at his feet for him to walk upon, saying that they were doing for him what had been done for Christ when He entered Jerusalem.

But then came a bard from the Highlands who fell at the boy-king's feet and in Gaelic tediously gave the names of all of Alexander's forebears for generations back to the days of Scota, the Egyptian Pharaoh's daughter from whom the Scots are said to take their name.

Palace of Scone: MOOT HILL

It is said that whenever Scottish kings were crowned here, the barons who swore fealty to them brought to the site inside their boots as much soil from their own land as they could manage. They deposited it to signify the union of all the land of Scotland on this site. After that custom, this is sometimes nicknamed Boot Hill.

◆ ◆ ◆

The coronation here in 1306 of Robert the Bruce was a simple affair—only four Scottish bishops and four earls attended. There was no crown (King Robert's ousted predecessor, John de Balliol, had gone off with that). Instead, a simple circlet of gold was laid on the Bruce's head by the Countess of Buchan, the sister of the Earl of Fife who, traditionally, should have done the honors, but had refused. The countess was willing to risk the displeasure of England's Edward I, who did not want a strong king in Scotland. Her brother was not.

But it was all such an unpretentious affair that the Bruce's wife sadly remarked, "It seems to me that we are but a summer King and Queen, whom the children crown with flowers in their sports." Happily for Scotland she was mistaken, since the Bruce valiantly led Scotland toward freedom from England.

Woodland Garden and Pinetum

As a youth working as the under-gardener here in the early years of the nineteenth century, David Douglas's affection for the trees around him grew as they did. As a grown man and full-fledged botanist traveling in North America, he discovered the fir tree that bears his name. Affectionately he sent seeds of it back to this garden and forest where he had been nurtured and trained.

STIRLING

Stirling Castle

Even James II's supporters were shocked by the king's murder here in 1452 of the Earl of Douglas. It was true that the pair were sworn enemies. Nonetheless, James had invited Douglas to his castle to discuss resolving their differences without a war, and he had promised him safe-conduct.

The Earl of Douglas took the king at his word and came to supper. Schooled since childhood in issuing such invitations (*See* Edinburgh, Edinburgh Castle: Banqueting Hall), the king asked Douglas when supper was over to break an alliance he had with two friends whom the king feared. Douglas declined.

"Traitor!" the king is reported to have shouted at his guest. "If you will not break it, this will." And drawing a dagger from beneath his cloak, he stabbed the earl. His court sprang to assist him in his murderous deed and tossed the body of the earl out the window.

But that was not the end of the matter. At the head of a band of six hundred men, Douglas's brother came to avenge the death. He dragged the document of safe-conduct tied to a horse's tail to show how little the king's word meant. And relentlessly the six hundred men set fire to Stirling Town.

◆　◆　◆

Among the guests whom James IV warmly welcomed here was the pretender, Perkin Warbeck of Flanders, who told the king that he was the Duke of York, the younger of the two princes Richard III was said to have murdered in the Tower of London. (See England, London, Tower of London: Bloody Tower.) Believing him, the ingenuous king provided him with both a pension and a pretty wife from the nobility. Then, to help pay for the invasion of England that Warbeck planned, the king sold all this castle's silver plate in the 1490s.

◆　◆　◆

Here a happy little Mary, Queen of Scots dashed up and down the long corridors and played with her four Marys—Mary Fleming, Mary Beaton, Mary Livingstone, and Mary Seton—who were to be her best friends, companions, and classmates for many years. The most loyal of all, Mary Seton, would still be her devoted confidante up to five years before Mary Stuart's death and Mary Seton's retirement to a convent in France.

◆　◆　◆

There were those who said that Mary, Queen of Scots, from the time of her coronation here, could come to no good end. The date selected for the coronation was, after all, the thirtieth anniversary of the disastrous Battle of Flodden when Scotland's James IV had gone to war against Henry VIII of England out of affection for France. When the battle ended on September 9, 1513, James was dead, along with thirteen Scottish earls and thirteen lords, an archbishop, a bishop, two abbots, three Highland chiefs, and thousands of men.

But it was on September 9, 1543, nonetheless, that the nine-month-old princess was crowned.

The prognosticators, of course, were right; but there were two moments of great joy for Mary within these palace walls.

In 1565, it was here that she fell in love with her handsome cousin, Henry Stuart, Lord Darnley. He came down with the measles, and the young queen, staying with him by day and often by night, took it upon herself to nurse him back to health. In the intimacy of the sickroom, he won her heart. From that liaison came her son James, who became James VI of Scotland; James I of England.

James's christening in the Royal Chapel here in 1566 brought Mary joy again, for it was a grand occasion. Though her love for Darnley was gone and he did not attend, she was delighted with the gold baptismal font that Elizabeth of England sent and the necklace of pearls and rubies from the King of France.

◆ ◆ ◆

It is no wonder that when James VI in the mid-eighteenth century was confronted here with 120 widows of the Clan Colquhoun (today called "Cahoon"), bearing the bloody clothes of their massacred husbands, he outlawed the Clan MacGregor that had done the deed and took away MacGregors' lands.

Mar's Wark (Broad Street)

Because the stone for this impressive Renaissance palace had been stolen from neighboring Cambuskenneth Abbey, it was cursed. Legend has it that the Earl of Mar, who was building the palace, died only two years after work on it had started in 1570. It has never been completed.

STONEHAVEN

Dunnottar Castle (2 miles south of Stonehaven)

The handsome, debonair Earl of Montrose and the Earl Marischal, who owned this extensive estate, had once been friends and comrades in arms. They had fought together for Presbyterianism. When the Earl of Montrose took up arms for Charles I and could not convince his friend to do likewise, Montrose attacked this property. From his battlements the Earl Marischal watched his woods and fields go up in smoke. Sadly looking on, he went so far as to venture that perhaps he had been wrong in rejecting Montrose's offer, since that would have saved his lands.

Overhearing him, a stern Presbyterian cleric took him to task for his weakness of spirit. As the pair regarded the smoldering ruins of this castle and its surroundings, the cleric remarked that the smell of the burning would assuredly prove to be "sweet-smelling incense in the nostrils of the Lord."

In 1651 the forces of antimonarchist Oliver Cromwell were besieging this castle, trying to force its surrender because they knew the Scottish crown, scepter, and sword of state were hidden here. The siege notwithstanding, certain courtesies were granted to Margaret Ogilvy, wife of the castle commander. For example, she could have visits from her old schoolmate, Mary Grainger, wife of the minister of neighboring Kinneff Church.

One day when Mrs. Grainger and her maid arrived, they carried with them two bundles of flax, presumably so Mrs. Ogilvy could spin and while away the time during her incarceration.

Of course the English soldiers who were on guard, searching for food or weapons, stuck their pikes through the bundles that the two women were carrying. Several days later, pretending that she had an unexpected need for any flax Mrs. Ogilvy had not yet spun, Mrs. Grainger returned for it with her maid. The soldiers did not bother with the bundles that were taken out. Indeed, said to have been quite entranced by the two visiting young women, the besieging general actually helped Mrs. Grainger onto her horse when it came time for her to leave. Little did he know that the scepter and sword of Scotland were inside the flax and that the crown was under her full skirt. And that night, once dark had come, the regalia was hidden beneath the pulpit of the Kinneff Church. There it remained for the next eight years until the Restoration came and it was joyfully taken out for the coronation of Charles II.

THE TROSSACHS

All along the shores of Loch Katrine and Loch Lomond, in the shadowed mountain passes and the tangled woods of silver birch and oak, beneath the craggy contours of Ben A'an and Ben Venue, the eighteenth-century outlaw-hero Rob Roy MacGregor stole from the rich and gave to the poor.

Fact and legend are so intertwined in the tales of Rob Roy (Walter Scott immortalized him in a book of that name) that nowadays there is really no telling one from the other. But at Glengyle at the head of Loch Katrine he is said to have been born. At age twenty-five during a cold, snowy winter, he is said to have daringly raided the village of Kippen and stolen a herd of cattle when Glengyle needed food. Cattle raids were common practice among the Highlanders of those days. After his first taste of raiding, rather than continuing in it, the clever Rob Roy set himself up in the business of "insuring" that the herds of the rich would be protected from raiders if he were paid for the protection. If he protected and was not

But it was not cattle-insuring that got him into trouble. It was, instead, entering into the cattle-buying business with a neighbor, the Duke of Montrose.

Rob Roy had established his wife and children in a pleasant little house in Cragroyston and had bought still more land at Inversnaid from the duke. Dealing over cattle and land as they did and both being successful men, they were soon discussing joint enterprises. The duke knew of cattle that he wanted. He proposed to Rob Roy that he go after them for the duke and gave him, accordingly, a sizable sum to make the purchase.

His supporters say that Rob Roy entrusted the money and the transaction to someone else, who absconded, thereby ruining Rob Roy's good name and turning him to his life of lawlessness.

The Duke of Montrose asked for his money back—or the cattle—and, getting neither, demanded retribution of the law. A proclamation was issued declaring that Rob Roy was a wanted man.

And it wasn't Rob Roy alone whom the duke went after. He ousted Rob's wife and children from their house on Loch Lomond and then burned it to the ground.

Notable for his strength and his valor, the outraged Rob Roy gathered a band of men about him to wreak his vengeance on the duke. In foray after foray, often at pistol point, they would demand the rents due Montrose from the tenants on his land. Sometimes they would steal his grain and distribute it to the poor.

In one of Rob Roy's most daring escapades, he and a sole companion surprised the duke's rent collector at Chappellarroch just after he had received money from tenants and was locking the sackful of it inside a cupboard. He remarked to the tenants assembled as he did so that he would willingly give the whole sack of money away if he could have Rob Roy's head in exchange.

Whereupon from outside came the voice of the outlaw positioning two men at each window of the house, two at each corner, and four at each door. Then Rob Roy and one of his men burst inside, pistols ready, swords in hand.

With the greatest of glee, the cheerful Rob announced that he had arrived with just what the factor had been looking for—his redbearded head, albeit still attached to his body. While he would not relinquish it in exchange for the tenants' rents, he would take the rents, if the factor pleased.

Since the factor thought that there were armed men at the doors, windows, and corners of the house, clearly there was nothing to do but to give over the rents. Gloomily, he unlocked the cupboard. Ever polite, Rob Roy expressed his thanks, handed out receipts for rent paid to any tenants who were present, and ordered the factor to put dinner on the table for all. Rob Roy promised to pay for it with money from the rent-collector's bag.

With dinner finished and the sack of money in his hand, Rob and his cohort readied to leave the house, but not before they had exacted an oath that no one would leave the premises for an hour. Since the factor thought the armed men were still in their positions around the house, he acquiesced.

Away Rob Roy and his companion fled on their horses. It wasn't until much later that the factor learned there had never been a band of men outside the house at all—only Rob Roy and his companion inside.

And that was hardly the end of the matter. Still later the audacious Rob Roy kidnapped the factor and several of his servants and held them for ransom at Rob Roy's Prison—a cavern at the base of Ben Lomond on Loch Lomond. The duke refused to pay the ransom. Noted for his softheartedness, his raids on the duke's property notwithstanding, Rob Roy released his prisoners.

By this time the Duke of Montrose had had more than he could bear. For five years Rob Roy had been pestering him. If neither magistrates nor soldiers could track down the outlaw, he knew he could—and he finally did in paid, of course, he took the cattle for himself.

1717. Not for long, however. Three days after Rob was captured, bound to one of his captors as they crossed the stream, he cut the strap binding him, plunged into the river, and swam away before he was missed.

Sometimes in these years on the loose Rob Roy lived in the cave that bears his name near Inversnaid; sometimes in Glen Shira on Loch Shira. Finally in 1722 he abandoned outlawry and made his peace with the duke. That wasn't enough, though. The government still called him an outlaw. Capturing him, they got him as far as a convict ship at Gravesend. It looked as if the life in store for the swashbuckling, independent-spirited man of the Trossachs would be one of slavery in Barbados.

But it all worked out in the end. A pardon arrived as the ship was pulling up anchor. Rob Roy came home again to the Trossachs—this time to the banks of the River Lochlarig, where he remained fairly peaceably until the end of his days.

Surprisingly for a man of his caliber, he lived a long life. Born in 1671, he lived until 1734. Though it is said that his wife belittled him for abandoning banditry, much of the spirit of his youth must have been retained. On his deathbed, learning that an erstwhile enemy had come to call, Rob demanded to be taken from his bed and given his dirk and pistols. No foeman was to see Rob Roy defenseless and unarmed.

With his wife and two sons, Rob Roy lies in the churchyard of Balquidder.

WESTER ROSS

Loch Maree

The followers of the seventh-century St. Maree for whom this lake is named and who had his cell on Isle Maree here could hardly be persuaded to eat of the sweet apples in the saint's orchard. It is said that he was so holy that when the apples he grew turned ripe, the figure of the cross was on them. It seemed sacrilegious somehow to consume them.

YARROW

St. Mary's Loch

It would be hard to assess the influence of this lovely loch on English letters. Sir Walter Scott featured it in *Marmion,* and William Wordsworth wrote about it in "Yarrow Revisited." Robert Louis Stevenson, the poet James Hogg, and the historian Thomas Carlyle all strolled its peaceful shores and sought inspiration in the Lowland hills around it.

3
WALES

ABERYSTWYTH

The Devil's Bridge (11½ miles east of Aberystwyth)

Year after year in the Middle Ages men tried without success to build a bridge across the roaring waters of the Mynach River here. But no one could. As the story goes, one day Marged, an old woman who lived alone with her cow and her dog by the riverbank, lost the cow. Looking across the chasm, Marged caught a glimpse on the other side of the river of the animal that was her livelihood. Somewhere upstream where the river was narrower the cow had crossed.

But it was a pelting rainstorm, and Marged hardly felt like walking endlessly to find the spot where her cow had crossed. Grumblingly, as she looked out across the yawning chasm with its plunging waters, she remarked that she would give anything for a bridge. And from across the way, a silken voice called back to her that, if she liked, a bridge could be supplied.

191

Marged peered beyond her cow and saw a man addressing her who was dressed like a monk. In view of the number of times constructing a bridge had already been tried and had failed, she was doubtful of the stranger's ability to do what others had been unable to do. But how much would it cost, and how long would it take? she asked.

The silken-voiced stranger promised the bridge within an hour. The only payment he requested was to have the first living thing that crossed the bridge once it was built. Marged was both skeptical and leery, but she needed her cow so she agreed to the stranger's offer. An hour later the bridge was done. The stranger stood beside her cow on the far side of the torrent that the bridge spanned. Smiling, he urged Marged to come after her cow. But Marged was taking no chances. Perhaps talking to her was a monk who had worked a miracle, or perhaps it was the devil himself. Instead of hurrying after the cow herself, she threw a crust of bread across the bridge and her dog ran after it. In fury the "monk" on the other side stamped his foot and disappeared in a cloud of smoke. As Marged had suspected, the bridge was the devil's handiwork. Regardless, the workmanship was good, and it still remains. And Marged got her cow back.

BANGOR

Penrhyn Castle

Made rich by the neighboring slate quarries, George Hay Dawkins Pennant proudly had this castle entirely rebuilt in the nineteenth century. He urged his architect, of course, to make use of the local slate. The architect designed, among other items, a four-poster bed made entirely of slate and weighing several tons. Visiting here, Queen Victoria was asked if she would like to sleep in it. She declined with only the vaguest politeness, remarking that she found the enormous bedstead "interesting but uninviting."

BEAUMARIS

Beaumaris Castle

In 1293, when he was having this castle built, Edward I was an old hand at castles. Caernarfon and Conwy were behind him. Contemporary accounts have him listening quietly on the ramparts at the end of a day's work to an English harpist playing.

BEDDGELERT

Legend has it that once where this village now stands, a twelfth-century prince, Llywelyn ab Iorwerth, and his wife went hunting one day. They left their favorite dog, a hound called Beddgelert, behind in the royal lodge guarding their infant son.

Returning home at the end of the hunt, the prince and princess were, as usual, greeted at the door to the lodge by Beddgelert. But this time the lodge door was wide open, and though he wagged his tail as always to greet them, Beddgelert was covered with blood.

When the prince rushed inside, he found his son's cradle overturned, blood-smeared, and empty.

With a cry of vengeance, the prince turned on the dog that he was certain had killed his infant son. Pulling his sword from its scabbard, Llywelyn thrust it through the hound. And as the dog's death cry was heard, so, too, was a cry from beneath the cradle. Turning it over, Llywelyn found both his crying child and the wolf that would have attacked the baby had it not been killed by Beddgelert.

To honor the brave dog he had mistrusted and killed, Llywelyn had a monument of stones placed here where he buried him so Beddgelert would not be forgotten.

CAERNARFON (CAERNARVON)

Caernarfon Castle

The body of a Roman, believed to be that of Magnus Maximus, the father of Constantine the Great was found here in 1283. Edward I took it as a sign. The discovery coincided with a story popular in Edward's day that recounted how Maximus had dreamed of finding a great fortified city in the mountains of Wales—a city with many-colored towers topped with eagles.

If he could build such a turreted fortification, Edward reasoned, it would be symbolic of his conquest of what had once been part of the Holy Roman Empire of Maximus and Constantine.

This castle, therefore, was constructed with towers encircled with rings of colored stone. One of them, the Eagle Tower, had its turrets topped with eagles of stone.

◆ ◆ ◆

In April 1284 a delighted Edward I hurried here from Rhuddlan Castle to see his newborn son who would become Edward II. And here all the chiefs of North Wales came a few days later to beg the English king who ruled them to appoint a native-born prince to govern their land. Tired of foreign rulers whose tongues they could not understand, they asked for one who spoke neither English nor French. If they had such a prince, all promised that they would willingly accept his jurisdiction over them.

Smiling broadly, the wily king told them he would be pleased to do as they wished. Whereupon Edward ordered his infant son brought to him.

Presenting the baby to the Welsh chieftains, Edward assured them that he was just what they had requested— "that he was a just-born native of their country, that his character was unimpeached, that he could not speak a word of English or French, and that, if they pleased, the first words that he uttered should be Welsh."

Little Edward was hardly what the Welshmen had expected. But with as good a grace as possible they approached the baby one by one, and, kissing his tiny hand, swore allegiance to him.

CARDIFF

Caerphilly Castle (5 miles north of Cardiff)

For weeks in 1326 Edward II and a handful of followers had been besieged in this castle by his vicious queen, Isabella, and her lover, Mortimer. There seemed some chance that the besieged might eventually wear down their attackers and drive them away. Using a furnace at the base of what today is its "leaning" tower, the king and his men were melting lead and pouring it down on those seeking to rout them out.

And so it was that an attack was made on the furnace itself. The red-hot metal was let run out. Then water was thrown on it from the moat. The result was an explosion which tipped the tower to the curious position in which it has stood ever since, making this a rival to Italy's leaning tower at Pisa.

Cardiff Castle

Imprisoned here for twenty-eight years by his brother Henry I, Duke Robert of Normandy could not see for his eyes had been put out. But his warders told him of a lovely oak that grew outside his prison tower. He wrote a poem about it. Along with his praise for the time-ravaged tree, he invoked misery on the hateful man who delights in discord. Few who heard this poem could doubt that he was writing about his brother.

CARMARTHEN

All still goes well in this little town reputed to be the birthplace of the sorcerer, Merlin. That is despite the fact that Merlin's Oak has been cut down. He had prophesied that when it was cut down, Carmarthen would cease to be.

Merlin's Hill (3 miles west of Camarthen)

In the chair the rocks make on this hillside, the magician Merlin, of King Arthur's day, is said to have sat and prophesied. He remains today inside this hill. Enchanted into entering it in the fifth century and kept imprisoned ever since, Merlin groans sometimes at twilight and shakes his chains.

CHEPSTOW

Chepstow Castle: MARTEN'S TOWER

A signer of the death warrant for Charles I, Henry Marten was kept imprisoned in this round tower for twenty years for that act. He apparently lived well here, with his family around him, and was free to walk around the town and countryside. An end to his incarceration was not especially welcome—or so he suggested on the epitaph he wrote for his own gravestone in the churchyard at St. Mary's here: "My time was spent in serving you and you. / And death's the pay, it seems, and welcome, too."

CHIRK

Chirk Castle

So renowned for hospitality was this castle in its heyday that a song was written about it. The song suggests that even if the brook that flows nearby became a brook of flowing wine or beer, and the hill that rises a stone's throw away were to be transformed to a hill of meat and bread, the supply would only satisfy a half-year's guests.

CLYRO

There are those who say it was in this town that a disagreeable member of the Baskerville family that dwelt here was torn to pieces by a ferocious hound. This inspired Sir Arthur Conan Doyle to write his "The Hound of the Baskervilles "

CONWY

Conwy Castle

There was no English merrymaking here on Christmas Day in 1294. Come to Wales to put down a rebellion, Edward I had lost all his supplies in an ambush and had been forced to take refuge behind these fifteen-foot thick castle walls. Of course, he had sent a messenger to order a new stock of supplies, but the river, clearly, was siding with the Welsh. It rose higher and higher, and there could be no passage on it. The English grew hungrier and thirstier as the weeks went by, and Christmas came and went in a dolorous fashion.

Not until New Year's would there be an English celebration. Then, at last, the waters fell; the English boats arrived and Edward and his men enjoyed their holiday festivities.

◆　◆　◆

It was the summer of 1399 when Richard II, away in Ireland, learned that his cousin Henry of Bolingbroke, whom he had banished the year before, had returned to England. Richard wasted no time in returning to protect his interests. But as he landed, his troops disbanded, and, virtually alone, he fled here in search of more men.

He had barely arrived when he found he had company—the Earl of Northumberland, a supporter of Bolingbroke's. The nervous king suggested that they hear Mass together and then sought a pledge of fealty from Northumberland. It was readily given, and Richard breathed easier. When Northumberland suggested that Richard leave the castle with him and assured him that no one meant him any harm, the agreeably surprised Richard did just as Northumberland requested. For Richard, that was the beginning of the end.

The next stop was a prearranged ambush. After that came imprisonment at Flint (*See* Flint, Flint Castle); a humiliating trip to London on a scrawny nag; forced abdication; further imprisonment in England; and a mysterious death, some say by violence; others by starvation.

◆ ◆ ◆

One Sunday in the 1400s while the garrison of this impregnable English castle was away at church, a Welsh carpenter let the forces of patriot Owen Glendower inside, and impregnable Conwy was taken.

◆ ◆ ◆

Until 1665 this handsome castle was even grander than it is today. But then, Edward, Earl of Conwy, to whom it had been given after the Restoration, had stone after stone removed and carried away to repair a castle that he owned in Ireland.

Conwy Castle: THE TERRACE

Though she devotedly followed her husband to many of his wars in harsh, foreign places, Edward I's queen, Eleanor of Castile, loved what was beautiful. Contemplating one day what to do to add a touch of color to this formidable castle, she decided that the pretty sweet peas of her native land might be the answer. So, forthwith, she had them imported and planted on this terrace. They were the first sweet peas ever to be planted in the British Isles.

DENBIGH

Denbigh Castle

For awhile Henry de Lacy, Earl of Lincoln, was quite happy building this castle as a fortification for Edward I in the thirteenth century. But then one of his sons fell into the well and drowned. Grief-stricken, De Lacy left the castle, never to return.

FISHGUARD

The seven-year-old French Republic in 1797 had great plans for its future. They included a full-scale invasion of

England. An early mini-invasion was organized. Several hundred convicts and galley slaves were released from their sentences to participate in it. Four vessels of them were sent across Bristol Channel with instructions, after landing, to burn Bristol, march into Wales, and burn Chester and Liverpool.

As it happened, the nervous raiders were put off by the sight of a Dublin packet boat. They decided that Wales would be an easier landing place than Bristol, so they changed course.

As soon as the French ships hove in sight, alerted militia and yeomen began to gather on shore, and their women with them. As the story goes, it was the red shawls of the women following their men that led to the French surrender.

After landing, the convicts and galley slaves had climbed to the top of Carreg Gwasted Point from which they could look down on their prey. At first, though they realized a battle was in prospect, when they saw only a black-clad army of men armed with muskets, the French felt certain they would be the victors. But then they saw behind the black-clads what appeared to be the red coats of the army, and their captain advanced to the leader of the Welsh and surrendered. By the time he saw that the army of "redcoats" was only an army of women in red shawls, it was too late.

FLINT

Flint Castle

For years Richard II and his greyhound, Mathe, had been inseparable. Whenever unleashed, Mathe would jump up affectionately on his master, put his paws on the king's shoulders, and lick his head and neck with enthusiasm. But that July day in 1399 when Richard surrendered here to his cousin, Henry of Bolingbroke, that didn't happen. (*See* Conwy, Conwy Castle.)

In the courtyard here where the two men stood, Mathe

leaped, instead, for the shoulders of Bolingbroke. When Bolingbroke asked the meaning of the fondness, the king replied that it meant much good fortune for Bolingbroke and none at all for Richard. Richard said that Mathe instinctively was paying court to the next king of England. And Richard and Mathe were right. Henry of Bolingbroke became Henry IV.

HARLECH

Harlech Castle

In 1468, Daffyd ap Ivan and forty hungry men's effort to hold this castle for the Lancastrians in the Wars of the Roses was valiant but failed. The troops of Henry IV battered relentlessly at the gates, but still the brave men of Harlech held on. Indeed, Daffyd is said to have defiantly sent a message to Henry recalling that once, in his past, Daffyd had held a castle in France against conquerors so long and so courageously that the old women of Wales heard of it and talked of it. Similarly, he told the king, he intended to hold Harlech Castle against Henry's men "till the old women of France hear about it."

And they have. So valorous was Daffyd's defense that the king agreed to pardon the garrison, and they proudly marched out. They are remembered to this day in the resounding marching song, "The March of the Men of Harlech."

HAVERFORDWEST

Roch Castle (8 miles to the northwest)

Because he had been warned that he would be killed by the bite of an adder, Adam de Rupe, the thirteenth-century builder of this house, refused ever to leave it. But it didn't matter. The soothsayer was right. An adder came in on a pile of wood and killed de Rupe just as had been prophesied.

HAWARDEN

Hawarden Castle Gardens

William Gladstone, who served four terms as Queen Victoria's prime minister, was cutting down trees here in 1868—his favorite occupation—when he learned that he was to become prime minister. He simply kept on chopping until his task was done. The queen never forgave him.

HOLYWELL

St. Winefride's Well

All Winefride wanted was to be left in peace to be a nun. Seventh-century Prince Caradoc was determined that she should be his bride. Furious when she spurned him, he struck her head off with his sword. Here where it fell a miraculous spring appeared, sending forth, it is said, two thousand gallons of clear water a minute.

LAUGHARNE

On November 5, 1953, in this "timeless, beautiful, barmy town, in this far, forgetful, important place of herons, cormorants, castle, churchyard, gulls, ghosts, geese, feuds, scares, scandals, cherry-trees, mysteries, jackdaws in the chimneys, bats in the belfry, skeletons in the cupboards, pubs, mud, cockles, flatfish, curlews, rain, and human, often all too human beings . . ." these prerecorded words of the poet Dylan Thomas were being broadcast when his wife, Caitlin, received word in their boathouse here that her husband lay ill in New York City. Four days later, he was dead.

LLANDAFF

Llandaff Cathedral

Time and again down through the centuries, this cathedral has been destroyed and rebuilt. In this century no cathedral in Great Britain but Coventry's has suffered such devastation. In 1941 a German landmine virtually blew Llandaff Cathedral to smithereens. As they have so often done since the twelfth century, the people of Llandaff saw to it that their church was once again rebuilt. This time its crowning artistic glory is a Christ in Majesty by Jacob Epstein.

LLANDDEWI BREFI

It is said that when sixth-century St. David came here to preach, a large crowd assembled and the short-of-stature patron saint of Wales could neither be seen nor heard. Taking out his handkerchief, St. David stood upon it, and it turned into a hill from which he most effectively sermonized.

LLANDUDNO

Gogarth Abbey Hotel

It was while visiting this seaside resort in 1862 that Charles Dodgson (Lewis Carroll) is said to have written much of *Alice's Adventures in Wonderland.*

Staying with his Oxford friends, the Liddells (*See* England, Oxford, Christ Church College), Dodgson strolled the beach with the youngest daughter, Alice, telling her stories. Later at the Liddell summer house that is now part of this hotel, he wrote the stories down and read them aloud in the evening to the adults.

LLANGOLLEN

Plas Newydd (Hill Street)

The eccentric Irish "Ladies of Llangollen," who "eloped" here when Lady Eleanor Butler was twenty-nine and Sarah Ponsonby was twenty-three, for fifty years never spent a night away from this black and white timbered mansion. But writers, artists, and actors, inventors, and military men of note were always honored to be invited to visit them. William Wordsworth (though his poem about the ladies referring to their years hardly pleased them) and Robert Southey came here to write; Charles Darwin, Sir Walter Scott, and the Duke of Wellington were guests. If the visitor was on a second visit, all that was asked of him (besides being entertaining) was a gift of a panel of carved oak to commemorate the event.

PEMBROKE

Carew Castle (4½ miles east of Pembroke)

Though Sir Rhys ap Thomas had taken an oath of fealty to Richard III and in it promised that only "over his prostrate body" would anyone opposed to Richard enter Sir Rhys's part of Wales, he was hardly a devoted subject. When word got out that Henry Tudor was on his way to wrest the kingdom from Richard's hands, Sir Rhys, the owner of this castle, took pains to lie beneath a bridge that Henry Tudor had to cross, so that he could no longer be held to his pledge of allegiance. And with great gusto he then joined Henry in his battle against Richard at Bosworth Field (*See* England, Market Bosworth).

When the battle was done, he celebrated by grandly redoing this castle for a five-day tournament for the happy royalty of Wales.

Pembroke Castle

From out of her husband's bed, the beautiful Nesta, eleventh-century Princess of Wales, is said to have been stolen by her stepson, Owain, visiting the castle that then stood on this site. Setting fire to the castle, the carefree Owain let his father escape by sliding down a drainpipe.

For Nesta, who earlier had been one of the six mistresses of Henry I, it all seems to have been a bit of a lark. She was soon "nesting" quite happily with Owain in his hunting lodge. Her husband, however, enlisted the aid of

Henry in getting her back. She remained with him equally happily until the end of his days, after which this "most beautiful woman in the world in her day" had liaisons with a constable and a sheriff before her radiance faded.

ST. DAVID'S

St. David's Cathedral

As he had done at Canterbury after the death of Thomas à Becket (*See* England, Canterbury, Canterbury Cathedral), a contrite Henry II is said to have walked here barefoot from the coast to seek further forgiveness at the shrine of sixth-century St. David.

SNOWDONIA NATIONAL PARK

Moel Hebog: GLENDOWER'S CHIMNEY

England's Henry IV was tired of the ravages of the Welsh prince, Owen Glendower, against the lords that he had sent to control Wales. Henry sent an army to capture Glendower. Valorous though the Welsh were, the king's army was larger. Glendower and his men were defeated. Glendower, however, managed an escape, though the English were soon after him. Quickly and stealthily, he made his way here to North Wales where, near Mount Snowdon, his red-haired friend Red Reece of Snowdon lived.

For a day or two Glendower remained undiscovered in Red Reece's house. Then word of his whereabouts reached Henry's men. When Glendower learned that the English were approaching, he readied to leave, but his host insisted that he would leave with him to show him the best departure route.

So the two men dressed, at Red Reece's urging, in the same dark cloaks and hats and left the back of Red Reece's house just as the English soldiers approached the front.

With their pursuers getting closer and closer, up the hill behind the house they scrambled until Red Reece urged Glendower to hide behind a cluster of rocks while he led the soldiers on. Owen hid. Reece raced on until his hat blew off, revealing his tell-tale red hair. The English turned around and went back after Glendower.

By this time, Glendower was heading toward this mountain. Though dark cliffs surrounded its summit, Glendower hoped he could in some way reach and get over them before his English pursuers had caught up with him. Unfortunately, it seemed unlikely. Much more likely was that he would be pinned against the cliffs by the English.

Just then he saw that a chimney-like cleft—three hundred feet from top to bottom—split the cliffs. A scramble to its top was his only possible avenue of escape.

Miraculously, he had gone halfway up the perilous climb before the English arrived. Their leader ordered them to follow, but schooled mountain-climbers though they were, they knew at a glance that the climb was too much for them. The panting, exhausted Glendower finally reached the chimney top and found a cave where he remained until the English had left the Colwyn Valley.

TINTERN

Tintern Abbey Ruins

Briefly escaped from imprisonment in 1327 at Berkeley Castle (*See* England, Berkeley, Berkeley Castle), Edward II found refuge for two nights here. In gratitude, he extended fishing rights on the nearby River Wye to Tintern Abbey's monks.

4
NORTHERN IRELAND

ARMAGH CITY (County Armagh)

Down on his luck, a seventeenth-century librarian here pawned the priceless ninth-century *Book of Armagh*, the life of St. Patrick. Instead of being a treasure in the county museum or in the library at Catholic St. Patrick's Cathedral here, today it is the property of Trinity College, Dublin, in the Republic of Ireland.

St. Patrick's Protestant Cathedral and St. Patrick's Catholic Cathedral

Walking in ancient days where this Protestant cathedral now stands, St. Patrick happened upon a doe with her fawn in the underbrush. The hungry companions with whom he walked would readily have killed both, but Patrick forbade them. Picking up the fawn, Patrick carried it on his shoulders to a safe place. The Protestant cathedral rises here where the fawn was found. The site of the Catholic cathedral is the place where St. Patrick took it.

BALLYCASTLE (County Antrim)

Bonamargy Friary

It is said that in the graveyard of this now-ruined friary, there was never time for the grass to grow, since there was so much warfare and so many burials in ancient times. So the fierce warrior Sorley Boye MacDonnell had his enormous coffin locked into a vault instead of being buried so it could never be disturbed.

BELFAST (County Antrim)

Grand Opera House

For more than twenty years this grand opera house that was a showpiece of Belfast at the turn of the century and through two world wars lay vacant. Sarah Bernhardt, as well as Pavlova and Orson Welles, had performed here. A victim of movies and television, however, it closed down in the 1950s.

Then in 1973 the Ulster Architectural Heritage Society and the Arts Council of Northern Ireland joined together to refurbish it. The long-locked doors were opened, the cobwebs swept away, and, in 1980, the old opera house reopened.

Harland & Wolff Shipyard

The great ocean liner *Titanic*, touted as "virtually unsinkable," left her berth here on April 2, 1912. But twelve days later, at 11:40 A.M. on April 14, on her maiden transatlantic voyage, she struck an iceberg and went down. One thousand five hundred and three lives were lost.

BELLEEK (County Fermanagh)

One sunny day in 1852, John Bloomfield, the owner of Castle Caldwell on Lower Lough Erne, remarked on the distinctive shine of the whitewash on his tenants' cottages. Asking the cottagers what the source of their whitewash was, he was told it was the naturally burnt lime of the region. He lost no time in making a further study of the matter. Delicate Belleek porcelain with its mother-of-pearl gleam was the result.

BUSHMILLS (County Antrim)

Bushmills Distillery

Peter the Great of Russia came in 1697 to this oldest distillery in the world while on a study tour of Europe. After sampling the "water of life" produced here, he is said to have exclaimed, "Of all beverages, the Irish is the best." So good was it, indeed, that in 1612, four years after the distillery's founding, Sir William Cockayne, the Lord Mayor of London, reportedly had bought so much whiskey from Bushmills that he had to sell part of his property to pay for it.

Dunluce Castle

Even in the best of seasons, the English-born Countess of Antrim, accustomed as she had been to the lively social life of the London court, felt isolated and unhappy in this windswept castle (now a ruin) above the sea. When storms whipped at the ramparts and sea waves growled and frothed below, she found this site unbearable. And, as it turned out, she was quite right to feel so.

One night in 1659 a great banquet was in progress here. Preparations for it had been going on for days. The castle was filled with guests, and the kitchen staff was hard at work on last-minute preparations. Suddenly, without warning, the kitchen slid into the sea one hundred feet below. Of the entire kitchen staff, only a tinker, mending pots, survived.

The countess left the castle, never to return.

Giant's Causeway (4 miles north of Bushmills)

As the story goes, it was the giant Finn McCool who
built this causeway of six-sided stepping stones in a rage
at a Scottish giant's boasting about how powerful he was.

The Scottish giant talked of all the giants whom he
had bested. Spoiling for a fight with Finn, the Scottish
giant warned that were it not for disliking the water so,
he would swim to Ireland and give Finn a thrashing, too.

That was too much for Finn. To show the Scottish
giant a thing or two, Finn constructed this basalt walk-
way over the Atlantic Ocean.

But no sooner was it finished than the giant of Scotland, with a leap and a bound, crossed it and, as he had
promised, came here to fight Finn.

However, a giant with the strength to build this mam-
moth causeway was a giant to be contended with, and the
Scottish giant lost to Finn. Afterward, however, the pair
became fast friends, with Finn prevailing upon his opponent to marry and settle here in Ireland. The Scottish
giant did, and he lived happily ever after. When both
giants died, there was no need for the causeway anymore,
so all except what remains today was allowed to sink into
the sea.

CAMP HILL (County Tyrone)

Ulster-American Folk Park: MELLON COTTAGE

One day in 1818, five-year-old Thomas Mellon, who,
with his descendants, endorsed many philanthropic
causes, became worried for his mother when he overheard angry words at the door of this cottage. He hurried
to get the sword that his father had once found under the
roof thatch. He was little, and it was big, but Thomas
dragged the sword to the door all the same. Mrs. Mellon
calmed both little Thomas and the neighbor. The raised
voice complaining about a Mellon cow straying next
door was lowered, and Thomas put the sword away.

CARRICKFERGUS (County Antrim)

At first, sightseers clambered into boats to view the action here that April day in 1778 when word got out that the privateer John Paul Jones (*See* Scotland, Edinburgh, Firth of Forth) with his American vessel *Ranger* was spoiling for a fight with the British sloop-of-war *Drake*. But it wasn't long before the sightseers went back. The battle that was about to take place, which became the new American nation's first naval victory, was a bloody one, and sightseers were wise to watch it from the shore.

For more than an hour the two ships fired at each other, until the *Drake's* captain was dead. She had lost most of her sails. Her hull was riddled with holes, and there was nothing to be done but to ask quarter.

Carrickfergus Castle

Because a prophecy had said that this province of Ulster would be conquered by a blond knight from a foreign land who rode a white horse and had birds on his shield, John de Courcy, a blond Anglo-Norman knight who rode a white horse and had painted birds on his shield, set sail from England to make his fortune here. In a bloody battle, he vanquished the town of Downpatrick and dreamed of how all Ulster would be his.

To assure that it would be, he started this enormous castle in the 1180s. But his dream never became reality. (*See* Downpatrick, Down Cathedral.)

◆ ◆ ◆

The ships of Protestant William III with an army of 36,000 sailed up to this castle in June 1690. Here William landed, en route to the battlefield at Boyne, where he would meet and defeat his father-in-law, the Catholic James II, who was seeking to regain his throne.

212 CASTLES, KEEPS, AND LEPRECHAUNS

DERRY (County Londonderry)

Protestant Cathedral of St. Colomb: CHURCHYARD

During the 1689 siege of this city, the cannonball that
now lies in this churchyard was sent thundering over the
walls with a note attached proposing capitulation and
giving the terms of surrender. But the Derry garrison
would have none of it. The cannonball has remained in
this churchyard where it fell.

The Walls

A miserable James II, Catholic king of England, sat with
his soldiers for a time outside these walls in the winter of
1688. He was in a fury that thirteen young Protestant
apprentices had slammed down the portcullis at the
Ferry Quay Gate, and no one would let him through. His
son-in-law, Protestant William of Orange, had been invited by some of England's powerful Protestant noblemen
to "relieve" James of the throne, which they felt he was
ruling with too Catholic a hand. Finally, damning residents here as "obstinate wretches," James left this city.

But in the spring he was back. For 105 days he besieged
those who had turned him away. Two thousand died of
illness or starvation, but still there was no surrender. The
local governor, however, escaped by climbing up a pear
tree near these walls and slipping over them to food and
safety. He has never been forgiven and is still hanged in
effigy here.

DEVENISH ISLAND (County Fermanagh)

On this rocky island the Hebrew prophet Jeremiah is
said to have been finally laid to rest. Fleeing Jerusalem
after it fell to the Babylonians, he was rescued from a
shipwreck off the Irish coast by King Brian Boru. One
story has it that Jeremiah carried with him both the Ark
of the Covenant (See Ireland, Tara) and the *Lia Fail* that
became the coronation stone of Ireland's kings.

Augustinian Abbey of St. Mary

It is said that sixth-century St. Molaise grew weary as he labored to build this abbey. When a bird burst into the most astounding song that he had ever heard, he stopped working to sit down and listen, enraptured.

He thought that it might have been an hour that he had rested, head bowed, while the bird trilled. But when it stopped singing and St. Molaise looked up, this abbey in its entirety stood before him. A hundred years had passed while the saint listened—not really to a bird, but to the Holy Spirit.

◆ ◆ ◆

It happened one day that St. Molaise, the founder of this abbey, was in need of a pen but had no quill readily at hand. Or so he thought until he raised one hand and opened it. Whereupon a responsive goose, flying overhead, dropped one of her feathers into his outstretched hand.

◆ ◆ ◆

The Battle of the Books was ended (*See* Republic of Ireland, Cooladrummon), and four thousand men were dead. Here, to the monastery founded by his schoolmate Molaise, the fiery Columba, who had started it all, had come still seething with anger even though he had won the battle. And while he sought to regain his composure in this quiet place by living under the discipline of monastic life, clearly he was not being successful.

The thoughtful Molaise pondered the problem of what to do with his old friend. Finally he deemed it wise to have Columba leave Ireland for a while.

And so, with more sternness than was customary, Molaise told Columba that he must start a missionary life elsewhere. Obediently, but not gracefully, he who would become St. Columba set sail for Scotland (*See* Scotland, Inner Hebrides, Iona) with a group of his followers.

DOWNHILL (County Londonderry)

Mussenden Temple

The fourth Earl of Bristol and the Bishop of Derry, Frederick Hervey was a remarkable eighteenth-century man. He was humorous, well-traveled, artistic, ecumenical, and enthusiastic in love. On the sand below his home, Downhill Castle, whose remains stand near here, he organized foot races between overweight Anglican clergymen and thin dissenters. He gleefully situated the race "track" where the sand was soft and where his plump fellow-Anglicans would have a hard time of it.

Because of the extensiveness of his travels and his love of luxury, Europe's Bristol Hotels took his name for their chain so he would be sure to spend his money in them.

His love of art led him to build a mausoleum modeled after a Roman temple for his brother when he died. His love for his cousin (and, some say, his mistress), Frideswide Mussenden, led him to erect this rotunda in her memory here on the cliff edge. And his ecumenical spirit led him to invite a Roman Catholic priest to celebrate Mass here once a week, since there was no Catholic church nearby.

DOWNPATRICK (County Down)

Down Cathedral

The Anglo-Norman knight John de Courcy is said to have done such good deeds as to bring the bones of St. Bridget, St. Columba, and St. Patrick together to lie in the graveyard here. However, he was more notable for his pride and cruelty in warfare (*See* Carrickfergus, Carrickfergus Castle) than for his kindliness. Unarmed, on Good Friday in 1204, he came here to do penance for his sins. While he knelt, he was set upon by his enemies.

Hearing the clatter of their arms behind him, the knight leapt to his feet and ran out into the graveyard, wrenching from the ground a wooden cross that marked a grave and using it to defend himself against his attackers. He drove them off, reportedly killing thirteen in the process. Truly repentant, perhaps, he then disappeared, abandoning both the mighty castle he had built at Carrickfergus and his dreams of one day conquering all of Ulster province.

EMDALE (County Down)

The romantic streak that marks the novels of the Brontë sisters, Charlotte, Emily, and Anne, clearly was an inheritance from their father, Patrick, born here as Patrick Brunty in 1777. An avid reader, Patrick was selected by this village's Presbyterian minister to study with him. In time, he became the schoolmaster at Drumballyroney School. But when Patrick kissed one of his pupils, the shocked church closed the school down.

ENNISKILLEN (County Fermanagh)

Castlecoole

Armar Lowry Corry, first Earl of Belmore, who built this great house from 1790 to 1796, wished it to be one of the most splendid structures in the country. He spared no pains or expense to have it so.

The Portland stone of which it was to be built was shipped to Ballyshannon where a new pier was built to unload it. From there, bullocks pulled it here on carts.

And in the end, the earl had the house he wished. A Frenchman visiting it the year after it was done, remarking on its beauty, compared it to a pagan temple to the gods.

LIMAVADY (County Londonderry)

In ancient days, a dog is said to have leapt across the River Roe here, bearing a note asking help for his master's clan from the clan across the river. Today a six-arched bridge crosses the gap the dog jumped. He is honored both by the name of this Georgian town, which translated from the Gaelic means "Dog's Leap," and by a carving of him on the wall of the parish church.

LOUGH NEAGH (Counties Antrim, Armagh, Tyrone, and Londonderry)

Surely it was the giant Finn McCool who dug out this 153-square-mile lake, the largest in all the British Isles. Clumping the dirt from it together in his hand, Finn skipped it out to sea to form the Isle of Man.

PORT NA SPANIAGH (County Antrim)

The storm howled for days off the Causeway Coast in October 1588. The Spanish Armada had been defeated, and those vessels that had survived were trying to head home, tossing about on the rough seas.

Among the ships was the galleon *Girona* with 1,300 men aboard. As the wind raged and the seas thundered over her decks, her captain, Don Alonzo Martinez, wondered if there might not be some respite offered at the waterfront castle of Catholic Sorley Boye MacDonnell. Don Alonzo thought he saw its chimneys in the distance.

But he didn't. What he saw were the stone chimneys of the Giant's Causeway, on which his vessel was dashed. Two hundred lives were lost, including his, and the treasure that the vessel was carrying—golden cameos and jeweled chains—remained on the bottom here until Belgian divers found it in 1967. The treasure is now in Belfast's Ulster Museum.

RATHLIN ISLAND (County Antrim)

Lying thirteen miles from Scotland and even closer to Ireland, over the centuries this island has been claimed by both the Irish and the Scots. But the Irish won it in 1617, thanks to the absence of snakes here. The Irish maintained in court that when St. Patrick ousted the serpents from the rest of Ireland, he ousted them from here, too. Their case was upheld.

◆   ◆   ◆

It did not matter that Robert the Bruce had been crowned the King of Scotland. Scotland was overrun with Englishmen, and there was no place where the king could go safely. The Bruce's wife, child, and two of his sisters were captives of the English. Two of his brothers had been killed.

So with a small band of followers, he left the mainland in the fall of 1306 for this little island off the coast of Ireland. All winter long, he and his men hid in the island's dank, dark caves.

One day the disconsolate Scottish king's eye was caught by a spider near at hand, spinning a web in a corner of the cave. It was not an easy task, for wind coming in from the mouth of the cave kept breaking the delicate web. Time and time again, however, the indefatigable spider would return to his work. Robert watched and thought of his defeats. He gained the strength to try once more to drive the English from his native land. When spring came, he was fighting back in Scotland.

SLEMISH MOUNTAIN (County Antrim)

For seven years, the youth who became St. Patrick served as a swineherd on this 1,437-foot-high mountain, where he was the slave of the pagan Miluic. But when he was twenty-three, Patrick had divine visions urging him to leave Slemish and prepare for a life as a Christian missionary. He did as he was bidden.

STRANGFORD (County Down)

Castle Ward

Bernard Ward, the first Lord Bangor, and his wife, Lady Anne, had distinctly different architectural tastes. And neither one would compromise. Lord Bangor was a devotee of the classical style, while Lady Bangor's preference was for the neo-Gothic that was popular in Ireland in the 1760s.

That is why this curious castle has such a split personality—a half-Palladian, half-Gothic façade. Inside there is more of the same. Though they lived together for a while there in their distinctly "his" and "hers" accommodations, in time their differences of taste got the better of their marriage, and they went their separate ways.

5
REPUBLIC OF IRELAND

ARAN ISLANDS (County Galway)

Inishmaan

To this barren island the playwright John Middleton Synge came at the turn of the century to write of the Irishness of its isolated inhabitants. Here he was told the tale of the off-islander who, having killed his father in a rage, sought refuge with relatives here who gave him sanctuary in a hole in the ground. Synge was told that the murderer was kept hidden there for weeks while the police searched for him. Then, finally, he made his escape to America.

Synge turned the local story into one of his most famous plays, *The Playboy of the Western World*.

Inishmore

In his youth, Enda, a prince in what is now County Dublin, was warlike in the tradition of his forebears. His sister, Fanchea, however, had dedicated her life to God

219

One day, returning bloody from battle, Enda was reproached by his devout sister and warned that unless he changed his ways, his final destination would be Hell.

The boastful prince, proud of his prowess on the battlefield, scoffed at his sister. He asked for one of the pretty novices in the care of Fanchea to be his bride. Fanchea replied that the choice of a bridegroom would be up to the girl. She approached her and offered her the prince's hand but was roundly turned down. The young woman said that her choice was to be the bride of Christ.

Enda would not, however, accept her refusal. Some months later he directed his sister to ask the young woman again if she would take him as her bridegroom. By this time, the girl had fallen ill and, pale and weak, lay close to death. Fanchea took her brother to the novice's bedside. She cruelly asked if the emaciated creature who lay before him was really the one he wished for as his wife. As he blanched, she warned of the fires of Hell that awaited him unless he turned to God.

Enda did turn to God. He came here to found Ireland's first monastery in the year 480 and became a saint for his piety. And it seems that the men he trained grew in piety, too, for on this island are the graves of 120 of his followers, and all of them are saints.

BALLINSKELLIGS BAY (County Kerry)

Warned by Noah's prophecy about the impending flood, Noah's grandson Bith and great-granddaughter Cessair, with forty-nine other women and two other men, sought to escape by going to an uninhabited, and therefore sinless, land. Taking ship, they landed here. What happened next, in view of the disparity in numbers between the sexes, has been a matter for much ribald conjecture.

BALLYVAUGHAN (County Clare)

The Burren

Living here on the slopes of Slieve Callan in the seventh century, St. Colman found the desolation of this barren landscape spiritually invigorating. All the same, he believed in a man's need for limited companionship, so he chose three pets to stay with him at all times—a cock to alert him to his times of prayer; a mouse to scurry over him and tickle him when he was asleep and should be awake; and a fly to be his bookmark, following his finger as it moved along the sentences and staying on the spot where he had stopped if he was called away for a while from his reading.

◆ ◆ ◆

Crossing these two hundred miles of desolate limestone rock in the 1650s, an officer of invading Oliver Cromwell's army is said to have remarked that the land lacked water enough to drown a man, wood enough to hang one, and even earth enough to bury one.

BANTRY (County Cork)

Bantry House

Looking out from this great house one windy morning three days before Christmas in 1796, Richard White, its owner, was startled to see fourteen frigates, transports, and other ships of war—all unmarked—bobbing at the mouth of Bantry Bay.

Clearly, they had not arrived on a social visit. White alerted the villagers that there might be something foul afoot, urging all able-bodied men to be ready to face an attack. He sent a messenger off to the English garrison at Cork fifty-two miles away to request troops to repulse any would-be invaders. At Cork, they scoffed a little at the idea that foreign ships bent on invasion could have made their way to the mouth of the bay unnoticed, but they did send troops. While the local militia awaited their arrival, they lined the shore to make it look as if there were more soldiers on hand than there actually were.

As it turned out, neither the troops from Cork nor the local militia were needed. Storm, fog, and dangerous reefs dissuaded the French invaders from coming ashore.

The Irish Protestant patriot Wolfe Tone, eager to see Ireland rid of English rule even if it meant allying his country with France, begged the French whom he had lured to Ireland to wait just a while for a change in the weather. But the French thought better of it, hauled up their anchors, and sailed away.

◆   ◆   ◆

The Viscount Berehaven who lived here in the mid-nineteenth century traveled all over Europe, but especially in France, to acquire *objets d'art* for this beloved house. The wealthy of France, fallen on hard times, would await the arrival of his well-known coach. He would fill it up with lamps, chests, and tapestries (Marie Antoinette's wedding tapestry among them) and bring them to Bantry House, where they remain today.

BELLACORICK (County Mayo)

The Musical Bridge

Woe betide anyone who tries to finish building this curious limestone bridge, which gets its name because music—of sorts—can be made by rubbing stones along its north parapet.

A century before construction of it began, but while building a bridge here was under discussion, a prophet warned that the work could never be finished and that anyone who tried to finish it was doomed. And sure enough, as recently as this century a country councilman thought to put an end to the local superstition but died just after laying the final stone.

BETTYSTOWN (County Meath)

One summer's day in 1850 a child who was playing on the beach here was entranced by something gleaming in the sand. The 3¼-inch wide, 8⅛-inch long pin, adorned with snakes and birds' heads and animals, turned out to be the silver Tara brooch, one of the finest pieces of eighth-century Irish metalwork that exists. It is now among the treasures in Dublin's National Museum.

BLARNEY (County Cork)

Blarney Castle

The lord of this castle during the reign of Elizabeth I, Cormac MacDermott MacCarthy, was a stubborn man, disinclined to change old ways. But he was also a man of infinite charm and a gifted tongue. When Elizabeth sought a change in the traditional method by which the lords of Ireland received the rights to their castles, he eloquently replied that of course he would do as she wished. He continued to say so time and again with increasing eloquence, but for all his fine talk, he never did actually accept her proposal.

An exasperated Elizabeth is said to have finally tired of his "fair words and soft speech" and remarked, "This is all Blarney; what he says he never means." Thus she gave to the world the word "blarney" and bequeathed to this site the notion that all who kiss the Blarney Stone 120 steps up the turret wall will receive the gift of gab.

BUNCRANA (County Donegal)

Marching through the streets of this village in his French uniform in 1798, along with three thousand French captives of the British, the Irish patriot Wolfe Tone (*see* Bantry, Bantry House) could easily have gone unnoticed. But a college classmate, Sir George Hill, recognized him and gleefully disclosed his identity by hurrying up to shake his hand and declaring in a loud voice, "My dear Tone."

Tone had gone abroad to seek French aid against the English and was just the man the English were looking for. He was hauled from the ranks of the French soldiers, court-martialed, and sentenced to be hanged.

Tone escaped the ignominy of hanging by cutting his own throat in Dublin's Newgate Jail, but he botched the job so that he hovered several days on the edge of death. During that time, cruel Sir George reportedly asked why the doctors didn't sew up his neck long enough to hang him properly.

BUTTEVANT (County Cork)

Kilcolman Castle

For eight years here the poet Edmund Spenser wrote happily, completing three books of his great allegory *The Faerie Queen*, while he supported himself as sheriff of Cork.

But in 1598, during one of the many rebellions that had swept Ireland, this castle was set on fire. Spenser, his wife, and three of their children managed to escape, but a fourth child died in the conflagration. The Spensers fled to England, but the poet never fully recovered, and *The Faerie Queen* was never ended.

CARRICK-ON-SUIR (County Tipperary)

Carrick-on-Suir Castle

"Black Tom," the tenth Earl of Ormonde, who had spent considerable time in London, was much enamored of his distant relation, Elizabeth I of England. And so, it seems, was she of him. All his life he dreamed she would visit him here. He designed the interior of his castle with stucco medallions of her head that he hoped would please her and with a stucco portrait of her in the entryway.

However, the state visit did not take place. But a persistent rumor has the "Virgin Queen" sharing accommodations with Black Tom before she became queen and proposes that she was the mother of one of his children.

Slievenamon

Legend has it that it was on this 2,368-foot-high mountain of the fairy women that the great giant warrior Finn McCool (See Northern Ireland, Bushmills, Giant's Causeway) in his old age selected Grainne, the young daughter of King Cormac, to be his bride.

Unable to decide which beautiful woman he would wed and desirous of having one who was quick and nimble as well as comely, he announced that he would seat himself on this mountaintop to admire the view and wait for the first woman to reach the top, and he would wed her.

The tall and slender Grainne proved the winner.

CASHEL (County Tipperary)

The Rock of Cashel

Plucking a shamrock from among the grasses on this limestone rock and holding it up in his fingers, St. Patrick explained to the multitude that had gathered how its three leaves were symbolic of the Trinity of Father, Son, and Holy Ghost, three in one. Ever since, the shamrock has been the symbol of Ireland.

As the story goes, the Devil is responsible for this great rock. Hurrying one day across the mountains that rise to the north, he took a giant bite from them to facilitate his passage. When he spat it out onto the plain, it became this rock. If transported, the rock would indeed just fit into the opening in Devil's Bit Mountain.

An aged and failing St. Patrick came here to Cashel of the Kings in 450 to baptize Aengus, King of Munster. Weak and unsteady, Patrick was forced to support himself with his crozier. He mistakenly thrust its spiked end through one of the king's feet while performing the baptism. But there was never a murmur from the king.

Only when the ceremony was over did St. Patrick notice the blood on the grass, raise his crozier, and realize what he had done.

Begging the king's pardon, St. Patrick asked Aengus why he had not cried out. The king replied that he had assumed the piercing of his foot was part of the baptism. The king said that even if he had not thought that, he would have been willing to bear the pain after learning of the sufferings of Christ.

CASTLEGREGORY (County Kerry)

The lord deputy of Ireland, Lord Leon Arthur Grey, along with Sir Walter Raleigh and the poet Edmund Spenser—all supporters of bloody extermination policies in Ireland—were passing through this pretty seaside town. Hugh Hoare, the owner of the castle that once stood here, offered these men dinner one evening. It seemed the politic thing to do, after all, if one had hopes of saving one's castle. But the patriotic mistress of the castle thought differently of the matter.

When it came time to offer the guests wine, it turned out that there was none to be had, for she had had all the wine poured out on the cellar floor.

When her husband learned what she had done (no one knows if his dinner guests still were present), he killed her in a fit of fury. Then before any charges could be brought, he conveniently dropped dead himself.

CASTLEPOLLARD (County Westmeath)

Tullynally Castle

They built again and again onto this grand castle whose battlements extend nearly a quarter of a mile. It has big turrets, little turrets, underground tunnels, and a furnace that was installed in the early days of the nineteenth century.

The Pakenham family that has owned this Gothic Revival structure since 1655 has, in virtually every new generation, added a turret or a wing, a stable or a garden. It is said that today it is the largest family-occupied castle in all the British Isles.

CELBRIDGE (County Kildare)

Castletown House

In the dining room of this elegant Irish Palladian house, the Devil is said to have stopped one day for dinner and, in a fit of pique, broken the hearthstone.

It happened in the mid-eighteenth century. Returning from the hunt, the great house's owner found a hungry-looking, dark-haired stranger on his grounds and, being hospitable, invited the passerby to stay for dinner.

As the story goes, while they were eating a napkin fell, and when the host bent to retrieve it, he saw that his guest had removed his boots to make what seemed to be cloven hooves more comfortable.

With an outcry, the host said that his guest should leave; he had no room for the Devil at his table. He also sent for a priest to exorcise the Devil should he refuse to quit the table peaceably.

The stranger refused. The summoned priest threw his breviary at him. It missed the Devil, who ducked, but broke the mirror behind him. Leaping over the dining table, the startled Devil landed on the hearth and broke it. Wreathed in sulphurous smoke, the stranger fled up the chimney.

CLARE ISLAND (County Mayo)

From this five-by-three-mile island the indomitable warrior queen Grace O'Malley (*See* Howth Castle) controlled the west coast of Ireland in the days of Elizabeth I, levying taxes on all ships that passed.

Grace was not to be trifled with. She bore a scar on her face from a childhood incident when she climbed to an eagle's nest and, the birds' clawing notwithstanding, destroyed the brood that had been attacking the sheep on her father's island. As a youngster, she also became an accomplished sailor.

Grace married several times—each time acquiring a castle from her marriage. Her first husband died. Before agreeing to marry the second one, she insisted that they contract so that either one, at the end of a year, could end the union. It was Grace, of course, who wanted to and did end the marriage by simply locking her husband out of the castle that she had acquired by marrying him.

It was through these marriages that Grace gained con-

trol of enough castles along the west coast of Ireland to
exact tribute of passersby. If they refused to pay, they had
Grace and her fleet to contend with.

On her death, she was buried here and her skull placed
in a niche on her tombstone. When in this century visiting scientists stole the skull, the boat in which they were
carrying it was struck by a storm as ferocious as Grace
O'Malley herself. Much shaken, they returned to the island and nervously replaced Grace's skull in its niche.

CLEW BAY (County Mayo)

After God had labored to create the world, it is said that
he threw the stones left over into Clew Bay. He may have
meant to pick them up, but didn't, and they have been
wrecking ships here ever since.

CLIFDEN (County Galway)

Derrygimlagh Bog

It had been a harrowing last few hours. Making what
would turn out to be the world's first successful transatlantic flight, Capt. John Alcock and Lt. Arthur Whit-
ten Brown struck fierce winds about dawn on June 12,
1919. Their plane bobbed uncontrollably. Suddenly it
began to spin and fall—lower and lower and lower—low
enough so that they could hear and see the ocean snarling. But almost miraculously, with only fifty feet to the
sea below, Alcock managed to get the plane out of its
dive. It rose to eleven thousand feet. But there, ice began
to form on its air intake. Its starboard engine had to be
shut down.

Alcock descended again in hopes that the warm air
below would melt the ice, and the engine could be started
once more. He was right. The ice melted. The dead engine was restarted. The little plane climbed, and at last
land was in sight. There seemed to be a green pasture
below them.

But there wasn't. It was Derrygimlagh Bog, but it made

a satisfactory landing place all the same.

It had been sixteen hours and twenty-eight minutes since the two young Englishmen had left St. John's, Newfoundland, on their historic flight.

CONG ABBEY (County Mayo)

For years after this abbey fell into disrepair, its most precious possession, the oaken, copper-plated Cross of Cong, richly decorated with gold filigree, was kept shut up by the church fathers here, except on Christmas and Easter, when it would be displayed.

But the place where it was being kept collapsed. A curate was finally convinced by art historians that the twelfth-century cross would be safer and would be viewed by more people in the National Gallery in Dublin than in the church here.

Parishioners, however, were outraged when they found their cross gone, and when a new priest came, they demanded its return.

At first, efforts were made to have the cross returned by legal means. When those failed, the priest set off for Dublin one day wearing his heaviest coat, browsed in the National Gallery, and, when he left, had the Cross of Cong secreted under his great coat.

He had barely reached the street, however, before he was apprehended and the cross returned to the museum. In a feeble attempt to mollify the parishioners, he was given a picture of the cross to carry home with him.

COOLADRUMMON (County Sligo)

It is said that when he was learning to read, Columba (who became St. Columba) was fed cake with the letters of the alphabet on it. That proved a fine method of instruction, for not only did Columba become a poet, but he also grew to love the beauty of the letters. Unfortunately, however, this love of letters later resulted in sixth-century Columba's exile from his native land. (*See*

Northern Ireland, Devenish Island, Augustinian Abbey of St. Mary)

One day while visiting his former teacher, St. Finian, Columba's eye fell on a manuscript of the Psalms, magnificently embellished and breathtaking in its beauty. The lover of letters could not take his eyes from it. Finian let Columba read it and examine it but—seeing the covetousness with which the younger priest looked at it—warned him that he was not to copy it. Columba listened with only one ear, and once he was hidden by night, he began the painstaking task of copying the manuscript.

But one evening as he stealthily worked, he was caught. A furious Finian demanded the copy he had made. Columba refused to surrender it. Finian took the matter to the high king, Dermot of Meath, to rule what was right and wrong.

Dermot's decision was that both the manuscript and the copy were the property of Finian. The royal decision notwithstanding, book-lover Columba took issue. A man of noble birth, Columba went to his father's tribe to ask their opinion and request their help. They of course found Columba in the right, and on this site ensued a battle known ever since as the Battle of the Books. Columba was its victor.

CROAGH PATRICK (County Mayo)

The wind howled and the rain spat on this 2,510-foot-high mountaintop for the forty days of Lent in 441. St. Patrick meditated joyously. As legend has it, when Easter had come—perhaps in gratitude for those days of satisfying contemplation—he gathered together all the poisonous creatures of Ireland, rang his bell, and hurled it from the mountaintop into the ocean. After it went all of Ireland's snakes and toads, forever banished from the Emerald Isle by his prayers.

CURRAGH PLAIN (County Kildare)

The devout Brigid (who became St. Brigid) wished to found a convent but needed land She chose a site on this lush land, now a center of horse breeding, and asked the local king if he would give it to her. He wouldn't. But Brigid was not to be discouraged. If he thought that she had requested too much, Brigid said, she would revise her request. All she needed was as much land as her cloak would cover.

Though understandably he questioned what she could do with such a small parcel, the king found that request reasonable enough and agreed to it. Brigid laid down her cloak. As the story goes, it miraculously grew and grew until she had sufficient land both for her convent and for a monastery.

DROGHEDA (County Louth)

There were those who said in hindsight that Sir Arthur Aston, the English Royalist who refused to surrender this city to Cromwell's Republican army in September 1649, should never have thought that his garrison of two thousand could hold out against Cromwell's eight thousand foot soldiers and four thousand cavalrymen. But Drogheda was behind a mile-and-a-half long, twenty-foot high wall. And it had a high hill on which St. Mary's steepled church rose—a good outlook for defenders and a good place from which to shoot down at the enemy.

Assessing the situation before the onslaught began, Sir Arthur is said to have remarked that "he who could take Drogheda could take Hell." The three-day slaughter of military men, women, and children by Cromwell's forces left nearly three thousand dead. And on September 13, 1649, those who remained shuddered and remarked that only a denizen of Hell could have wreaked such relentless cruelty.

DRUMCLIFFE (County Sligo)

Benbulbin

As the legend goes, on the slopes of this mountain the warrior Diarmuid, beloved of Princess Grainne who was destined to be the wife of the great giant Finn McCool

(*See* Carrick-on-Suir, Slievenamon), was gored by a wild boar that Finn had sent him to hunt. Having decided to wed Grainne himself, Finn refused to heal the wound with his magical powers and left Diarmuid to die.

Drumcliffe Churchyard

Before William Butler Yeats died in France in 1939, he left explicit instructions that he was to be buried here at the foot of 1,730-foot high Benbulbin in this county that he had known all his life which was "more beautiful than other places."

Lissadell House

Though he loved immensely this house above the sea with its backdrop of mountains and its gardens, Sir Robert Gore-Booth mortgaged his estate for the benefit of his hungry neighbors when the potato famine struck in 1846.

His granddaughter, Constance de Markievicz (*See* Dublin, Kilmainham Jail), was of the same mettle, and in the 1916 struggle for Irish independence she helped dig trenches for the revolutionaries on Dublin's Stephen's Green. Her friend, the poet William Butler Yeats, immortalized Constance and her sister, Eva, in verse as the "two girls in silk kimonos, both beautiful, one a gazelle."

DUBLIN (County Dublin)

To rid itself of the reputation of having one of the most dangerous harbors in the world, the city fathers here employed a brilliant English hydrographer in 1800 to carry out the first systematic and accurate charting of Dublin Bay. He produced the first relief tinting to bring out the forms of the surrounding hills.

A grateful Board of Ireland Navigation Company honored the hydrographer for his outstanding work in 1801.

Not quite the villain depicted in book and film—Captain William Bligh of the *Bounty* was a highly respected scientist.

Abbey Theatre (Lower Abbey Street)

When John Middleton Synge's *Playboy of the Western World* opened in 1907 at the Abbey Theatre that then stood on this spot, a week of street and theatre fighting followed. Referring to a woman's underclothes, Synge had used the word "shift," which was deemed unfit for the public stage.

Brazen Head Hotel (20 Lower Bridge Street)

Only after dark when he could not be recognized did the fiery young patriot Robert Emmet dare leave his upstairs room here during that long winter of 1802. At other times his fellow patriots would come here and together they would plot revolution against England—revolution that they dreamed would bring freedom to Ireland. Instead, it brought death by hanging a year later to twenty-five-year-old Emmet.

Christ Church Cathedral (Christ Church Place)

England's Henry VII was a nervous king, fearful that he might lose the crown that had become his through his victory over Richard III on Bosworth Field (*see* England, Market Bosworth). To assure that this wouldn't happen, he held captive Edward Plantagenet, the Earl of Warwick, a possible claimant.

One day word spread that Edward had escaped from the Tower of London where he had been kept since he was four years old. Not long after that, a priest arrived in Dublin with a fifteen-year-old boy in tow. He insisted that the boy was the long-imprisoned Edward, whom he had rescued. The youth was greeted with such enthusiasm that a coronation was held for him here in 1487.

Once crowned, he embarked for England with the priest to lay claim to his throne. But, sadly for him, after a skirmish at Stoke his small band of supporters was defeated, and he was captured. The real Edward was, meanwhile, paraded through the streets of London by the king to prove he had never escaped from the Tower at all. In time, the imposter was unmasked as Lambert Simnel, the son of an English baker.

◆   ◆   ◆

A secret passage ran under this church that was begun in the twelfth century. In the eighteenth century a British officer, after attending a funeral here, "disappeared" from the church. It was not until some weeks later that his remains were found. He had been accidentally shut inside the secret passage, which has been kept closed ever since.

Christ Church Cathedral: TOMB OF STRONGBOW'S SON

Though no burial is a pleasant occasion, the commitment here of the young son of the powerful Anglo-Norman warrior, Strongbow, was an even sadder interment than most. It was at the hand of his father that the youth had died. He was sliced in two when Strongbow, watching him in battle, decided that the youth was not courageous enough. (*See* Waterford.)

Custom House

This striking Palladian structure on the River Liffey almost didn't get built. Residents of neighboring areas thought it would turn their streets into slums. Businessmen were opposed to the edifice that would sprawl along the river. There was enough consternation about it that its designer, the English architect James Gandon (*See* Dublin, The Four Courts), began to wear a sword to work and spread the word that he was deft at using it.

Dublin Castle

When Justice holding her scales was put atop the gate here, its designer failed to foresee that Dublin's rains could affect the dispensation of justice. Depending on the direction from which the wind and rain came, the scales would tip—hardly impartially—in one direction or the other. If Justice were to keep its good name, officials deemed it wise after a while to drill holes in the scales to let the water through.

Dublin Castle: BEDFORD TOWER

From a safe in the library of this fifteenth-century clock tower, the diamonds, rubies, and emeralds that were the crown jewels of Ireland mysteriously disappeared in the summer of 1907.

Accused of the theft but not convicted of it was ne'er-do-well Frank Shackleton, an employee in the castle's College of Arms. He was known to have been in financial straits, to have borrowed money from a moneylender, and to have had it repaid by his brother, the Antarctic explorer Sir Ernest Shackleton. Sir Ernest's reputation, happily, was never besmirched by his brother's questionable one.

The jewels have never been found. Sir Arthur Conan Doyle, who was asked to look for them, turned the theft into the Sherlock Holmes adventure, "The Bruce-Partington Plans."

Dublin Castle: THE RECORD TOWER

For three years, teenaged "Red" Hugh O'Donnell, son of the chieftain of the Donegal clan (*See* Rathmullen), was imprisoned in this castle tower, for he was viewed as a threat to Queen Elizabeth I. Then one winter night in 1591 he and several companions managed to squeeze through the bars of his jail and descend by rope to the ground. But the weather was bitter and, in order to slip through the bars, the youths had had to leave their outer clothing behind. Though they were able to get as far as the Wicklow Hills, once there, cold and exhaustion stopped them. They were recaptured and brought back here. This time "Red" Hugh was shackled.

But a seer had said that the boy would be a power to contend with and, a year later, "Red" Hugh escaped again. A file was smuggled in to him on Christmas Eve and, in the drinking and revelry of the evening, no one heard the sawing of the shackles.

Once again with two companions, "Red" Hugh slipped through the window bars and slid to the ground on a rope of bed sheets. Although it was snowing, they swam the moat to where an accomplice was to be waiting with saddled horses. The accomplice was there, but the horses weren't. All the same, two of the boys made their way through the back streets of the city and up into the mountains, while the third was recaptured.

But again cold and exhaustion slowed the escapees. Their guide hid them in a cave near Glendalough to go in search of help. When they were found wrapped in each other's arms, they were almost unconscious from the cold. Indomitable—at least for a while longer (*See* Kinsale)—"Red" Hugh survived, though his companion didn't.

Fishamble Street

When George Frederick Handel's "Messiah" was first performed, it was at the Music Hall that stood on this street in 1742. So large a crowd was expected for the premiere of the oratorio that the women planning to attend were asked not to wear their hoop skirts that night, and the men were asked not to carry swords.

The Four Courts (Inn's Quay)

Catherine the Great of Russia was eager to have the outstanding English architect James Gandon come to St.

Petersburg to continue to design in the Western architectural tradition that her predecessor Peter the Great had introduced. But Dublin wanted him, too. Happily, Dublin won him. This lantern-domed restored masterpiece that was to house the Exchequer, Common Pleas, King's Bench, and Chancery courts is part of his legacy.

General Post Office (O'Connell Street)

Easter Monday 1916 was a sunny holiday, so little attention was paid to the 150 men who stood on the steps of this imposing building. Very few passersby stopped to hear the poet and fiery orator Padraig Pearse as he declared the establishment of a sovereign Irish Republic, independent of England. Many Dubliners were simply out for a holiday stroll or a bicycle ride, and if they looked up at all at the group assembled on these post office steps, it was with idle curiosity.

Then shots began to ring out from other parts of the city—The Four Courts, Jacob's Biscuit Factory, Boland's Bakery, the College of Surgeons, Dublin Castle, the Imperial Hotel, St. Stephen's Green. At first, even these were not take seriously since small arms practice was common. But the shooting did not let up.

When it ended five days later, downtown Dublin was in shambles—179 buildings had been destroyed, 450 people were dead and 2,614 wounded, and 90 of the proud insurrectionists who had stood on these steps had been sentenced to death.

But the first step had been taken that would, as the rebel martyrs had hoped and predicted, result one day in an independent Republic of Ireland.

The Grand Canal: LOCKS 5 AND 8

It is said that it is the water from these locks, coming down from St. James's Well in County Kildare, that is pumped out to be used in the brewing of Guinness beer and that imparts its particular flavor to it.

Kilmainham Jail (Inchicore Road)

Though his last days were spent in disrepute, in 1881 the moderate political leader and Protestant Charles Stewart Parnell was a favorite of Irish Catholics and Protestants alike. He was even nicknamed "the Uncrowned King." While he was imprisoned here, suspected of rousing farmers to unrest, package after package came to him from adoring ladies of Ireland. There were Kelly green Irish tea cosies, socks, and even a green satin quilt.

But when it was discovered a few years later that he had been having an affair with a married woman, overnight the adulation came to an end.

◆   ◆   ◆

Thirty-six-year-old Padraig Pearse, poet, educator, and president of the Irish Provisional Government (*See* Dublin, General Post Office), spent most of the night writing before his execution here on May 3, 1916. The Easter Monday Rising seeking freedom for Ireland had failed. But "we die," Pearse wrote in his last poem that night, "in bloody protest for a glorious thing."

◆   ◆   ◆

For days in 1916 Constance de Markievicz (*See* Drumcliffe, Lissadell House) waited, condemned to death, while one after the other her comrades (except for Eamon de Valera) in the battle against British rule in Ireland (*See* Dublin, General Post Office) were led into the gravel courtyard here and shot by firing squad. President of the Irish Provisional Government, Padraig Pearse, was shot. Commander of the Irish Republican Army and Commandant-General of rebel forces in Dublin, James Connolly was carried wounded to the courtyard and executed on the chair where he sat.

Altogether fifteen Irish patriots were felled by firing squad bullets while the countess waited, expecting her fate to be the same. But then she was told that because she was a woman she would be sentenced to life imprisonment instead. Because he was born in America, de Valera was saved from execution as well.

The Hugh Lane Municipal Gallery of Modern Art
(Parnell Square)

In the beginning, Dublin said it didn't want the Bonnards, Monets, Degas, Utrillos, and Vuillards that Sir Hugh Lane, nephew of the playwright Lady Gregory (*See* Gort, Coole Park), was offering the city. Irish painters were good enough for them, the Dublin city councilmen said, so in his will Sir Hugh left his art collection to the National Gallery in London. Being a devoted Irishman, however, and just in case his countrymen had a change of heart, he left a codicil to the will that would give the works to Dublin if it agreed to build an appropriate gallery for them.

Sir Hugh drowned when the *Lusitania* went down in 1916 (*See* Kinsdale, Great Sovereign Rock), and London's National Gallery acquired the paintings. But by this time Dublin *did* have an interest. The codicil, the Dublin councilmen said, clearly indicated that Dublin had been Sir Hugh's first choice as the home for his collection. But the codicil had had only one witness. A court suit ensued. Not until 1959 in a compromise agreement was it decided that the collection was to go back and forth between Dublin and London.

Marsh's Library (Upper Kevin Street)

The ghost of cantankerous Narcissus Marsh who founded this seventeenth-century library (*See* Dublin, Trinity College) that is Ireland's oldest, is said to haunt it.

His niece, who was his housekeeper, had as much as she could take of him after a while and eloped, leaving a note in a book explaining her actions to her uncle. But the furious, distraught Marsh never found it and is said to walk among these dark oak stacks, still in a fury, opening and slamming shut book after book. There are some twenty thousand of them in which his niece might have left her letter.

70 Merrion Square

Terrified regularly by a nightmare of being buried alive, that teller of tales of the grotesque, Sheridan le Fanu, died here in 1873 of an overdose of laudanum taken to ward off that dream.

Mornington House (24 Upper Merrion Street)

Arthur Wellesley, Duke of Wellington, tended to shudder in later years when reminded that he was born here. Never proud of being an Irishman, he was wont to exclaim that "being born in a stable doesn't make one a horse."

The National Gallery Of Ireland (Merrion Square)

When he was a boy, George Bernard Shaw skipped school to come here. When he grew up and became a renowned playwright, he claimed that he owed his education to this gallery. Gratefully, he left it a third of his estate.

The National Gallery of Ireland: PORTRAIT OF WOODROW WILSON

Horrified by the bloodshed on the Continent where he was at the outbreak of World War I, the American painter John Singer Sargent presented a blank canvas to this museum, offering to fill it for a donation of £2,000 to the International Red Cross. Sir Hugh Percy Lane (*See* Dublin, The Hugh Lane Municipal Gallery of Modern Art) made the donation, commissioning this portrait of Woodrow Wilson.

Phoenix Park Monument

The trees were just starting to bud here that May evening in 1882 when Lord Frederick Cavendish, chief secretary for Ireland, and his under-secretary, T. H. Burke, walking home near this monument of the mythical phoenix bird, were set upon by seven men armed with surgeon's amputating knives and hacked to death.

Their murderers fled in a taxi and an open car, both driving at furious speed.

A secret society whose members called themselves the National Invincibles claimed honor for the evil deed, but few honored them for it.

For weeks—to all but a handful of the bloodthirsty—the murder site seemed to have spoiled this pretty park, one of the British Isles' largest. And for months the Invincibles who had wielded the surgeon's knives remained undiscovered. Then two more political murders, again with long knives, were attempted in Dublin. A special police inquiry began, and finally informers led to the Phoenix Park murderers. Five men were found guilty of the crime and hanged.

St. George's Church (Hardwicke Place)

In the church that occupied this site in 1806, bright-eyed thirty-three-year-old Kitty Pakenham became the bride of thirty-seven-year-old Sir Arthur Wellesley, who would in time become the Duke of Wellington, Napoleon's conqueror at Waterloo.

They had first met some nine years earlier. They talked of marriage then, but the young soldier's prospects were not considered good enough, in her family's eyes, to make him an acceptable marriage prospect. Besides, he played the violin, they knew, when his mind ought to have been on military matters. So the love-smitten soldier had burned his violin and talked his older brother into buying a captaincy for him—all for the love of Kitty.

Assignments abroad, however, had kept the couple apart. Sir Arthur had thrived in India, and Kitty Pakenham, bright eyes notwithstanding, was all but forgotten. Other women were enticing, too Then, at thirty-seven,

Sir Arthur was back here in Dublin, and Kitty Pakenham seemed to have been waiting. The proper thing, therefore, was to woo her again. This time, like it or not (and he was not too sure he did), he wooed and won her.

St. Patrick's Cathedral (Patrick Street)

Over the years this monumental church has suffered many mishaps and indignities. It was begun in the twelfth century. In the fourteenth century its spire blew off, and it was set on fire. In Oliver Cromwell's time horses were stabled in it. In the seventeenth century one roof was taken off and a new one put on. By the beginning of the nineteenth century, a new roof over the nave was needed.

In 1863 Sir Benjamin Lee Guinness, whose father Arthur had started the Guinness Brewery, took it upon himself as a charitable act to have the church restored. Finally, when it was all done, a service in honor of its completion was held. The dean is said to have announced that his text for the service would be Hebrews II—a chapter that does not exist in the Bible but whose number, II, appears on every bottle or can of Guinness stout.

St. Patrick's Cathedral: DEANERY GARDEN

On the night of the burial of his beloved "Stella" (*See* Dublin, St. Patrick's Cathedral: Grave of Stella), a heartsick Jonathan Swift, the dean of the cathedral, left his room in the deanery for another room from which he would not see the lights from her funeral.

St. Patrick's Cathedral: GRAVE OF STELLA

It remains one of the literary world's great mysteries—the love of Jonathan Swift, author of *Gulliver's Travels* and dean of this cathedral from 1713 to 1745, for Esther Johnson, whom he called "Stella" and to whom he wrote his tender *Journals* of fanciful baby talk.

Some believe that they were actually man and wife. Others surmise that, their devotion to each other notwithstanding, they could not share a bed because they were related. And over the years, depending on the view of their relationship that was taken by the new deans of the cathedral, the grave of Stella has been kept near Swift's or has been moved farther away from it.

St. Patrick's Cathedral: GRAVE OF JONATHAN SWIFT

Underneath this great cathedral flows the Poddle River. In 1835, a year of torrential rains, the river overflowed, dislodging the flagstones of the cathedral floor and the coffins of Jonathan Swift and "Stella," the woman he loved. Since the coffins had been disturbed by natural causes, it did not seem too macabre, before putting them back, to take a look at their remains to see "for scientific purposes," what the skull looked like of so great a man as Swift.

Called upon to do the examination was Sir William Wilde, archeologist, antiquarian, and father of the writer Oscar Wilde, and the most famous surgeon, oculist, and expert on diseases of the ear in his day. It was Wilde who dispelled the rumors that Swift's "madness" (*See* Dublin, St. Patrick's Hospital) might have been the result of syphilis. He diagnosed the problem that had made the theologian-satirist inclined to fits of rage as a disease of the semicircular canals of the inner ear that caused deafness and dizziness. Wilde also examined "Stella's" skull, exclaiming at its beauty and symmetry and at the exquisiteness of her teeth.

St. Patrick's Cathedral: THE SOUTH TRANSEPT—OLD CHAPTER DOOR

The altercation between the Earls of Kildare and Ormonde should never have happened in the house of God, but it did. The argument grew heated. Both men were surrounded by their armed supporters. Bloodshed seemed imminent, so the Duke of Ormonde took sanctuary in the Chapter House.

Gradually tempers were soothed, and, through the closed door, the earls' differences were settled. But to make sure they both held to their agreement, there had to be a handshake. To make sure there was before they were face-to-face again, the hole was cut in this door to facilitate it.

St. Patrick's Hospital (Steven's Lane)

The pain of Menière's disease, the ailment of the inner ear that had plagued the theologian-satirist Jonathan Swift, was increasing. Sometimes it resulted in Swift's having fits of violent rage. Sometimes he was felled by its excruciating headaches. Sometimes he foamed at the mouth and vomited, and his manservant made extra money by showing off his renowned master in his stricken state. Swift knew that it was clearly time to write his will.

Long interested in mental hospitals, Swift directed that most of the money that he left should go toward the founding of this hospital "for idiots and lunatics," which, today, is a rich repository of Swift memorabilia.

Trinity College (College Green)

The obstreperous students here proved, happily, to be too much for Narcissus Marsh, who was provost of this college just before the turn of the eighteenth century. Longing to spend more time in tranquility among his books, he left his college post and founded Marsh's Library. (See Dublin, Marsh's Library.)

St. Werburgh's Church (Werburgh Street)

When it came time in 1798 to bury the Irish patriot Lord Edward Fitzgerald, there was only one proper mourner here, and the interment took place in the dark of night. Espousing the cause of a free Ireland as he did, and having gone to France to seek Napoleon's aid for the Irish cause, by English standards Lord Edward was a traitor. He died, a victim of the wounds received in his capture on the very day Napoleon decided that invading Egypt was an enterprise dearer to him than helping Ireland.

Persona non grata that Lord Edward was, no one except one aunt dared to appear at his funeral. (His family had already, for safety's sake, left Dublin.) His coffin was a plain, unmarked one. But a hidden bystander recognized the aunt and, realizing whom it was she mourned, marked the coffin with Edward's initials after she had gone. In later years, this enabled his descendants to find his body and honor it with proper burial.

DUNGARVAN (County Waterford)

The Englishman George Longe had a perfect way of convincing Queen Elizabeth I that Ireland was the place for the establishment of a glass factory. Wood was needed to fire the glass furnaces, and England wished to conserve its woods. Longe pointed out in his request to have a glass factory that in Ireland woods were a place in which the Irish could hide. If they were cut down for his furnaces, he said tantalizingly, in time of rebellion there would be fewer hiding places. He received permission for his glass company.

GALWAY CITY (County Galway)

The Claddagh

In the days when this was a whitewashed fisherman's village ruled by its own king, a goldsmith named Joyce plied his trade here and fashioned the Claddagh ring on which two hands hold a crowned heart. Soon this design became the fashion in wedding rings.

As the story goes, when he was a boy, Joyce was kidnapped by Algerian pirates. Landed in Tunis, he was put to work at a jeweler's. In 1689, however, when William III became king of England, all Englishmen being held captive by the Moors were returned home. But Joyce was both so attractive a youth and so skilled a jeweler that his Moorish employer offered his daughter to him as a bride if he would stay. She was beautiful and Joyce yearned for her, but he yearned more for his homeland. So he returned here, bringing with him the design for the Claddagh ring he had made in his captivity.

The Collegiate Church of St. Nicholas (off Shop Street)

About to embark for the New World, Christopher Columbus with one of his crewmen, the Irishman Rice de Culvey, stopped here to worship and to seek inspiration, perhaps, from the spirit of St. Brendan the Navigator, who was said to have crossed the Atlantic himself in the sixth century.

Eyre Square

The Eyre family that prospered here left three fine gifts to this city—this square that bears their name, a five-foot-long eighteenth-century silver mace, and a seventeenth-century ceremonial sword. But the mace and the sword did considerable traveling before they were finally returned here in 1960 and put on display in the bank at No. 19.

They were a gift to the city. But when the city fell on hard times in 1840 and lacked the necessary funds to pay the mayor, city fathers presented him with the mace and sword instead. Both stayed in his family for nearly a century. Then they were sold to an art dealer who, in turn, sold them to the newspaper publisher William Randolph Hearst.

During his lifetime, Hearst kept them at his California ranch. Before his death, however, he stipulated that once he was gone they should be returned here where they belonged.

Lynch Memorial Window (Market Street)

Of course it was tragic, but as James Lynch FitzStephen saw it, there was nothing he could do but execute the sentence imposed.

In 1493, FitzStephen was not only a prosperous businessman with a good trade in imported French and Spanish wines, but he was also the mayor of Galway. When his son Walter stabbed to death a Spanish house guest after the guest had flirted with the woman Walter loved, the law decreed the death sentence.

But there were few men in Galway so popular as Walter, and the hangman refused to officiate. No one else would either. That left it up to James Lynch FitzStephen himself, who, therefore, hanged his own son from a prison window. Ever since, Lynch's name has been used to describe a lawless mob-hanging, though of course, that was exactly the opposite of what happened here.

GLEN COLUMBKILLE (County Donegal)

The Spaniard's Church

Although the building of Catholic churches in Ireland was forbidden in the eighteenth century, now and again there was a let-up in restrictions. As the story goes, this church was built in 1725 with money left by a shipwrecked Spanish sailor. After receiving the last rites, he told the priest who attended him to take the money from his belt and build a church.

GLENDALOUGH (County Wicklow)

Surely the gentle St. Kevin—in the palm of whose hand a blackbird built her nest and around whom a lake monster gently swam while the saint prayed—would not, as the poet Thomas Moore has him, have sought to avoid temptation by hurling the temptress, pretty Kathleen, into this lake. But there are those who insist that when he found he yearned for Kathleen as much as she yearned for him, this sixth-century celibate fled to this solitary place. When Kathleen followed him and he woke on his narrow ledge above the lake to find her bending over him, he pushed her, and she fell to a drowning death.

GLENGARIFF (County Cork)

Cromwell's Bridge

It is said that an impatient Oliver Cromwell, having trouble fording the river here, ordered a bridge to be built within an hour by the local citizenry. For every hour his crossing was delayed, he warned, a man would be hanged. Needless to say, the bridge was finished in short order, and its now-ruined state may well bear witness to the haste with which it was constructed.

GORT (County Galway)

Coole Park

On the trunk of the copper beech autograph tree here, the writers and artists whom Lady Augusta Gregory nurtured with money and affection in pre-World War I years carved their initials—playwrights George Bernard Shaw and J. M. Synge, the poet W. B. Yeats and his brother, artist Jack Yeats, the artist Augustus John, and the poet John Masefield. In the house that stood here then (but was torn down in 1941 for its stone), Lady Gregory nursed and encouraged frail young Yeats. It was at the end of the park, in Coole Lake, that he saw the fifty-nine swans that inspired him to write one of his best-known poems, "The Wild Swans at Coole."

Thoor Ballylee

Legend had it that a cure for all evils was to be found at Feakle, so the poet William Butler Yeats came looking for

Republic of Ireland   249

it. He didn't find that, but he did find this square Norman tower abutting two whitewashed cottages. Though they were in disrepair, he liked them and in 1917 bought them. He was newly married, and the tower appealed to him especially as a gift for his wife. He wrote:

"I, the poet William Yeats
With old mill-boards and sea-green slates,
And smith work from the Gort forge,
Restored this tower for my wife George,
And may these characters remain
When all is ruin once again."

HOWTH (County Dublin)

Howth Castle

Returning from a visit to Queen Elizabeth I of England, Grace O'Malley, the uncrowned Queen of the West (*See* Clare Island), tried to stop here for lunch.

The voyage from London to her castle on Clare Island was a long one, so Grace decided to put in here for a rest. At any castle in her part of Ireland, luncheon would willingly have been offered, but it wasn't here. In a rage, Grace kidnapped the heir to this castle.

His father begged for the return of the boy, offering virtually everything that he had as a ransom, Grace said she wanted no ransom. All she wanted was a little hospitality. Grace did not release her captive until the boy's father agreed that the gates of Howth Castle would forever be open at mealtime and that a place would always be kept for a guest. And until recent years, this had been so.

INISHBOFIN (County Donegal)

Working a field sometime in the last century, a farmer and a young farmhand unearthed some of the nine tons of treasure said to have been buried here in the sixteenth century by Grace O'Malley, the Queen of the West. (*See* Clare Island and Howth.)

Determined to keep the treasure for himself, the farmer swore the boy to secrecy and promptly set about using some of the money to build a boat and to send his son to maritime school. Once the son was a captain, he was given much of the remaining treasure to take with him on his father's vessel to buy rum in the West Indies. The plan was that he would buy it cheaply there and sell it at a sizable profit here on his return.

But the night that he sailed away was a stormy one. The son would have liked to wait until the storm abated. His greedy father, however, would have none of that, and the ship put out to sea.

As the son had predicted, the storm worsened. Realizing his error in judgment, the father sent another boat to tell his son to return. But the second vessel missed him, and the son and his ship went down that night, treasure and all.

INISHCLORAUM (County Roscommon)

Toward the end of her exhausting and astonishing life of wars and cattle-stealing, legendary Queen Maeve of the national epic "The Raid of Coolaney" retired here to enjoy the peace of this island in Lough Ree.

But peace did not last long. As she splashed in a cool fresh-water pool one day, an enemy hurled a stone at the once-mighty queen and killed her.

KELLS (County Meath)

It is remarkable that the Book of Kells has survived at all.

First, it had to be protected from marauding Norseman who attacked the Monastery of St. Columba on Iona (*See* Scotland, Inner Hebrides, Iona), where it was begun. Then in 807 it had to make the sea journey here, one of a handful of items (including the bones of St. Columba) that the monks saved.

For a century after that, while the monks built a new settlement in this quiet place, it remained safe. The artists of this new monastic community worked to complete their splendid illuminated book.

But in the tenth century this monastery was discovered by the Norsemen and raided. Happily, the Book of Kells was saved again.

Next, in the eleventh century, it was mysteriously stolen. Mysteriously recovered just a few months later, it had been buried with its cover of gold and wood torn off, but the manuscript itself was intact.

The devoted monks brought it back here where it stayed until Oliver Cromwell's troops arrived from England in the seventeenth century.

The Cromwellian forces' record of destruction was even worse than the Norsemen's, so the governor of Kells, fearing the worst for the precious illuminated manuscript, spirited it away to Trinity College, Dublin, where it has remained ever since.

KILKENNY (County Kilkenny)

The Black Abbey

From 1348 to 1349 the Black Death raged through Kilkenny visiting every house. Keeping solemn track of its visitation was Friar Clyn of this abbey. Sensing that he too was about to be felled by the plague, he wrote in his last entry that he was leaving his parchment scroll to be kept by whomever chanced to survive.

Someone did survive, for there is a next entry in another hand.

Cathedral of St. Canice

It made no difference to the invading troops of Oliver Cromwell that this medieval church was one of the finest in Ireland. Indeed, that meant that there was more in it to destroy and pillage. And that was exactly what they did, turning this cathedral into a stable for their horses, breaking its finest stained glass windows, and using the baptismal font as their horses' watering trough.

Kyteler's Inn

"Pretty as a picture" was the way Alice Kyteler, who owned this inn in the fourteenth century, was described when she was a young woman. And she was surely pretty enough to win four husbands. The richest banker in Kilkenny, the first one, died only a few months after they were married, but a second husband quickly wooed and won her. Though he died sooner than might have been expected, a third man fell for Alice's charms and made her his bride. He too met an untimely death, but Dame Alice soon had a fourth husband.

Even though her feminine charms were so great that the men who married her all seemed oblivious of how short-lived their predecessors had been, her children, reaching adulthood, began to wonder what had happened to their fathers. They went to the bishop and expressed fear for their own lives.

When the bishop came here for a talk with Dame Alice, he was met by her tavern help, who tied him up and carried him off to Kilkenny Prison. The bishop protested, but Dame Alice's riches and influence had the last say. It was months before the bishop was released. It was no time at all after that, however, that he was seeking vengeance. An ecclesiastical court was set up that promptly accused Alice, her oldest son, William, and her maid, Petronella, of sorcery and witchcraft. It was said that they had brewed poisonous potions from the stewed entrails of black roosters, the hair and nails of unbaptized children, and dead men. The two women were tried, found guilty, and sentenced to be burned at the stake.

Petronella was burned, but Dame Alice, clearly the more powerful witch of the pair, escaped to England. Since he was a man, William's sentence was lighter. He was ordered to reroof the church with lead, but, being a penny-pincher, he never did.

KILLORGLIN (County Kerry)

The Puritan army of Oliver Cromwell was encamped near here in 1649 when it is said that a young goat herder on the mountain where they had made their camp heard the murmur of English words. He crept close to listen and see what the enemy was up to. He discovered that the campers were laying plans to creep down on the town before dawn, surprise its sleeping inhabitants, and take it. Down the young herdsman scurried to his father in town with the news of what he had heard. But his father pooh-poohed him. At other times, up in the mountains watching the goats, the imaginative boy had insisted that he had seen a serpent with a mane (a most unlikely story since St. Patrick rid Ireland of snakes [*See* Croagh Patrick]) and a leprechaun mending shoes. It seemed just as unlikely that he had fallen on an English encampment, and the father sent the boy back to his goats with a harsh warning to stop all the nonsense.

The young herdsman took matters into his own hands. Grabbing the lead goat of his herd by the horns, he led it and all the goats that followed it right to the enemy camp. There, with a shout, he loosed the goats into the camp. The startled, sleepy Englishmen, thinking that it was men who were attacking, began to fire their guns. The gunfire alerted the town that the enemy was coming, and realizing that their arrival would no longer be a surprise, the Cromwellians fled. In gratitude to the goats, each August ever since, one has been brought down into town from the mountain. With its horns garlanded with ribbons, it is hoisted to the top of a specially built tower, supplied with food and water, and left to "preside" over the merrymaking of a three-day Puck Fair.

KINSALE (County Cork)

The Battle of Kinsale was over. For ten weeks in that winter of 1601 the Spaniards, whom the Irish had asked to help them fight England, had held this pretty seacoast town. But the English besieged the town again and again, and the nervous Spanish general Don Juan del Aguila surrendered.

Disheartened but not ready to give up all hope, dynamic "Red" Hugh O'Donnell (*See* Dublin, Dublin Castle: The Record Tower), a leader of the Irish troops in the combat, embarked for Spain to ask more help from Philip III.

But "Red" Hugh never got there. An English agent was sent after him to make sure that he didn't, and twenty-eight-year-old "Red" Hugh died of poison.

The Irish mission failed, and the gleeful English transformed this town into an Englishmen's community, with all Irishmen forbidden to live within the city walls.

◆ ◆ ◆

Catholic James II of England could not have been more pleased with the reception that he received here when he arrived on March 19, 1689, from exile in France. There was speech-making in his honor and dancing along the road that he took to Dublin. Coats were laid beneath his horse's hooves. Women greeted him with kisses as the savior of Ireland. But less than a year and a half later, his joyousness ended with his defeat by his Protestant son-in-law, William of Orange, at the Battle of the Boyne.

◆ ◆ ◆

In the harbor here one day in 1703 the restless Scot, Alexander Selkirk (*See* Scotland, Lower Largo), joined the crew of the vessel *Cinque Ports*. Some months later, following an altercation with the captain, Selkirk was to be put ashore—alone—on the Pacific island of Juan Fernández, where he remained for the next four years and four months, living the solitary life that writer Daniel Defoe was to turn into *Robinson Crusoe.*

Charles Fort

The ghost of the White Lady is said to walk around the walls of this seventeenth-century fort at night.

When she was alive, her name was Wilful, and she was the daughter of the governor of this fort.

As the story goes, on her wedding day Wilful was strolling the battlements with her new husband when she saw pretty white flowers growing on the rocks below. She remarked on them to a sentry who, wishing to please the pretty lady, said that he would go after them for her if her bridegroom would take his place on the wall. That seemed a reasonable request, so the bridegroom donned the sentry's coat and took his musket while the sentry found a rope and let himself down after the flowers.

But the enterprise took longer than anticipated. Dusk fell. With the onset of it, Wilful's new husband urged her to go indoors, and she dutifully obeyed. Tired after the events of his wedding day and after his hours of parading in the sentry's garb, the bridegroom found a cozy wall as protection from the wind and settled down beside it. Soon he was fast asleep.

Meanwhile, the governor began his nightly rounds of sentry posts. When he found the sleeping "sentry," the governor was furious at such a breach of discipline and shot the "sentry" dead. Only when the body was carried indoors did he discover his mistake. Learning what had happened, Wilful flung herself from these battlements, around which her weeping ghost is still said to walk.

Great Sovereign Rock

Recalling that it was off this rock in May of 1916 that the transatlantic liner *Lusitania* was struck by a German torpedo and one thousand five hundred lives were lost, the superstitious tend not to blame the torpedo alone. They remember that in ancient days the King of Kinsale is said to have stood here and thrown a dart out to sea as far as he could. He said that where it landed was the seaward bound of his kingdom, and it was not to be crossed without permission.

KINVARA (County Galway)

Dun Guaire Castle

One Sunday, in the fort that stood here in the sixth century, generous King Guaire was just sitting down to his dinner when it disappeared. Whisked out the windows of his castle went his plates full of food. Though dumbfounded, Guaire rose to the occasion as a king should and galloped off after the floating dinner. He found his plates, all right, at an isolated hermitage where a saint named Colman lived. But the dinner was all gone. Hungry St. Colman, just ending a fast and seeing a dinner hovering in his window, had thanked God for it and then dined like a king.

So impressed was Guaire by the miracle that he not only forgave the hermit for finishing his feast, but gave him land on which to build a monastery.

KNOCK (County Mayo)

Knock Basilica

On a misty, rainy night in 1879, fourteen townspeople here insisted that they had seen the Virgin Mary dressed in white with a gold crown on her head, accompanied by St. Joseph and St. John. Although the rain drenched the viewers, it did not seem to touch the Virgin and the saints. To commemorate the event and to accommodate the crowds that soon flocked here in hopes of having a glimpse of the Blessed Mother, this fifteen-thousand-seat basilica was built.

LETTERFRACK (County Galway)

Kylemore Abbey

One sunny day in 1862 Mitchell Henry, a young surgeon from Manchester, and his County Down bride, Margaret Vaughan, picnicked here in the wooded Pass of Kylemore on their honeymoon.

Margaret looked up across the pass and noticed a tiny cottage in the distance. Breathlessly, she murmured of the loveliness of its site and said she could not imagine a prettier place to live.

So Henry wrote to the cottage owner and inquired if the little shooting box his wife had seen was for sale.

It was. The Henrys bought it, and on the nine thousand acres that went with it they built this Gothic Revival building that they called their castle and surrounded it with spacious gardens.

The Henrys could not have been happier until Margaret was cajoled by a friend to take a tour of Egypt, where she was stricken with a fever and died. The heartbroken Mitchell brought her body back and buried it here. But after that, he no longer took any joy in the house. He seemed to lose interest too in his work. When one of the nine children he and Margaret had had was killed in a pony cart accident, it was more than he could bear. The castle the Henrys had built with such love was put on the market and bought by an American. During World War I it became an abbey.

LISMORE (County Waterford)

Lismore Castle

Only fourteen years after arriving in Ireland from England, wearing just a diamond ring, a gold bracelet, a doublet, breeches, and a shirt and carrying £28, adventurer Richard Boyle had made sufficient wealth to buy this castle for £1,500 from Sir Walter Raleigh. Here he begat seven daughters and seven sons, the last of whom became the scientist Robert Boyle. Here the once-penurious Richard amassed much of the wealth that made him, when he died, one of Ireland's wealthiest men.

◆ ◆ ◆

The grand style in which Richard, the first Earl of Cork, and his wife and offspring lived here in the seventeenth century had its drawbacks. It is said that one night the lady of the house, rising from bed, fell, gashing herself on her silver chamber pot.

◆ ◆ ◆

Jilted by the poet Byron, Lady Caroline Lamb came here in melancholy spirits in 1812 to recover. But she was quite put out with the grand surroundings which were not at all in keeping with her mournful mood.

Lismore Castle: GREAT ROOM

Impressive, surely, is the view from the main window here, for if one looks out, the eye plunges directly to the Blackwater River below. So impressive, indeed, is the view that, spending a night at Lismore during the Battle of the Boyne, James II is said to have jumped back from the window in terror after looking out.

MALAHIDE (County Wicklow)

Malahide Castle

In the 1920s invaluable manuscripts of the eighteenth-century James Boswell, biographer of Samuel Johnson and others, turned up everywhere in this twelfth-century castle that belonged to his great-great-grandson. There were manuscripts stuffed in desk drawers and in a box used for croquet mallets. There were even manuscripts in an old stable.

The discovery began when Yale University Boswell scholar Chauncey B. Tinker put an ad in the *London Times Literary Supplement* seeking previously unknown Boswell manuscripts. An anonymous reply led him to this castle. Getting an invitation here for a glimpse of the treasures took him five years and required the intercession of the U.S. consul-general in Dublin. Then, over tea, Professor Tinker was allowed a glimpse of a few of the old family papers, which his host and hostess told him "weren't fit for print."

And it was three years after that before the great-great-grandson, James Boswell Talbot, was willing to sell them—and then only after endless negotiations with another American—Samuel Johnson collector Lieutenant Colonel Ralph Heyward Isham. Colonel Isham had most casually, at first, let his interest in the papers be known and been invited to spend several days here. Once arrived and having made friends with the Talbots, he incidentally pointed out that the family papers might be of some value. In time the Talbots agreed, and arrangements for a sale to Colonel Isham got under way.

Even as late as 1950, after the death of Lord Talbot and the passing of this castle into other hands, Boswell letters and journals were still being uncovered in the turrets and garrets of this venerable structure. Today they are safely kept in climate-controlled conditions at Yale University.

MAYNOOTH (County Kildare)

Carton House

Visiting here, Queen Victoria was so delighted with the jaunting car in which her host, the Duke of Leinster, drove her about that after she had left, the duke had a copy of it made for her.

NEWGRANGE (County Meath)

It was a dreadful battle that took place near here at Tailltee in ancient days between the De Danann inhabitants of the Emerald Isle and the Milesian invaders from Spain. Three De Danann kings, three De Danann queens, and many warriors were lost in the conflict.

Those who survived fled into the hills. But in the end, it all turned out quite happily for Ireland.

When they had finally recouped their strength, the De Danann gathered here at Brugh na Boinne to decide if they could live as a conquered people. Legend has it that they decided they couldn't and dug their way instead into this large earth mound, fanning out from it to found their own underground kingdom all across Ireland. They have lived here ever since as fairies and their cobbler relatives, leprechauns, fiddling and dancing and guarding the gold in the earth from those who inhabit its surface.

RATHMULLEN (County Donegal)

Into this port one day in 1588 came a "Spanish" merchant ship carrying a cargo of wine. The ship dropped anchor, and the captain graciously invited the gentry of the town to come aboard his vessel for a wine-tasting. They did—and fourteen-year-old "Red" Hugh O'Donnell (whose father was the independent chieftain of the Donegal clan) was among them. While the guests enjoyed their wine in the captain's cabin, they suddenly found themselves surrounded by armed men. Although the others were allowed to depart, "Red" Hugh wasn't. A seer had prophesied that the golden-haired Irish youth would bring woe to England, and Queen Elizabeth was nervous about him. The disguised ship took the boy straight to Dublin where, for the next three years, he was imprisoned in the castle. (*See* Dublin, Dublin Castle: The Record Tower.)

ROSS CASTLE (County Kerry)

Under normal circumstances, this fourteenth-century island castle would have suffered greatly in 1652 from Cromwellian forces, for a sizable body of Irish forces had taken refuge in it after a defeat at the Battle of Knocknaclasky in County Cork. They were prepared to fight to the death. But when the defenders saw a boatful of soldiers rowing toward them across Lough Leane, they meekly surrendered. An old prophecy had it that once strange ships sailed on the lakes of Killarney, all would be lost at Ross Castle. Learning of the ancient prophesy, the attacking English general had a boat hauled overland to the lake. The superstitious defenders were taken in by it.

◆ ◆ ◆

His riches and his powers could do nothing to prevent it: Prince O'Donoghue of this castle was growing old. But perhaps, the prince thought, necromancy could help. So for seven weeks he immured himself in a tower here with books on magic. He boiled brews and mixed potions that, he hoped, would restore his youth. And when, finally, he allowed his worried wife to come see him, he told her the only solution to his problem was if she agreed to cut him into pieces no larger than a three-year-old child. She was to leave them in a tub for seven weeks behind the locked tower door, and when she opened it, she would find her husband alive and well and in one piece—but only the size of that three-year-old.

When his wife looked hesitant, the prince decided he had best test her mettle. He would read to her, he said, from his book of magic. No matter what she saw or heard while he read, she must not cry out.

Dutifully, she listened to the prince's terrifying readings, and as he read, strange things began to happen.

First, the castle seemed to shake as if it would fall down. But the prince's wife stayed stoically silent. Not until she saw her own child laid out dead did she cry out. Then one piercing scream followed another as she watched her distraught husband leap from the tower window into Lough Leane, followed by his table and his magic books.

The castle shook again. Where the prince and his household goods had sunk, there were only bubbles on the lake. But nowadays, they say, he and all that went with him may be seen in stone on the lake floor. As he wished, the prince has not withered and wasted away as mortal flesh does.

SANDYCOVE (County Dublin)

Martello Tower

For James Joyce, it was a terrifying night—so terrifying that after only six days here he left and never returned—except in his imagination, which made this the setting for the opening of *Ulysses*.

Twenty-two-year-old Joyce was sharing living quarters in this tower with his old friend Oliver St. John Gogarty (who became the "stately, plump Buck Mulligan" of *Ulysses*) and a friend of Gogarty's, Samuel Trench. Having a nightmare in which he was being chased by a black panther, Trench fired a revolver at what he thought was the panther. When the panther did not seem, to the still-dreaming Trench, to have been killed, he continued to scream, and Gogarty, waking, fired more shots at the fireplace to satisfy his friend. A startled Joyce got out of bed, dressed, and left the tower for more tranquil lodgings.

SKELLIG MICHAEL (County Kerry)

Only one monk, Etgall, remained in his beehive hut on this rocky island in 825 when Norse treasure hunters arrived in search of jewels and gold. Angered when they found nothing and no one but the gaunt hermit, they took him away with them. He died, some say, of hunger (unused as he was to their strange food). But others say he died of homesickness for his beloved barren island of wheeling birds.

SLANE (County Meath)

The four Conyngham sisters could neither live with each other nor without each other. Their wise brother built the four Georgian houses, each an exact duplicate of the other, that face each other in the center of town. That way they could spy on each other, visit each other, but not annoy others with their scolding and arguments.

STATION ISLAND (County Donegal)

Lough Derg

For forty days and forty nights St. Patrick is said to have
fasted here until he had a vision of Purgatory. Thereafter
in the Middle Ages, pilgrims would come and, after fasting and prayers, be let down at night by the monks into
the cavern that was said to be the entrance to Purgatory.
The pilgrims would remain several hours. Because of
the darkness, their reduced mental and physical strength
from the fasting, and their imaginations, the pilgrims
would return with incredible tales of what they had seen.

TARA (County Meath)

It was Easter Eve 453. The Druidic priests had just lit
their bonfire to welcome spring and on that night each
year, the law decreed, no other bonfire was to be built in
the land. Suddenly, in the distance, on the Hill of Slane
flames from another bonfire leaped into the sky. The
enraged priests turned to the king. Who had broken the
law, they asked, and would he be punished?

Messengers were sent to neighboring Slane, and they
returned with word that it was the priest called Patrick
who preached Christianity who had built the fire. It must
be extinguished, the priests warned. If it were not put out
that night, it would never die. The messengers were sent
back with a chariot to fetch the Christian priest.

Patrick came, but he left his bonfire burning. Here in
this holy place of Druid worship, he preached of the
Resurrection. The king listened. The Druids listened.

When Patrick was done, King Lagohaire asked them if
they could refute what Patrick had said. None could to
Lagohaire's satisfaction. The Druids' warnings notwithstanding, therefore, Lagohaire neither punished Patrick
nor forbade his continued preaching. And the fear of the
Druids was realized. The fire of Christianity in Ireland
has never been put out.

◆   ◆   ◆

In a London secondhand bookshop, an English amateur archeologist of the 1920s read with fascination that the Ark of the Covenant, (*See* Northern Ireland, Devenish Island), might be buried on this hill that was sacred to the Irish as long ago as the Bronze Age. And so, with fellow amateur archeologists, he arrived here, and a fruitless dig began that did much to disrupt these ancient earthworks.

TRALEE (County Kerry)

Rose of Tralee Memorial

There was no question but that William Pembroke Mulchinock loved Mary O'Connor, the cobbler's beautiful daughter. The problem was that he was gentry and she wasn't, and marriage would have been unacceptable. Versifier that he was, however, young Willie Mulchinock couldn't help writing poems about the dark-haired colleen whom his mother had hired as a serving girl and who had captured his heart. But when one of his poems fell into his mother's hands, Willie was shipped off to County Galway to meet the daughter of a family friend who was of his class.

As his mother had hoped, her impressionable son fell in love quite as readily with Alice Keogh of Ballinasloe as he had fallen for Mary O'Connor of Tralee. He forgot Mary, married Alice, and sailed for America. There in 1851 he published a book of poems. America was pleasant enough, William found, but his yearning for Ireland never left him. One day he proposed to Alice that they go home.

Alice said no. Willie decided he would go alone. On the day that he reached Tralee, as it happened, a funeral was in progress. Willie was told it was Denis O'Connor, the cobbler, who had died. And, remembering his love of long ago, Willie asked whatever had become of the cobbler's daughter. She too was dead, he was told—dead of a broken heart after the man she loved had left her for another and gone to America.

Memories of every pleasant moment that he had had with Mary O'Connor flooded back, and William Mulchinock followed her father's funeral procession to Clogherbrien Graveyard. There, beside the gravestone of Mary O'Connor, he wrote the only poem he is remembered for—about "Mary, the Rose of Tralee."

TRIM (County Meath)

Trim Castle

In this enormous castle with its eleven-foot-thick walls, a nervous Richard II of England pettishly imprisoned the young son of his enemy, Henry of Bolingbroke. On a six-week visit here in Ireland, Richard had learned that Bolingbroke was seeking his throne and was being supported by the populace. So Richard clapped young Henry, who was at hand, into this prison.

But it did no good. Henry of Bolingbroke became Henry IV, and his imprisoned son became the gallant warrior Henry V. (*See* Wales, Conwy, Conwy Castle.)

WATERFORD (County Waterford)

As the story goes, Ireland's woes all began with a woman.

The forty-four-year-old wife of twelfth-century warrior-king Tiernan O'Rourke, Devorguilla was a flirt. And she flirted so seductively with another warrior-king, Diarmuid MacMurrough, that he abducted her.

Now, Devorguilla was so beguiling that, regardless of her indiscretions and her age, her husband wanted her back. In time he got her back, forgiving her entirely. But MacMurrough was made to pay for the abduction.

O'Rourke raided his lands and turned his people against him, persuading them to banish him from his kingdom for misconduct.

Having lost both his mistress and his lands, the en-

raged MacMurrough sailed off to England to seek the
help of Henry II in regaining what he had lost.

Henry had been coveting Ireland for quite some time.
Although Henry was busy when MacMurrough arrived,
he sent MacMurrough to his nobles for help. Providing it
willingly was an Anglo-Norman knight, Richard Fitz-
gilbert de Clare, the Earl of Pembroke, who came to be
called "Strongbow" for his prowess in battle. All Strongbow ostensibly wanted for aiding MacMurrough was his
daughter Aoife in marriage, along with the right of succession in MacMurrough's kingdom of Leinster for their
offspring.

Delighted with the arrangement, and assured that
Strongbow would follow him, MacMurrough boldly
sailed home. Here, after a few skirmishes, he reclaimed
part of his land. He also soothed his rival O'Rourke by
paying reparations for the abduction of Devorguilla.
Then he waited for Strongbow, who wasn't long in coming.

Strongbow chose this port as the best place to land,
noting that there were two possible approaches to the
harbor, one using the village of Crooke, the other the
promontory of Hook Head. He is said to have remarked
(thereby introducing a new phrase to the English lan-
guage) that he would take Waterford "by Hook or by
Crooke."

In advance of his own arrival, he sent a noble young
friend, ten knights, and seventy archers. They landed
near Wexford, where their small force was met not only
by the Irish but by three thousand Danes, the original
settlers here.

Intrigued by the new green land that could be theirs,
MacMurrough's Norman supporters were not about to be
stopped—the overwhelming numbers ready to attack
them notwithstanding.

Seeing a herd of cattle, they corralled them, sent them
head-on toward the enemy, and, following in their wake,
the Norman archers devastated the Irish and the Danes
seeking to escape the horns of the angry beasts.

A little later Strongbow himself arrived. Ireland's centuries of anguish under English rule had started—thanks to the aging coquette, Devorguilla.

◆ ◆ ◆

In this eleventh-century round tower with its ten-foot-thick walls, Aoife, the daughter of King Diarmuid Mac-Murrough of the Province of Leinster, became the bride in 1171 of the Anglo-Norman knight Strongbow. She was her father's gift in exchange for Strongbow's help in regaining his lost kingdom.

Apparently Aoife felt relatively kindly toward Strongbow, arranged marriage and his bad temper notwithstanding (*See* Dublin, Christ Church Cathedral: Tomb of Strongbow). When he died only six years after their wedding, she remarked of her redheaded spouse that "a great tooth had fallen."

Waterford Glass Factory

Over the years Waterford glass has had its ups and downs. Begun in 1759, the first glass house here on the River Suir survived only eight years. But in 1780 production was started again of Waterford glass, which is said to ring sweeter than any other glass and to be warmer to the touch.

But still there were problems with duties that England insisted on for Irish glass. Not until the end of World War II did Waterford glass truly come into its own. That was when Bernard Fitzpatrick, a Dublin jeweler and silversmith who in pre-war years had often visited European glass factories, saw his old Czech friend Charles Bacik, a glass manufacturer whose factory seemed likely to fall into Communist hands. He proposed that Bacik come to Ireland and enter the glass business. Bacik needed little persuading. By the early 1950s more than thirty European glass blowers and cutters, down on their luck in their war-ravaged homelands, had come here to work. Waterford glass was thriving.

WEXFORD (County Wexford)

Market Square

One night in 1798 the farmers of this town, a priest at their head and pitchforks as their only weapons, ambushed and disarmed the British so boldly and cleverly that even the enemy exclaimed at it. The statue here honors that event.

Selskar Abbey

"Pretending" sorrow, most thought, for the murder in Canterbury Cathedral of Thomas à Becket, Archbishop of Canterbury (See England, Canterbury, Canterbury Cathedral), Henry II of England spent Lent of 1172 doing penance within this now-ruined abbey's walls.

YOUGHAL (County Cork)

Entering this port in the sixteenth century after a storm had dismasted his vessel and shredded his sails, a down-at-the-heels pirate is said to have stolen masts, sails, and shrouds from local vessels. The infuriated fishermen of Youghal would have none of that. They banded together and, in the dark of night before he could sail away, captured the pirate, his crew, and the ship—getting back, in the long run, considerably more than they had lost.

Myrtle Grove

Under the yew trees in front of this now-private house, Sir Walter Raleigh, mayor of Youghal in 1588, decided one day to smoke the pipe he had been given by the Indians in the New World. Legend has it that a loyal servant, seeing the curls of smoke rising around his master's head and never having seen a pipe before, drenched Sir Walter's head with a tankard of ale—the liquid nearest at hand—to put out the fire.

Also brought here by Raleigh from the New World and planted in this back garden was the first potato ever seen in Ireland.

St. Mary's Collegiate Church

It is said that not far from this church, the sprightly 147-year-old Countess of Desmond climbed a cherry tree one summer day in 1604 when she had a longing for the sweet red fruit. She fell down and was killed and is remembered with a monument here.

INDEX